Anonymous

The Tax-payer's manual:

Containing the acts of Congress imposing direct and excise taxes

Anonymous

The Tax-payer's manual:
Containing the acts of Congress imposing direct and excise taxes

ISBN/EAN: 9783337714925

Printed in Europe, USA, Canada, Australia, Japan

Cover: Foto ©ninafisch / pixelio.de

More available books at **www.hansebooks.com**

THE
TAX-PAYER'S MANUAL:

CONTAINING

THE ACTS OF CONGRESS

IMPOSING

DIRECT AND EXCISE TAXES;

WITH COMPLETE MARGINAL REFERENCES,

AND

AN ANALYTICAL INDEX

SHOWING

ALL THE ITEMS OF TAXATION, THE MODE OF PROCEEDING,
AND THE DUTIES OF THE OFFICERS.

WITH

AN EXPLANATORY PREFACE.

NEW YORK
D. APPLETON AND COMPANY,
443 & 445 BROADWAY.
1862

CONTENTS.

EXPLANATION OF THE TAX LAWS.
THE EXCISE LAW.
ANALYTICAL INDEX OF THE EXCISE TAX.
THE DIRECT TAX LAW.
THE ACT TO COLLECT TAXES IN INSURRECTIONARY DISTRICTS.
INDEX TO THE TWO LATTER ACTS.

EXPLANATION OF THE TAX LAWS.

Two internal tax laws have been passed by Congress, and are known as the "Direct Tax" law and the "Excise Tax" law.

The "Direct Tax" law was passed August 5th, 1861. It increased the duties on certain articles imported from foreign countries, laid duties on many articles then exempt from duty, such as teas, &c., and also imposed a tax of twenty millions of dollars on all the States and Territories. This tax was apportioned among the several States and Territories, and the Legislature of each loyal State assumed and undertook to pay the portion assigned to it. At the time of the passage of the act, the Government of the United States was indebted to each of the States for sums of money advanced to pay the expenses of enlisting and equipping volunteers called out by the President during that year. This indebtedness was cancelled by offsetting against it the amount of tax called for from each State, with a discount of fifteen per centum from the tax. If the balance was in favor of the Government, the State paid it over; if it was in favor of the State, the Government paid it. Thus the only effect of this portion of the "Direct Tax" law upon tax-payers, was the assessment and collection of a small State tax for 1862, in those States where there had previously been none, and an increase in the State tax in others. So much of this "Direct Tax" law as imposed a tax of twenty millions of dollars was modified by Congress on July 1st, 1862, so as to authorize the levy and collection of one tax to that amount, and to provide that no other tax should be levied under the act until April 1st, 1865.

To supply the place of this suspended act, the "Excise Tax" law was passed. According to the provisions of a subsequent act, it takes effect July 21st, 1862. According to the notification of the Secretary of the Treasury, or Commissioner of Internal Revenue, the officers required will not be prepared to execute the act before September 1st, 1862. The peculiar features of this "Excise Tax" law are as follows:

It imposes a tax upon all spirits, ale, beer, porter, and other fermented liquors, distilled or brewed after August 1st, 1862.

It requires all persons engaged in certain trades or occupations to obtain a license, as distillers, brewers, wholesale dealers, retail dealers, bankers, tavern-keepers, eating-houses, brokers, confectioners, tobacconists, livery stable keepers, lawyers, physicians, apothecaries, manufacturers, agents, &c. &c.

It imposes a tax, either specific or ad valorem, upon an immense number of articles manufactured by the industry of the mass of the people, and which are largely consumed by them.

It levies a specific tax on spring carriages, pleasure boats, each head of slaughtered cattle, hogs, and sheep; an ad valorem tax on the gross receipts of all railroads, passenger and ferry boats; on the interest paid on railroad bonds; dividends paid by railroad companies, banks, trust companies, and savings institutions; on the salaries of all officers and persons in the service of the United States; on the gross receipts for all advertisements in news and periodical publications.

It also levies an ad valorem tax on so much of the incomes, gains, and profits of all persons as exceeds $600.

It requires a stamp duty to be paid upon nearly all written papers relative to the transfer from one to another of anything of value, such as contracts, checks, drafts, bills of exchange, bonds, certificates of stocks, conveyances, leases, telegraphic despatches, insurance policies, mortgages, power of attorney, freight bills, &c., &c.

It also requires a stamp duty to be paid on every bottle, phial, box, pot, or other enclosure containing medicines or preparations of persons claiming to have any secret formula; also on the endless variety of perfumery and cosmetics.

It levies an ad valorem duty upon all legacies and distributive shares of personal property.

The act makes it the duty of all persons to furnish a list of property to the assessor; and the process for the collection of the tax, upon non-payment, is very prompt and summary.

On the 7th of June, 1862, Congress passed an Act for the collection of direct taxes in insurrectionary districts. It is designed to carry out the Act of August, 1861. It makes the tax a lien upon the land in all insurrectionary States, and provides for its forfeiture to the United States, and a summary sale of the same "in fee simple, free and discharged from all prior liens, incumbrances, right, title, and claim whatsoever." It is the last Act in this Manual.

This Act goes into effect September 1st, 1862.

EXCISE TAX.

AN ACT

To provide internal revenue to support the government and to pay interest on the public debt.

Be it enacted by the Senate and House of Representatives of the United States of America in Congress assembled, That, for the purpose of superintending the collection of internal duties, stamp duties, licenses, or taxes imposed by this act, or which may be hereafter imposed, and of assessing the same, an office is hereby created in the Treasury Department to be called the office of the Commissioner of Internal Revenue; and the President of the United States is hereby authorized to nominate, and, with the advice and consent of the Senate, to appoint, a Commissioner of Internal Revenue, with an annual salary of four thousand dollars, who shall be charged, and hereby is charged, under the direction of the Secretary of the Treasury, with preparing all the instructions, regulations, directions, forms, blanks, stamps, and licenses, and distributing the same, or any part thereof, and all other matters pertaining to the assessment and collection of the duties, stamp duties, licenses, and taxes which may be necessary to carry this act into effect, and with the general superintendence of his office, as aforesaid, and shall have authority, and hereby is authorized and required, to provide proper and sufficient stamps or dies for expressing and denoting the several stamp duties, or the amount thereof in the case of percentage duties, imposed by this act, and to alter and renew or replace such stamps from time to time, as occasion shall require; and the Secretary of the Treasury may assign to the office of the Commissioner of Internal Revenue such number of clerks as he may deem necessary, or the exigencies of the public service may require, and the privilege of franking all letters and documents pertaining to the duties of his office, and of receiving free of postage all such letters and documents, is hereby extended to said commissioner.

Office of Commissioner of Internal Revenue created.

Salary.
Duties.

Powers.

Clerks.
To have franking privilege.

GENERAL PROVISIONS.

Sec. 2. *And be it further enacted,* That, for the purpose of assessing, levying, and collecting the duties or taxes hereinafter prescribed by this act, the President of the United States be, and he is hereby, authorized to divide, respectively, the States and Territories of the United States and the District of Columbia into convenient collection districts, and to nominate, and, by and with the advice and consent of the Senate, to appoint an assessor and a collector for each such district, who shall be residents within the

Collection districts to be designated.

Assessor and collector appointed for each district.

EXCISE TAX.

same: *Provided,* That any of said States and Territories and the District of Columbia may, if the President shall deem it proper,

Limitation of the number of districts be erected into and included in one district: *Provided,* That the number of districts in any State shall not exceed the number of representatives to which such State shall be entitled in the present Congress, except in such States as are entitled to an increased representation in the Thirty-Eighth Congress, in which States the number of districts shall not exceed the number of representatives to which any such State may be so entitled: *And provided, fur-*

Additional districts in California. *ther,* That in the State of California the President may establish a number of districts not exceeding the number of senators and representatives to which said State is entitled in the present Congress.

Assessors to divide their districts into assessment districts and appoint assistant assessors. SEC. 3. *And be it further enacted,* That each of the assessors shall divide his district into a convenient number of assessment districts, subject to such regulations and limitations as may be imposed by the Commissioner of Internal Revenue, within each of which he shall appoint one assistant assessor, who shall be resident therein; and each assessor and assistant assessor so appointed, and accepting the appointment, shall, before he enters on the duties of his appointment, take and subscribe, before some competent magistrate, or some collector, to be appointed by virtue of this act, (who is hereby empowered to administer the same,) the

Oath of assessor and assistant assessor. following oath or affirmation, to wit: "I, A B, do swear, or affirm, (as the case may be,) that I will bear true faith and allegiance to the United States of America, and will support the Constitution thereof, and that I will, to the best of my knowledge, skill, and judgment, diligently and faithfully execute the office and duties of assessor for, (naming the assessment district,) without favor or partiality, and that I will do equal right and justice in every case

Certificate of. in which I shall act as assessor." And a certificate of such oath or affirmation shall be delivered to the collector of the district for which such assessor or assistant assessor shall be appointed. And every assessor or assistant assessor acting in the said office without

Penalty for not taking oath. having taken the said oath or affirmation shall forfeit and pay one hundred dollars, one moiety thereof to the use of the United States, and the other moiety thereof to him who shall first sue for the same, with costs of suit.

Collector to give bond. SEC. 4. *And be it further enacted,* That before any such collector shall enter upon the duties of his office, he shall execute a bond for such amount as shall be prescribed by the Commissioner of Internal Revenue, under the direction of the Secretary of the

Five sureties Treasury, with not less than five sureties to be approved as sufficient by the Solicitor of the Treasury, containing the condition that said collector shall faithfully perform the duties of his office according to law, and shall justly and faithfully account for and pay over to the United States, in compliance with the order or

Its condition. regulations of the Secretary of the Treasury, all public moneys which may come into his hands or possession; which bond shall be filed in the office of the First Comptroller of the Treasury. And such collectors shall, from time to time, renew, strengthen, and increase their official bond, as the Secretary of the Treasury may direct.

Collector to appoint deputy collectors. SEC. 5. *And be it further enacted,* That each collector shall be authorized to appoint, by an instrument of writing under his hand,

How. as many deputies as he may think proper, to be by him compen-

Number. sated for their services, and also to revoke any such appointment, giving such notice thereof as the Commissioner of Internal Revenue shall prescribe; and may require bonds or other securities and accept the same from such deputy; and each such deputy shall have the like authority, in every respect, to collect the duties and taxes levied or assessed within the portion of the district assigned to him which is by this act vested in the collector himself; but each collector shall, in every respect, be responsible both to the United States and to individuals, as the case may be, for all moneys collected, and for every act done as deputy collector by any of his deputies whilst acting as such, and for every omission of duty: *Provided,* That nothing herein contained shall prevent any collector from collecting himself the whole or any part of the duties and taxes so assessed and payable in his district. *Bonds of deputies. Powers. Collector responsible for deputies. Collector may collect the taxes.*

SEC. 6. *And be it further enacted,* That it shall be the duty of any person or persons, partnerships, firms, associations, or corporations, made liable to any duty, license, stamp, or tax imposed by this act, when not otherwise and differently provided for, on or before the first day of August, eighteen hundred and sixty-two, and on or before the first Monday of May in each year thereafter, and in all other cases before the day of levy, to make a list or return to the assistant assessor of the district where located, of the amount of annual income, the articles or objects charged with a special duty or tax, the quantity of goods, wares, and merchandise made or sold, and charged with a specific or ad valorem duty or tax, the several rates and aggregate amount according to the respective provisions of this act, and according to the forms and regulations to be prescribed by the Commissioner of Internal Revenue, under the direction of the Secretary of the Treasury, for which such person or persons, partnerships, firms, associations, or corporations are liable to be assessed under and by virtue of the provisions of this act. *Citizens, Partners, Firms, Associations, Corporations to make lists.*

SEC. 7. *And be it further enacted,* That the instructions, regulations, and directions, as hereinbefore mentioned, shall be binding on each assessor and his assistants, and on each collector and his deputies, in the performance of the duties enjoined by or under this act; pursuant to which instructions the said assessors shall, on the first day of August, eighteen hundred and sixty-two, and on the first Monday of May in each succeeding year, and from time to time thereafter, in accordance with this act, direct and cause the several assistant assessors to proceed through every part of their respective districts, and inquire after and concerning all persons being within the assessment districts where they respectively reside, owning, possessing, or having the care or management of any property, goods, wares, and merchandise, articles or objects liable to pay any duty, stamp, or tax, including all persons liable to pay a license duty, under the provisions of this act, (by reference as well to any lists of assessment or collection taken under the laws of the respective States, as to any other records or documents, and by all other lawful ways and means, especially to the written list, schedule, or return required to be made out and delivered to the assistant assessor by all persons owning, possessing, or having the care or management of any property, as aforesaid, liable to duty or taxation,) and to value and enumerate the said objects of taxation, respectively, in the manner prescribed by this act, and in conformity with the regulations and instructions before mentioned. *Duty of assessors and assistant assessors. Assessments, when to be made. Who liable to be taxed. How assessors may find out.*

4   EXCISE TAX.

Duty of assessors in cases of failure of persons to make list.

SEC. 8. *And be it further enacted*, That if any person owning, possessing, or having the care or management of property, goods, wares, and merchandise, articles or objects liable to pay any duty, tax, or license, shall fail to make and exhibit a written list when required, as aforesaid, and shall consent to disclose the particulars of any and all the property, goods, wares, and merchandise, articles and objects liable to pay any duty or tax, or any business or occupation liable to pay any license, as aforesaid, then, and in that case, it shall be the duty of the officer to make such list, which, being distinctly read, consented to, and signed, by the person so owning, possessing, or having the care and management as aforesaid, shall be received as the list of such person.

Penalty for delivering fraudulent list.

SEC. 9. *And be it further enacted*, That if any such person shall deliver or disclose to any assessor or assistant assessor appointed in pursuance of this act, and requiring a list or lists, as aforesaid, any false or fraudulent list or statement, with intent to defeat or evade the valuation or enumeration hereby intended to be made, such person so offending, and being thereof convicted on indictment found therefor in any circuit or district court of the United States held in the district in which such offence may be committed, shall

Fine and costs.

be fined in a sum not exceeding five hundred dollars, at the discretion of the court, and shall pay all costs and charges of prosecution; and the valuation and enumeration required by this act shall, in all such cases, and in all cases of under valuation or under statement in such lists or statements, be made, as aforesaid, upon lists, according to the form prescribed, to be made out by the as-

Duty of assessors when list fraudulent or undervalued.

sessors and assistant assessors, respectively; which lists the said assessors and assistant assessors are hereby authorized and required to make according to the best information they can obtain, and for the purpose of making which they are hereby authorized to enter into and upon all and singular the premises respectively; and from

No appeal.

the valuation and enumeration so made there shall be no appeal.

Assistant assessors to notify absent persons.

SEC. 10. *And be it further enacted*, That in case any person shall be absent from his or her place of residence at the time an assistant assessor shall call to receive the list of such person, it shall be the duty of such assistant assessor to leave at the place of residence of such person, with some person of suitable age and discretion, if such be present, otherwise to deposit in the nearest post

Duty of absent persons.

office a written note or memorandum, addressed to such person, requiring him or her to present to such assessor the list or lists required by this act within ten days from the date of such note or memorandum.

Penalty for neglecting or refusing to give list when required.

SEC. 11. *And be it further enacted*, That if any person, on being notified or required, as aforesaid, shall refuse or neglect to give such list or lists within the time required, as aforesaid, it shall

Assessor's duty.

be the duty of the assessor for the assessment district within which such person shall reside, and he is hereby authorized and required,

Enter premises.

to enter into and upon the premises, if it be necessary, of such persons so refusing or neglecting, and to make, according to the best information which he can obtain, and on his own view and information, such lists of property, goods, wares, and merchandise, and all articles or objects liable to duty or taxation, owned or possessed, or under the care or management of such person, as are required by this act, including the amount, if any, due for license;

Sickness an excuse. 50 per cent. to be added.

and in case of refusal or neglect to make such lists, except in cases of sickness, the assessors shall thereupon add fifty per centum to the amount of the items thereof; and the lists, so made an' ub-

EXCISE TAX. 5

scribed by such assessor, shall be taken and reputed as good and sufficient lists of the persons and property for which such person is to be taxed for the purposes of this act; and the person so failing or neglecting, unless in case of sickness or failure to receive the notice, shall, moreover, forfeit and pay the sum of one hundred dollars, except where otherwise provided for, to be recovered for the use of the United States, with costs of suit. *Assessor's list sufficient.*

Fine $100.

SEC. 12. *And be it further enacted,* That whenever there shall be in any assessment district any property, goods, wares, and merchandise, articles, or objects, not owned or possessed by, or under the care or management of, any person or persons within such district, and liable to be taxed as aforesaid, and no list of which shall have been transmitted to the assistant assessor in the manner provided by this act, it shall be the duty of the assistant assessor for such district, and he is hereby authorized and required, to enter into and upon the premises where such property is situated, and take such view thereof as may be necessary, and to make lists of the same, according to the form prescribed, which lists, being subscribed by the said assessor, shall be taken and reputed as good and sufficient lists of such property, goods, wares, and merchandise, articles, or objects, as aforesaid, under and for the purposes of this act. *Assistant assessors to make list of goods, &c., of non-residents.*

Such lists good.

SEC. 13. *And be it further enacted,* That the owners, possessors, or persons having the care or management of property, goods, wares, and merchandise, articles or objects, not lying or being within the assessment district in which they reside, shall be permitted to make out and deliver the lists thereof required by this act (provided the assessment district in which the said objects of duty or taxation are situated is therein distinctly stated) at the time and in the manner prescribed to the assistant assessor of the assessment district wherein such persons reside. And it shall be the duty of the assistant assessor who receives any such list to transmit the same to the assistant assessor where such objects of taxation are situate, who shall examine such list; and if he approves the same, he shall return it to the assistant assessor from whom he received it, with his approval thereof; and if he fails to approve the same, he shall make such alterations therein as he may deem to be just and proper, and shall then return the said list, with such alterations therein or additions thereto, to the assistant assessor from whom he received the said list; and the assistant assessor, where the person liable to pay such tax resides, shall proceed in making the assessment of the tax upon the list by him so received, in all respects as if the said list had been made out by himself. *Persons to make lists of property owned in other districts.*

Duty of assistant assessors relative to said lists.

To approve or alter.

SEC. 14. *And be it further enacted,* That the lists aforesaid shall, where not otherwise specially provided for, be taken with reference to the day fixed for that purpose by this act, as aforesaid, and where duties accrue at other and different times, the lists shall be taken with reference to the time when said duties become due; and the assistant assessors, respectively, after collecting the said lists, shall proceed to arrange the same, and to make two general lists—the first of which shall exhibit, in alphabetical order, the names of all persons liable to pay any duty, tax, or license under this act residing within the assessment district, together with the value and assessment, or enumeration, as the case may require, of the objects liable to duty or taxation within such district for which each such person is liable, or for which *Lists, how taken.*

Assistant assessors to make two general lists.

List of persons liable to pay tax and amount.

EXCISE TAX.

List of non-residents owning property in the district.

any firm, company, or corporation is liable, with the amount of duty or tax payable thereon; and the second list shall exhibit, in alphabetical order, the names of all persons residing out of the collection district, owners of property within the district, together with the value and assessment or enumeration thereof, as the case may be, with the amount of duty or tax payable thereon as aforesaid. The forms of the said general list shall be devised and prescribed by the assessor, under the direction of the Commissioner of Internal Revenue, and lists taken according to such forms shall be

Lists to be sent to the assessor in thirty days.

made out by the assistant assessors and delivered to the assessor within thirty days after the day fixed by this act as aforesaid, requiring lists from individuals; or where duties, licenses, or taxes accrue at other and different times, the lists shall be delivered from time to time as they become due. And if any assistant assessor shall fail to perform any duty assigned by this act within the time prescribed by his precept, warrant, or other legal instructions, not being prevented therefrom by sickness, or other unavoidable

Penalty for neglect of duty.

accident, every such assistant assessor shall be discharged from office, and shall, moreover, forfeit and pay two hundred dollars, to be recovered for the use of the United States, with costs of suit.

Assessors to advertise where lists may be examined.

SEC. 15. *And be it further enacted,* That the assessors for each collection district shall, by advertisement in some public newspaper published in each county within said district, if any such there be, and by written or printed notifications, to be posted up in at least four public places within each assessment district, advertise all persons concerned of the time and place within said county when and where the lists, valuations, and enumerations made and taken

Lists open for 15 days.

within said county may be examined; and said lists shall remain open for examination for the space of fifteen days after notice

Time and place for hearing appeals.

shall have been given as aforesaid. And said notifications shall also stat when and where within said county, after the expiration of said fifteen days, appeals will be received and determined relative to any erroneous or excessive valuations or enumerations by the assistant assessors. And it shall be the duty of the assessor for each collection district, at the time fixed for hearing such appeal as aforesaid, to submit the proceedings of the assistant

Assessors to submit lists.

assessors, and the lists taken and returned as aforesaid, to the inspection of any and all persons who may apply for that purpose. And the said assessor for each collection district is hereby authorized, at any time within fifteen days from and after the expiration of the time allowed for notification as aforesaid, to hear and deter-

To determine appeals.

mine, in a summary way, according to law and right, upon any and all appeals which may be exhibited against the proceedings

Proviso.

of the said assistant assessors: *Provided,* That the question to be determined by the assessor, on an appeal respecting the valuation or enumeration of property, or objects liable to duty or taxation, shall be, whether the valuation complained of be or be not in a just relation or proportion to other valuations in the same assessment district, and whether the enumeration be or be not cor-

Appeals to be in writing.

rect. And all appeals to the assessor, as aforesaid, shall be made in writing, and shall specify the particular cause, matter, or thing respecting which a decision is requested; and shall, moreover, state the ground or principle of inequality or error complained of.

Assessor to re-examine & equalize valuations.

And the assessor shall have power to re-examine and equalize the valuations as shall appear just and equitable; but no valuation or enumeration shall be increased without a previous notice, of at least

Notice on an increase of valuation.

five days, to the party interested, to appear and object to the same,

EXCISE TAX. 7

if he judge proper; which notice shall be given by a note in writing, to be left at the dwelling-house, office, or place of business of the party by such assessor or an assistant assessor.

SEC. 16. *And be it further enacted,* That the said assessors of each collection district, respectively, shall, immediately after the expiration of the time for hearing appeals, and, from time to time, as duties, taxes, or licenses become liable to be assessed, make out lists containing the sums payable according to the provisions of this act upon every object of duty or taxation in and for each collection district, which lists shall contain the name of each person residing within the said district, owning or having the care or superintendence of property lying within the said district which is liable to the said tax, or engaged in any business or pursuit requiring a license, when such person or persons are known, together with the sums payable by each; and where there is any property within any collection district liable to the payment of the said duty or tax, not owned or occupied by or under the superintendence of any person resident therein, there shall be a separate list of such property, specifying the sum payable, and the names of the respective proprietors, where known. And the assistant assessor making out any such separate list shall transmit therefrom to the assistant assessor, where the persons liable to pay such tax reside or shall have their principal place of business, copies of the list of property held by persons so liable to pay such tax, to the end that the taxes assessed under the provisions of this act may be paid within the collection district where the persons liable to pay the same reside, or may have their principal place of business. And in all other cases the said assessor shall furnish to the collectors of the several collection districts, respectively, within ten days after the time of hearing appeals, and from time to time thereafter as required, a certified copy of such list or lists for their proper collection districts; and in default of performance of the duties enjoined upon assessors by this section they shall severally and individually forfeit and pay the sum of five hundred dollars to the use of the United States, and, moreover, shall forfeit their compensation as assessors: *Provided,* That it shall be in the power of the Commissioner of Internal Revenue to exonerate any assessor as aforesaid from such forfeitures, in whole or in part, as to him shall appear just and equitable.

Assessors to make lists of persons liable to taxation, and amount payable.

Separate list of non-residents.

Assistant assessors to transmit the list to district where persons reside.

All taxes to be paid within the district where persons reside.

Lists for collectors.

Penalty for neglect of duty.

Proviso.

SEC. 17. *And be it further enacted,* That there shall be allowed and paid to the several assessors and assistant assessors, for their services under this act—to each assessor three dollars per day for every day employed in making the necessary arrangements and giving the necessary instructions to the assistant assessors for the valuation; and five dollars per day for every day employed in hearing appeals, revising valuations, and making out lists agreeably to the provisions of this act; and one dollar for every hundred taxable persons contained in the tax list, as delivered by him to said collectors, and forwarded to the Commissioner of Internal Revenue; to each assistant assessor three dollars for every day actually employed in collecting lists and making valuations, the number of days necessary for that purpose to be certified by the assessor and approved by the Commissioner of Internal Revenue; and one dollar for every hundred taxable persons contained in the tax list, as completed and delivered by him to the assessor. And the said assessors and assistant assessors, respectively, shall also be allowed their necessary and reasonable charges for stationery

Compensation of assessors.

Compensation of assistant assessors.

Stationery to be allowed.

and blank books used in the execution of their duties, and the compensation herein specified shall be in full for all expenses not otherwise particularly authorized: *Provided,* The Secretary of the Treasury shall be, and he is hereby, authorized to fix such additional rates of compensation to be made to assessors and assistant assessors in the States of California and Oregon and the Territories as may appear to him to be just and equitable, in consequence of the greater cost of living and travelling in those States and Territories, and as may, in his judgment, be necessary to secure the services of competent and efficient men, provided the rates of compensation thus allowed shall not exceed the rates paid to similar officers in such States and Territories respectively.

Additional rates of compensation may be allowed in California, Oregon, and the Territories.

In cases where a collection district embraces more than a single congressional district the Secretary of the Treasury may allow the assessor such compensation as he may deem necessary.

Other cases.

SEC. 18. *And be it further enacted,* That each collector, on receiving a list, as aforesaid, and from time to time as such lists may be received from the said assessors, respectively, shall subscribe three receipts; one of which shall be given on a full and correct copy of such list, which list shall be delivered by him to, and shall remain with, the assessor of his collection district, and shall be open to the inspection of any person who may apply to inspect the same; and the other two receipts shall be given on aggregate statements of the lists aforesaid, exhibiting the gross amount of taxes to be collected in his collection district, one of which aggregate statements and receipts shall be transmitted to the Commissioner of Internal Revenue, and the other to the First Comptroller of the Treasury; and all lists received from time to time, as aforesaid, shall be in like form and manner transmitted as aforesaid.

Duty of collector on receipt of lists from assistant assessors.

To give three receipts.

SEC. 19. *And be it further enacted,* That each of said collectors shall, within ten days after receiving his annual collection list from the assessors, respectively, as aforesaid, give notice, by advertisement published in each county in his collection district, in one newspaper printed in such county, if any such there be, and by notifications to be posted up in at least four public places in each county in his collection district, that the said duties have become due and payable, and state the time and place within said county at which he will attend to receive the same, which time shall not be less than ten days after such notification; and all persons who shall neglect to pay the duties and taxes so as aforesaid assessed upon them to the collector within the time specified, shall be liable to pay ten per centum additional upon the amount thereof, the fact of which liability shall be stated in the advertisement and notifications aforesaid. And with regard to all persons who shall neglect to pay as aforesaid, it shall be the duty of the collector, in person or by deputy, within twenty days after such neglect, to make a demand personally, or at the dwellings or usual places of business of such persons, if any they have, for payment of said duties or taxes, with the ten per centum additional aforesaid. And with respect to all such duties or taxes as are not included in the annual lists aforesaid, and all taxes and duties the collection of which is not otherwise provided for in this act, it shall be the duty of each collector, in person or by deputy, to demand payment thereof, in manner aforesaid, within ten days from and after receiving the list thereof from the assessor; and if the annual and other duties shall not be paid within ten days from and

Collectors to advertise when and where taxes are payable.

Taxes, when payable.

Penalty for neglect to pay taxes.

Collector or his deputy to demand payment personally within twenty days after neglect.

10 per cent. additional.

Other taxes, when payable.

EXCISE TAX.

after such demand therefor, it shall be lawful for such collector or his deputies to proceed to collect the said duties or taxes, with ten per centum additional thereto, as aforesaid, by distraint and sale of the goods, chattels, or effects of the persons delinquent as aforesaid. And in case of such distraint it shall be the duty of the officer charged with the collection to make, or cause to be made, an account of the goods or chattels which may be distrained, a copy of which, signed by the officer making such distraint, shall be left with the owner or possessor of such goods, chattels, or effects, or at his or her dwelling, with some person of suitable age and discretion, with a note of the sum demanded, and the time and place of sale; and the said officer shall forthwith cause a notification to be published in some newspaper within the county wherein said distraint is made, if there is a newspaper published in said county, or to be publicly posted up at the post office, if there be one within five miles, nearest to the residence of the person whose property shall be distrained, and in not less than two other public places, which notice shall specify the articles distrained, and the time and place for the sale thereof, which time shall not be less than ten nor more than twenty days from the date of such notification, and the place proposed for sale not more than five miles distant from the place of making such distraint: *Provided,* That in any case of distraint for the payment of the duties or taxes aforesaid the goods, chattels, or effects so distrained shall and may be restored to the owner or possessor, if prior to the sale payment of the amount due or tender thereof shall be made to the proper officer charged with the collection of the full amount demanded, together with such fee for levying, and such sum for the necessary and reasonable expense of removing, advertising, and keeping the goods, chattels, or effects so distrained as may be prescribed by the Commissioner of Internal Revenue; but in case of non-payment or tender, as aforesaid, the said officers shall proceed to sell the said goods, chattels, or effects at public auction, and shall and may retain from the proceeds of such sale the amount demandable for the use of the United States, with the necessary and reasonable expenses of distraint and sale, and a commission of five per centum thereon for his own use, rendering the overplus, if any there be, to the person whose goods, chattels, or effects shall have been distrained: *Provided,* That there shall be exempt from distraint the tools or implements of a trade or profession, one cow, arms, and provisions, and household furniture kept for use, and apparel necessary for a family.

SEC. 20. *And be it further enacted,* That in all cases where the property liable to distraint for duties or taxes under this act may not be divisible, so as to enable the collector by a sale of part thereof to raise the whole amount of the tax, with all costs, charges, and commissions, the whole of such property shall be sold, and the surplus of the proceeds of the sale, after satisfying the duty or tax, costs, and charges, shall be paid to the owner of the property, or his, her, or their legal representatives, or if he, she, or they cannot be found, or refuse to receive the same, then such surplus shall be deposited in the treasury of the United States, to be there held for the use of the owner, or his, her, or their legal representatives, until he, she, or they shall make application therefor to the Secretary of the Treasury, who, upon such application, shall, by warrant on the treasury, cause the same to be paid to the applicant. And if the property advertised for

[margin notes: Collector or his deputies to collect by distraint. Make list of property distrained. Notice to owner or agent. Advertise. Ten days public notice of sale. Property to be restored on payment of tax and fees. Sale of property and disposition of surplus proceeds. Property exempt from distraint. Property not divisible, all to be sold. Disposal of surplus.]

10   EXCISE TAX.

Property not sold for the tax and fees to be purchased for United States.
sale as aforesaid cannot be sold for the amount of the duty or tax due thereon, with the costs and charges, the collector shall purchase the same in behalf of the United States for an amount not exceeding the said tax or duty, with the costs and charges thereon. And all property so purchased may be sold by said collector under such regulations as may be prescribed by the Commissioner of Internal Revenue. And the collector shall render a distinct account of all charges incurred in the sale of such property, and shall pay into the treasury the surplus, if any there be, after defraying the charges.

Sale of real estate.
SEC. 21. *And be it further enacted,* That in any case where goods, chattels, or effects sufficient to satisfy the duties imposed by this act upon any person liable to pay the same shall not be found by the collector or deputy collector, whose duty it may be to collect the same, he is hereby authorized to collect the same by seizure and sale of real estate; and the officer making such

Notice to be given of time and place of sale to the owner.
seizure and sale shall give notice to the person whose estate is proposed to be sold, by giving him in hand, or leaving at his last and usual place of abode, if he has any such within the collection district where said estate is situated, a notice, in writing, stating what particular estate is proposed to be sold, describing the same with reasonable certainty, and the time when and place where said officer proposes to sell the same; which time shall not be less

Time of sale.
than ten nor more than twenty days from the time of giving said notice; and the said officer shall also cause a notification to the same effect to be published in some newspaper within the county where such seizure is made, if any such there be, and shall also

Advertise.
cause a like notice to be posted up at the post office nearest to the place of residence of the person whose estate shall be so seized, and in two other public places within the county; and the place of said sale shall not be more than five miles distant from the estate seized. At the time and place appointed, the officer making such seizure shall proceed to sell the said estate at public auction, offering the same at a minimum price, including the amount of duties with the ten per centum additional thereon, and all charges for advertising, and an officer's fee of ten dollars. And if no person offers for said estate the amount of said minimum, the officer

May be purchased for the United States.
shall declare the same to be purchased by him for the United States, and shall deposit with the district attorney of the United States a deed thereof, as hereinafter specified and provided; otherwise the same shall be declared to be sold to the highest bidder.

Sale may be adjourned five days.
And said sale may be adjourned by said officer for a period not exceeding five days, if he shall think it advisable so to do. If the amount bid shall not be then and there paid, the officer shall forthwith proceed to again sell said estate in the same manner. If the amount bid shall be then and there paid, the officer shall give his receipt therefor, if requested, and within five days thereafter

Deed to be made according to State laws.
he shall make out a deed of the estate so sold to the purchaser thereof, and execute the same in his official capacity, in the manner prescribed by the laws of the State in which said estate may [be]

Deed to recite facts of seizure and sale.
situated, in which said deed shall be recited the fact of said seizure and sale, with the cause thereof, the amount of duty for which said sale was made, and of all charges and fees, and the amount paid by the purchaser, and all his acts and doings in relation to said seizure and sale, and shall have the same ready for delivery to said purchaser, and shall deliver the same accordingly, upon request therefor. And said deed shall be prima facie evi-

dence of the truth of the facts stated therein; and if the proceedings of the officer as set forth have been substantially in pursuance of the provisions of this act, shall be considered and operate as a conveyance to the purchaser of the title to said estate, but shall not affect the rights of third persons acquired previously to the claim of the United States under this act. The surplus, if any, arising from such sale shall be disposed of as provided in this act for like cases arising upon sales of personal property. And any person whose estate may be seized for duties, as aforesaid, shall have the same right to pay or tender the amount due, with all proper charges thereon, prior to the sale thereof, and thereupon to relieve his said estate from sale, as aforesaid, as is provided in this act for personal property similarly situated. And any collector or deputy collector may, for the collection of duties imposed upon any person by this act, and committed to him for collection, seize and sell the lands of such person situated in any other collection district within the State in which said officer resides; and his proceedings in relation thereto shall have the same effect as if the same were had in his proper collection district; and the owners, their heirs, executors, or administrators, or any person having an interest therein, or any person on their behalf, shall have liberty to redeem the land sold as aforesaid, within one year from and after recording the said deed, upon payment to the purchaser, or in case he cannot be found in the county where the lands are situate, to the collector for the use of the purchaser, his heirs, or assigns, of the amount paid by the purchaser, with interest on the same at the rate of twenty per centum per annum. And it shall be the duty of every collector to keep a record of all sales of land made in his collection district, whether by himself or his deputies, in which shall be set forth the tax for which any such sale was made, the dates of seizure and sale, the name of the party assessed, and all proceedings in making said sale, the amount of fees and expenses, the name of the purchaser, and the date of the deed; which record shall be certified by the officer making the sale. And it shall be the duty of any deputy making sale, as aforesaid, to return a statement of all his proceedings to the collector, and to certify the record thereof. And in case of the death or removal of the collector, or the expiration of his term of office from any other cause, said record shall be deposited in the office of the clerk of the district court of the United States for the district within which the said collector resided; and a copy of every such record, certified by the collector, or by the clerk, as the case may require, shall be evidence in any court of the truth of the facts therein stated. And when any lands sold, as aforesaid, shall be redeemed as hereinbefore provided, the collector or clerk, as the case may be, shall make an entry of the fact upon the record aforesaid, and the said entry shall be evidence of such redemption. And the claim of the government to lands sold under and by virtue of the foregoing provisions shall be held to have accrued at the time of seizure thereof.

SEC. 22. *And be it further enacted,* That if any collector shall find upon any lists of taxes returned to him for collection property lying within his district which is charged with any specific or ad valorem tax or duty, but which is not owned, occupied, or superintended by some person known to such collector to reside or to have some place of business within the United States, such collector shall forthwith take such property into his custody, and

12 EXCISE TAX.

Advertise the tax for 30 days. shall advertise the same, and the tax charged upon the same, in some newspaper published in his district, if any shall be published therein, otherwise in some newspaper in an adjoining district, for the space of thirty days; and if the taxes thereon, with all charges for advertising, shall not be paid within said thirty days, such collector shall proceed to sell the same, or so much as is necessary, *Sale.* in the manner provided for the sale of other goods distrained for the non-payment of taxes, and out of the proceeds shall satisfy all taxes charged upon such property, with the costs of advertising and selling the same. And like proceedings to those provided in the preceding section for the purchase and resale of property which cannot be sold for the amount of duty or tax due thereon shall be had with regard to property sold under the provisions of *Surplus.* this section. And any surplus arising from any sale herein provided for shall be paid into the treasury, for the benefit of the owner of the property. And the Secretary of the Treasury is authorized, in any case where money shall be paid into the treasury for the benefit of any owner of property sold as aforesaid, *Payment of surplus, on proof.* to repay the same, on proper proof being furnished that the person applying therefor is entitled to receive the same.

Collectors to transmit monthly statements of collections. SEC. 23. *And be it further enacted,* That the several collectors shall, at the expiration of each and every month, after they shall, respectively, commence their collections, transmit to the Commissioner of Internal Revenue a statement of the collections made by them, respectively, within the month, and pay over monthly, or at such time or times as may be required by the Commissioner of Internal Revenue, the moneys by them respectively collected within the said term, and at such places as may be designated and required by the Commissioner of Internal Revenue; and each of the said collectors shall complete the collection of all sums annually assigned to him for collection, as aforesaid, shall pay over the same into the treasury, and shall render his final account to the Treasury Department as often as he may be required, and *Collections to be completed in six months.* within six months from and after the day when he shall have received the collection lists from the said assessors or assistant assessors, as aforesaid. And the Secretary of the Treasury is *Depositories.* authorized to designate one or more depositories in each State, for the deposit and safe-keeping of the moneys collected by virtue of this act; and the receipt of the proper officer of such depository to a collector for the money deposited by him shall be a sufficient voucher for such collector in the settlement of his accounts at the Treasury Department; and the Commissioner of Internal Revenue may, under the direction of the Secretary of the Treasury, prescribe such regulations with reference to such deposits as he may deem necessary.

Collectors charged with amount of taxes receipted for SEC. 24. *And be it further enacted,* That each collector shall be charged with the whole amount of taxes by him receipted, whether contained in lists delivered to him by the assessors, respectively, or delivered or transmitted to him by assistant assessors from time to time, or by other collectors; and shall be *Credited with amount sent to other collectors, and taxes of absconding persons.* credited with the amount of duties or taxes contained in the lists transmitted in the manner above provided to other collectors, and by them receipted as aforesaid; and also for the duties or taxes of such persons as may have absconded, or become insolvent, prior to the day when the duty or tax ought, according to the provisions of this act, to have been collected: *Provided,* That it shall be proved to the satisfaction of the First Comptroller of

EXCISE TAX.

the Treasury that due diligence was used by the collector, and that no property was left from which the duty or tax could have been recovered. And each collector shall also be credited with the amount of all property purchased by him for the use of the United States, provided he shall faithfully account for, and pay over, the proceeds thereof upon a resale of the same as required by this act. *(Credited with amount of property purchased for United States.)*

SEC. 25. *And be it further enacted,* That if any collector shall fail either to collect or to render his account, or to pay over in the manner or within the times hereinbefore provided, it shall be the duty of the First Comptroller of the Treasury, and he is hereby authorized and required, immediately after such delinquency, to report the same to the Solicitor of the Treasury, who shall issue a warrant of distress against such delinquent collector and his sureties, directed to the marshal of the district, therein expressing the amount of the taxes with which the said collector is chargeable, and the sums, if any, which have been paid. And the said marshal shall, himself, or by his deputy, immediately proceed to levy and collect the sum which may remain due, by distress and sale of the goods and chattels, or any personal effects of the delinquent collector, giving at least five days' notice of the time and place of sale, in the manner provided by law for advertising sales of personal property on execution in the State wherein such collector resides; and, furthermore, if such goods, chattels, and effects cannot be found sufficient to satisfy the said warrant, the said marshal or his deputy shall and may proceed to levy and collect the sum which remains due, by distress and sale of the goods and chattels, or any personal effects, of the surety or sureties of the delinquent collector, giving notice as hereinbefore provided. And the bill of sale of the officer of any goods, chattels, or other personal property, distrained and sold as aforesaid, shall be conclusive evidence of title to the purchaser, and prima facie evidence of the right of the officer to make such sale, and of the correctness of his proceedings in selling the same. And for want of goods and chattels, or other personal effects of such collector or his sureties, sufficient to satisfy any warrant of distress, issued pursuant to the preceding section of this act, the lands and real estate of such collector and his sureties, or so much thereof as may be necessary for satisfying the said warrant, after being advertised for at least three weeks in not less than three public places in the collection district, and in one newspaper printed in the county or district, if any there be, prior to the proposed time of sale, may and shall be sold at public auction by the marshal or his deputy, who, upon such sale, shall, as such marshal or deputy marshal, make and deliver to the purchaser of the premises so sold a deed of conveyance thereof, to be executed and acknowledged in the manner and form prescribed by the laws of the State in which said lands are situated, which said deed so made shall invest the purchaser with all the title and interest of the defendant or defendants named in said warrant existing at the time of seizure thereof. And all moneys that may remain of the proceeds of such sale after satisfying the said warrant of distress, and paying the reasonable costs and charges of sale, shall be returned to the proprietor of the lands or real estate sold as aforesaid. *(Penalty for collectors failing to account for the taxes. Marshal to levy on the property of collector or sureties. May levy on property of surety. Bill of sale conclusive evidence. Levy on real estate. Notice of sale to be given three weeks. Marshal to give deed to purchaser. Disposal of surplus.)*

SEC. 26. *And be it further enacted,* That each and every collector, or his deputy, who shall exercise or be guilty of any extor- *(Penalty for extortion or oppression by collector.)*

Damages, how recovered.

tion or wilful oppression, under color of this act, or shall knowingly demand other or greater sums than shall be authorized by this act, shall be liable to pay a sum not exceeding double the amount of damages accruing to the party injured, to be recovered by and for the use of the party injured, with costs of suit, and shall be dismissed from office, and be disqualified from holding such office thereafter; and each and every collector, or his deputies, shall give receipts for all sums by them collected and retained in pursuance of this act.

Collectors, &c., may inspect breweries and distilleries, &c., during daytime.

SEC. 27. *And be it further enacted,* That a collector or deputy collector, assessor or assistant assessor, shall be authorized to enter, in the daytime, any brewery, distillery, manufactory, building, or place where any property, articles, or objects, subject to duty or taxation under the provisions of this act, are made, produced, or kept, within his district, so far as it may be necessary for the purpose of examining said property, articles, or objects, or inspecting the accounts required by this act from time to time to be made. And every owner of such brewery, distillery, manufactory, building, or place, or persons having the agency or superintendence of the same, who shall refuse to admit such officer, or to suffer him to examine said property, articles, or objects, or to inspect said accounts, shall, for every such refusal, forfeit and pay the sum of five hundred dollars.

Penalty for refusing to admit such officer.

Penalty for obstructing collectors and rescuing property.

SEC. 28. *And be it further enacted,* That if any person shall forcibly obstruct or hinder a collector or deputy collector in the execution of this act, or of any power and authority hereby vested in him, or shall forcibly rescue, or cause to be rescued, any property, articles, or objects, after the same shall have been seized by him, or shall attempt or endeavor so to do, the person so offending shall, for every such offence, forfeit and pay the sum of five hundred dollars.

In case of sickness of collector his duties may devolve on a deputy.

SEC. 29. *And be it further enacted,* That in case of the sickness or temporary disability of a collector to discharge such of his duties as cannot under existing laws be discharged by a deputy, they may be devolved by him upon one of his deputies: *Provided,* That information thereof be immediately communicated to the Secretary of the Treasury, and shall not be disapproved by him: *And provided, further,* That the responsibility of the collector or his sureties to the United States shall not be affected or impaired thereby.

Proviso.

Sureties still held.

Oldest deputy collector to act in case of disability of collector.

SEC. 30. *And be it further enacted,* That in case a collector shall die, resign, or be removed, the deputies of such collector shall continue to act until their successors are appointed; and the deputy of such collector longest in service at the time immediately preceding may and shall, until a successor shall be appointed, discharge all the duties of said collector; and for the official acts and defaults of such deputy a remedy shall be had on the official bond of the collector, as in other cases; and of two or more deputy collectors, appointed on the same day, the one residing nearest the residence of the collector at the time of his death, resignation, or removal, shall in like manner discharge the said duties until the appointment of a successor; and any bond or security taken of such deputy by such collector, pursuant to the fifth section of this act, shall be available to his heirs or representatives to indemnify them for loss or damage accruing from any act of the proper deputy so continuing or so succeeding to the duties of such collector.

Bond of collector still in force.

Bond of deputy to be available to heirs, &c., for loss.

EXCISE TAX.

SEC. 31. *And be it further enacted*, That it shall be the duty of the collectors aforesaid, or their deputies, in their respective districts, and they are hereby authorized, to collect all the duties and taxes imposed by this act, however the same may be designated, and to prosecute for the recovery of the same, and for the recovery of any sum or sums which may be forfeited by virtue of this act; and all fines, penalties, and forfeitures which may be incurred or imposed by virtue of this act shall and may be sued for and recovered, in the name of the United States, or of the collector within whose district any such fine, penalty, or forfeiture shall have been incurred, in any proper form of action, or by any appropriate form of proceeding, before any circuit or district court of the United States for the district within which said fine, penalty, or forfeiture may have been incurred, or before any other court of competent jurisdiction; and where not otherwise and differently provided for, one moiety thereof shall be to the use of the United States, and the other moiety thereof to the use of the person who, if a collector or deputy collector, shall first inform of the cause, matter, or thing whereby any such fine, penalty, or forfeiture was incurred. *[Collectors to collect all duties and taxes imposed. Fines, &c., may be sued for. Informer has a moiety.]*

SEC. 32. *And be it further enacted*, That if any person, in any case, matter, hearing, or other proceeding in which an oath or affirmation shall be required to be taken or administered under and by virtue of this act, shall, upon the taking of such oath or affirmation, knowingly and willingly swear or affirm falsely, every person so offending shall be deemed guilty of perjury, and shall, on conviction thereof, be subject to the like punishment and penalties now provided by the laws of the United States for the crime of perjury. *[Penalty for false swearing.]*

SEC. 33. *And be it further enacted*, That separate accounts shall be kept at the treasury of all moneys received from internal duties or taxes in each of the respective States, Territories, and collection districts; and that separate accounts shall be kept of the amount of each species of duty or tax that shall accrue, so as to exhibit, as far as may be, the amount collected from each source of revenue, with the moneys paid to the collectors and deputy collectors, and to the other officers employed in each of the respective States, Territories, and collection districts, an abstract in tabular form of which accounts it shall be the duty of the Secretary of the Treasury, annually, in the month of December, to lay before Congress. *[Separate accounts to be kept for States, Territories, and collection districts.]*

SEC. 34. *And be it further enacted*, That there shall be allowed to the collectors appointed under this act, in full compensation for their services and that of their deputies in carrying this act into effect, a commission of four per centum upon the first hundred thousand dollars, and two per centum upon all sums above one hundred thousand dollars; such commissions to be computed upon the amounts by them respectively paid over and accounted for under the instructions of the Treasury Department: *Provided*, That in no case shall such commissions exceed the sum of ten thousand dollars per annum, except as hereinafter provided. And there shall be further allowed to each collector his necessary and reasonable charges for stationery and blank books used in the performance of his official duties, which, after being duly examined and certified by the Commissioner of Internal Revenue, shall be paid out of the treasury: *Provided*, That the Secretary of the Treasury be authorized to make such further allowance as may *[Compensation to collectors. Not to exceed $10,000. Stationery and blank books. Secretary of the Treasury may]* be reasonable in cases in which, from the territorial extent of the district or from the amount of internal duties collected, it may seem just to make such allowance; but the whole compensation shall not exceed ten thousand dollars, except in collection districts embracing more than one congressional district.

<small>make additional allowance.</small>

<small>Right of aggrieved parties in cases of distraint.</small>

SEC. 35. *And be it further enacted*, That when any duty or tax shall have been paid by levy and distraint, any person or persons or party who may feel aggrieved thereby may apply to the assessor of the district for relief, and exhibit such evidence as he, she, or they may have of the wrong done, or supposed to have been done, and after a full investigation the assessor shall report the case, with such parts of the evidence as he may judge material, including also such as may be regarded material by the party aggrieved, to the Commissioner of Internal Revenue, who may, if it shall be made to appear to him that such duty or tax was levied or collected, in whole or in part, wrongfully or unjustly, certify the amount wrongfully and unjustly levied or collected, and the same shall be refunded and paid to the person or persons or party as aforesaid, from any moneys in the treasury not otherwise appropriated, upon the presentation of such certificate to the proper officer thereof.

<small>Report to the commissioner.</small>

<small>Tax be refunded when wrongfully levied.</small>

<small>Bills of sale conclusive evidence.</small>

SEC. 36. *And be it further enacted*, That in all cases of distraint and sale of goods, or chattels, for non-payment of taxes provided for in this act, the bill of sale of such goods or chattels given by the officer making such sale to the purchaser thereof shall be conclusive evidence of the right of the officer to make such sale, and of the correctness of his proceedings in selling the same.

<small>Duty of President in States and Territories where this act cannot be executed.</small>

SEC. 37. *And be it further enacted*, That if for any cause, at any time after this act goes into operation, the laws of the United States cannot be executed in a State or Territory of the United States, or any part thereof, or within the District of Columbia, it shall be the duty of the President, and he is hereby authorized, to proceed to execute the provisions of this act within the limits of such State or Territory, or part thereof, or District of Columbia, so soon as the authority of the United States therein shall be re-established, and to collect the sums which would have been due from the persons residing or holding property, goods, wares, or merchandise, object or article therein liable to any duty, license, or tax, with interest at the rate of six per centum per annum thereon from the time such duty, license, or tax ought to have been paid until paid in the manner and under the regulations prescribed in this act, so far as applicable, and where not applicable the assessment and levy shall be made and the time and manner of collection regulated by the instructions and directions of the Commissioner of Internal Revenue, under the direction of the Secretary of the Treasury.

<small>To collect soon after as possible.</small>

<small>Interest 6 per cent.</small>

<small>Officers to perform duties imposed by act of August 6, 1861, in States where that tax has not been assumed.</small>

SEC. 38. *And be it further enacted*, That the officers who may be appointed under this act, except within those districts within any State or Territory which have been or may be otherwise specially provided for by law, shall be, and hereby are, authorized, in all cases where the payment of such tax has not been assumed by the State, to perform all the duties relating to or regarding the assessment and collection of the direct tax imposed by an act entitled "An act to provide increased revenue from imports to pay interest on the public debt, and for other purposes," approved August fifth, eighteen hundred and sixty-one, or any direct tax which may be hereafter enacted: *Provided*, That the sum of nineteen

EXCISE TAX. 17

thousand three hundred and twelve dollars, direct tax, laid upon the Territory of Nebraska by said act, shall be paid and satisfied by deducting said amount from the appropriation for legislative expenses of the Territory of Nebraska for the year ending thirtieth of June, eighteen hundred and sixty-three, and no further claim shall be made by said Territory for legislative expenses for said year : *Provided, further,* That the State of Tennessee shall have until the first day of December next to assume the payment of her portion of said tax. Direct tax of Nebraska credited.

Tennessee.

SPIRITS, ALE, BEER, AND PORTER.

SEC. 39. *And be it further enacted,* That it shall be the duty of the collectors, within their respective districts, to grant licenses for distilling, which licenses shall contain the date thereof, the sum paid, and the time when the same will expire, and shall be granted to any person, being a resident of the United States, who shall desire the same, by application, in writing, to such collector, upon payment of the sum or duty payable by this act upon each license requested. And at the time of applying for said license, and before the same is issued, the person so applying shall give bond to the United States in such sum as shall be required by the collector, and with one or more sureties, to be approved by said collector conditioned that in case any additional still or stills, or other implements to be used as aforesaid, shall be erected by him, his agent or superintendent, he will, before using, or causing or permitting the same to be used, report in writing to the said collector the capacity thereof, and information from time to time of any change in the form, capacity, ownership, agency, or superintendence, which all or either of the said stills or other implements may undergo ; and that he will, from day to day, enter, or cause to be entered, in a book to be kept for that purpose, the number of gallons of spirits that may be distilled by said still or stills, or other implements, and also of the quantities of grain or other vegetable productions, or other substances put into the mash tub, or otherwise used by him, his agent, or superintendent, for the purpose of producing spirits, which said book shall be open at all times during the day (Sundays excepted) to the inspection of the said collector, who may make any memorandums or transcripts therefrom ; and that he will render to the said collector, on the first, tenth, and twentieth days of each and every month, or within five days thereafter, during the continuance of said license, an exact account, in writing, taken from his books, of the number of gallons of spirits distilled and sold, or removed for consumption or sale, by him, his agent, or superintendent, and the proof thereof, and also of the quantities of grain or other vegetable productions, or other substances, put into the mash tub, or otherwise used by him, his agent, or superintendent, for the purpose of producing spirits, for the period or fractional part of a month then next preceding the date of said report, which said report shall be verified by affidavit in the manner prescribed by this act; and that he will not sell or permit to be sold, or removed for consumption or sale, any spirits distilled by him under and by virtue of his said license, until the same shall have been inspected, gauged, and proved, and the quantity thereof duly entered upon his books as aforesaid ; and that he will, at the

EXCISE TAX.

And pay the duties.

time of rendering said account, pay to the said collector the duties which by this act are imposed on the spirits so distilled; and the said bond may be renewed or changed, from time to time, in regard to the amount and sureties thereof, according to the discretion of the collector.

Bond may be renewed.

Distiller to state place and capacity of still.

SEC. 40. *And be it further enacted*, That the application in writing made by any person for a license for distilling, as aforesaid, shall state the place of distilling, the number and capacity of the still or stills, boiler or boilers, and the name of the person, firm, company, or corporation using the same; and any person making a false statement in either of the said particulars shall forfeit and pay the sum of one hundred dollars, to be recovered with costs of suit.

Penalty for false statement.

Duty on spirits distilled after August 1, 1862.

SEC. 41. *And be it further enacted*, That, in addition to the duties payable for licenses herein provided, there shall be paid, on all spirits that may be distilled and sold, or removed for consumption or sale, of first proof, on and after the first day of August, eighteen hundred and sixty-two, the duty of twenty cents on each and every gallon, which shall be paid by the owner, agent, or superintendent of the still or other vessel in which the said spirituous liquors shall have been distilled; which duty shall be paid at the time of rendering the accounts of spirituous liquors so chargeable with duty, required to be rendered by this act: *Provided*, That the duty on spirituous liquors and all other spirituous beverages enumerated in this act shall be collected at no lower rate than the basis of first proof, and shall be increased in proportion for any greater strength than the strength of proof.

20 cents per gallon.

When payable.

First proof the basis.

Standard for first proof.

SEC. 42. *And be it further enacted*, That the term first proof used in this act and in section six of the act of March second, eighteen hundred and sixty-one, entitled "An act to provide for the payment of outstanding treasury notes, to authorize a loan, to regulate and fix the duties on imports, and for other purposes," shall be construed, and is hereby declared to mean, that proof of a liquor which corresponds to fifty degrees of Tralles' centesimal hydrometer, adopted by regulation of the Treasury Department, of August twelfth, eighteen hundred and fifty, at the temperature of sixty degrees of Fahrenheit's thermometer; and that in reducing the temperatures to the standard of sixty, and in levying duties on liquors above and below proof, the table of commercial values, contained in the manual for inspectors of spirits, prepared by Professor McCulloh, under the superintendence of Professor Bache, and adopted by the Treasury Department, shall be used and taken as giving the proportions of absolute alcohol in the liquids gauged and proved according to which duties shall be levied.

Tables of Prof. McCulloh adopted.

Inspectors to be appointed by collector.

Oath.

SEC. 43. *And be it further enacted*, That there shall be designated by the collector in every assessment district where the same may be necessary one or more inspectors, who shall take an oath faithfully to perform their duties in such form as the Commissioner of Internal Revenue shall prescribe, and who shall be entitled to receive such fees as may be fixed and prescribed by said commissioner. And all spirits distilled as aforesaid by any person licensed as aforesaid shall, before the same is used, or removed for consumption or sale, be inspected, gauged, and proved by some person so as aforesaid designated for the performance of such duties, and who shall mark upon the cask or other package containing such spirits, in a manner to be prescribed by said com-

Fees.

Duty of inspectors.

All distilled spirits to be inspected.

EXCISE TAX.

missioner, the quantity and proof of the contents of such cask or package, with the date of inspection and the name of the inspector. And any person who shall attempt fraudulently to evade the payment of duties upon any spirits distilled as aforesaid, by changing in any manner the mark upon any such cask or package, shall forfeit the sum of five hundred dollars for each cask or package so altered or changed, to be recovered as hereinbefore provided. And the fees of such inspector shall in all cases be paid by the owner of the spirits so inspected, gauged, and proved. And any such inspector who shall knowingly put upon any such cask or package any false or fraudulent mark shall be liable to the same penalty hereinbefore provided for each cask or package so fraudulently marked. And any person who shall use any cask or package so marked, for the purpose of selling spirits of a quality different from that so inspected, shall be subject to a like penalty for each cask or package so used. *[Penalty for fraud to evade payment of duties. Owners to pay fees of inspectors. Penalty for fraudulent marking.]*

SEC. 44. *And be it further enacted,* That the owner or owners of any distillery may erect, at his or their own expense, a warehouse of iron, stone, or brick, with metal or other fire-proof roof, to be contiguous to such distillery; and such warehouse, when approved by the collector, is hereby declared a bonded warehouse of the United States, and shall be used only for storing distilled spirits, and to be under the custody of the collector or his deputy. And the duty on the spirits stored in such warehouse shall be paid when and as it is sold or removed from such warehouse for sale. *[Distiller may erect fire-proof warehouse. Declared bonded warehouse. Duty paid when spirits sold.]*

SEC. 45. *And be it further enacted,* That every person who, on the first day of August, eighteen hundred and sixty-two, shall be the owner of any still, boiler, or other vessel, used or intended to be used for the purpose of distilling spirituous liquors, as hereinbefore provided, or who shall have such still, boiler, or other vessel under his superintendence, either as agent for the owner or on his own account, and every person who, after said day, shall use or intend to use any still, boiler, or other vessel, as aforesaid, either as owner, agent, or otherwise, shall from day to day make true and exact entry, or cause to be entered, in a book to be kept by him for that purpose, the number of gallons of spirituous liquors distilled by him, and also the number of gallons sold, or removed for consumption or sale, and the proof thereof, which book shall always be open in the daytime, Sundays excepted, for the inspection of the said collector, who may take any minutes, memorandums, or transcripts thereof, and shall render to said collector, on the first, tenth, and twentieth days of each and every month in each year, or within five days thereafter, a general account in writing, taken from his books, of the number of gallons of spirituous liquors distilled and sold, or removed for consumption or sale, and the proof thereof, for the period or fractional part of a month preceding said day, or for such portion thereof as may have elapsed from the date of said entry and report to the said day which shall next ensue; and shall also keep a book, or books, in a form to be prescribed by the Commissioner of Internal Revenue, and to be open at all seasonable hours for inspection by the collector and assessor of the district, wherein shall be entered, from day to day, the quantities of grain, or other vegetable productions, or other substances put into the mash tub by him, his agent, or superintendent, for the purpose of producing spirits; and shall verify or cause to be verified the said *[Daily record of quantity of spirits made, sold, &c., to be kept. Record open to collector. Render tri-monthly accounts from said record. Record of quantity of grain, &c., used, to be kept.]*

To be verified by oath.	entries, reports, books, and general accounts, by oath or affirmation, to be taken before the collector or some other officer authorized by the laws of the State to administer the same according to the form required by this act, where the same is prescribed;
Pay duties.	and shall also pay to the collector the duties which by this act ought to be paid on the spirituous liquors so distilled and sold, or removed for consumption or sale, and in said accounts mentioned, at the time of rendering an account thereof.
Collector may grant permits for removal of spirits after inspection.	SEC. 46. *And be it further enacted,* That the collector of any district may grant a permit to the owner or owners of any distillery within his district to send or ship any spirits, the product of said distillery, after the quantity and proof thereof shall have been ascertained by inspection according to the provisions of this act, to any place without said district and within the United States; and in such case the bill of lading or receipt (which shall be in
Shipper.	such form as the Commissioner of Internal Revenue may direct) of the same shall be taken in the name of the collector of the district in which the distillery is situate, and the spirits aforesaid shall be
Consignee.	consigned, in such bill of lading or receipt, to the collector of the district in which the place is situate, whither the spirits is sent or shipped, and the amount of duties upon said spirits shall be stated in the receipt; and upon the arrival of the spirits, and upon the demand of the collector aforesaid, the agent of the distillery (and the name of the agent, for the convenience of the collector,
Who pay duties in case of removal.	shall always appear in the bill of lading or receipt) shall pay the duties upon the said spirits, with the expense of freight, and every other expense which has accrued thereupon; and the said collector, upon the payment of the duties aforesaid, shall deliver the bill of lading or receipt and the spirits to the agent of the said distillery; and if the duties are not paid as aforesaid, then the said
Spirits stored till duties paid.	spirits shall be stored at the risk and cost of the owner or agent thereof, who shall pay an addition of ten per centum thereupon; and all the general provisions of this act, in reference to liens,
Costs.	penalties, and forfeitures, as also in reference to the collection, shall apply thereto, and be enforced by the collector of the district in which the spirits may be: *Provided,* That no permit shall be
Not less than fifty barrels to be permitted.	granted, under this section, for a quantity less than fifty barrels: *And provided, further,* That the Commissioner of Internal Revenue, under the direction of the Secretary of the Treasury, may make such further regulations and require such further securities as he may deem proper, in order to protect the revenue and to carry out the spirit and intent of this section.
Spirits and coal oil may be removed for exportation.	SEC. 47. *And be it further enacted,* That distilled spirits may be removed from the place of manufacture for the purpose of being exported, or for the purpose of being re-distilled for export, and refined coal oil may be removed for the purpose of being exported, after the quantity of spirits or oil so removed shall have been ascertained by inspection, according to the provisions of this act, upon and with the written permission of the collector or deputy collector of the district, without payment of the duties thereon previous to such removal, the owner thereof having first
Bonds to be given.	given bond to the United States, with sufficient sureties, in the manner and form and under regulations prescribed by the Commissioner of Internal Revenue, and in at least double the amount of said duties, to export the said spirits or oil or pay the duties thereon within such time as may be prescribed by the Commissioner, which time shall be stated in said bond: *Provided,* That any per-

son desiring to give such bond shall first make oath, before the collector or deputy collector to whom he may apply for a permit to remove any such spirits or oil, in manner and form to be prescribed by said Commissioner, that he intends to export such liquors or oil, and that he desires to obtain said permit for no other purpose whatever; and any collector or deputy collector is hereby authorized to administer such oath: *And provided, further,* That no such removal shall be permitted where the amount of duties does not exceed the sum of three hundred dollars, nor in any case where the person desiring such permission has failed to perform the obligation of any bond previously given to the United States for the removal of any such articles, until the same shall have been fully kept and performed. And the collector of the district in which any such bond may be given is authorized to cancel said bond on payment of said duties, with interest thereon, at a rate to be fixed by said Commissioner, and all proper charges, if said liquors or oil shall not have been exported, or upon satisfactory proof that the same have been duly exported as aforesaid. And in case of the breach of the obligation of any such bond, the same shall be forthwith forwarded by the collector of the district to the Commissioner of Internal Revenue, to be by him placed in the hands of the First Comptroller of the Treasury, who shall cause the same proceedings to be taken thereon for the purpose of collecting the duties, interest, and charges aforesaid, as are provided in this act in case of a delinquent collector. *Oath.*

Amount of spirits above $300 in value.

Duties to be paid when not exported.

SEC. 48. *And be it further enacted,* That the entries made in the books of the distiller, required to be kept in the foregoing section, shall, on the first, tenth, and twentieth days of each and every month, or within *five* days thereafter, be verified by oath or affirmation, to be taken as aforesaid, of the person or persons by whom such entries shall have been made, which oath or affirmation shall be certified at the end of such entries by the collector or officer administering the same, and shall be, in substance, as follows: "I do swear (or affirm) that the foregoing entries were made by me on the respective days specified, and that they state, according to the best of my knowledge and belief, the whole quantity of spirituous liquors distilled and sold, or removed for consumption or sale, at the distillery owned by ———, in the county of ———, amounting to ——— gallons, according to proof prescribed by the laws of the United States."

Entries in distillers' books to be verified by oath.

Oath.

SEC. 49. *And be it further enacted,* That the owner, agent, or superintendent aforesaid, shall, in case the original entries required to be made in his books by this act shall not have been made by himself, subjoin to the oath or affirmation of the person by whom they were made the following oath or affirmation, to be taken as aforesaid: "I do swear (or affirm) that, to the best of my knowledge and belief, the foregoing entries are just and true, and that I have taken all the means in my power to make them so."

Entries made by other persons to be verified.

Oath.

SEC. 50. *And be it further enacted,* That on and after the first day of August, eighteen hundred and sixty-two, there shall be paid on all beer, lager beer, ale, porter, and other similar fermented liquors, by whatever name such liquors may be called, a duty of one dollar for each and every barrel containing not more than thirty-one gallons, and at a like rate for any other quantity or for fractional parts of a barrel, which shall be brewed or manufactured and sold or removed for consumption or sale within the United States or the Territories thereof, or within the District of

Duty on beer, lager beer, porter, &c.

$1 per barrel, &c.

22   EXCISE TAX.

<small>To be paid by brewer.</small> Columbia after that day; which duty shall be paid by the owner, agent, or superintendent of the brewery or premises in which such fermented liquors shall be made, and shall be paid at the time of rendering the accounts of such fermented liquors so chargeable with duty, as required to be rendered by the following section <small>Fractional parts of barrels, how accounted.</small> of this act: *Provided,* That fractional parts of a barrel shall be halves, quarters, eighths, and sixteenths, and any fractional part containing less than one-sixteenth shall be accounted one-sixteenth; more than one-sixteenth, and not more than one-eighth, shall be accounted one-eighth; more than one-eighth, and not more than one-quarter, shall be accounted one-quarter; more than one-quarter, and not more than one-half, shall be accounted one-half; more than one-half shall be accounted one barrel.

<small>Record of quantity of grain, &c., used, and quantity made, sold, &c., of fermented liquors.</small> SEC. 51. *And be it further enacted,* That every person who, on said first day of August, eighteen hundred and sixty-two, shall be the owner or occupant of any brewery or premises used or intended to be used for the purpose of brewing or making such fermented liquors, or who shall have such premises under his control or superintendence as agent for the owner or occupant, or shall have in his possession or custody any vessel or vessels intended to be used on said premises in the manufacture of beer, lager beer, ale, porter, or other similar fermented liquors, either as owner, agent, or otherwise, shall, from day to day, enter or cause to be entered in a <small>Open to inspection.</small> book to be kept by him for that purpose, and which shall be open at all times, except Sundays, between the rising and setting of the sun, for the inspection of said collector, who may take any minutes or memorandums or transcripts thereof, the quantities of grain, or other vegetable productions or other substances, put into the mash tub, or otherwise used for the purpose of producing beer or for any other purpose, and the quantity or number of barrels and fractional parts of barrels of fermented liquors made and sold, or removed for consumption or sale, keeping separate account of the several kinds and descriptions; and shall render to said collector, on the first <small>Render monthly accounts to the collector.</small> day of each month in each year, or within ten days thereafter, a general account, in writing, taken from his books, of the quantities of grain, or other vegetable productions or other substances, put into the mash tub, or otherwise used for the purpose of producing beer, or for any other purpose, and the quantity or number of barrels and fractional parts of barrels of each kind of fermented liquors made and sold, or removed for consumption or sale, for one <small>Verified on oath.</small> month preceding said day, and shall verify, or cause to be verified, the said entries, reports, books, and general accounts, on oath or affirmation, to be taken before the collector or some officer authorized by the laws of the State to administer the same according to the form required by this act where the same is prescribed; and <small>Pay duties.</small> shall also pay to the said collector the duties which, by this act, ought to be paid on the liquor made and sold, or removed for consumption or sale, and in the said accounts mentioned, at the <small>Removal for storage, how authorized.</small> time of rendering the account thereof, as aforesaid. But where the manufacturer of any beer, lager beer, or ale, manufactures the same in one collection district, and owns or hires a depot or warehouse for the storage and sale of such beer, lager beer, or ale in another collection district, he may, instead of paying to the collector of the district where the same was manufactured the duties chargeable thereon, present to such collector or his deputy an invoice of the quantity or number of barrels about to be removed for the purpose of storage and sale, specifying in such invoice, with

reasonable certainty, the depot or warehouse in which he intends to place such beer, lager beer, or ale; and thereupon such collector or deputy shall indorse on such invoice his permission for such removal, and shall at the same time transmit to the collector of the district in which such depot or warehouse is situated a duplicate of such invoice; and thereafter the manufacturer of the beer, lager beer, or ale so removed shall render the same account, and pay the same duties, and be subject to the same liabilities and penalties as if the beer, lager beer, or ale so removed had been manufactured in the district. The Commissioner of Internal Revenue may prescribe such rules as he may deem necessary for the purpose of carrying the provisions of this section into effect.

Sec. 52. *And be it further enacted*, That the entries made in the books required to be kept by the foregoing section shall, on said first day of each and every month, or within ten days thereafter be verified by the oath or affirmation, to be taken as aforesaid, of the person or persons by whom such entries shall have been made, which oath or affirmation shall be certified at the end of such entries by the collector or officer administering the same, and shall be, in substance, as follows: *Original entries to be verified by oath.*

"I do swear (or affirm) that the foregoing entries were made by me on the respective days specified, and that they state, according to the best of my knowledge and belief, the whole quantity of fermented liquors either brewed or brewed and sold at the brewery owned by ———, in the county of ———, amounting to —— barrels." *Oath.*

Sec. 53. *And be it further enacted*, That the owner, agent, or superintendent aforesaid, shall, in case the original entries required to be made in his books shall not have been made by himself, subjoin to the oath or affirmation the following oath or affirmation, to be taken as aforesaid: *Entries made by other persons to be verified.*

"I do swear (or affirm) that, to the best of my knowledge and belief, the foregoing entries are just and true, and that I have taken all the means in my power to make them so." *Oath.*

Sec. 54. *And be it further enacted*, That the owner, agent, or superintendent of any vessel or vessels used in making fermented liquors, or of any still, boiler, or other vessel used in the distillation of spirits on which duty is payable, who shall neglect or refuse to make true and exact entry and report of the same, or to do, or cause to be done, any of the things by this act required to be done as aforesaid, shall forfeit for every such neglect or refusal all the liquors and spirits made by or for him, and all the vessels used in making the same, and the stills, boilers, and other vessels used in distillation, together with the sum of five hundred dollars, to be recovered with costs of suit; which said liquors or spirits, with the vessels containing the same, with all the vessels used in making the same, may be seized by any collector of internal duties, and held by him until a decision shall be had thereon according to law: *Provided*, That such seizure be made within thirty days after the cause for the same may have occurred, and that proceedings to enforce said forfeiture shall have been commenced by such collector within twenty days after the seizure thereof. And the proceedings to enforce said forfeiture of said property shall be in the nature of a proceeding in rem, in the circuit or district court of the United States for the district where such seizure is made, or in any other court of competent jurisdiction. *Penalty for neglect to make true reports.* *Fine.* *Seizure.* *Proviso.*

SEC. 55. *And be it further enacted,* That in all cases in which the duties aforesaid, payable on spirituous liquors distilled and sold, or removed for consumption or sale, or beer, lager beer, ale, porter, and other similar fermented liquors, shall not be paid at the time of rendering the account of the same, as herein required, the person or persons chargeable therewith shall pay, in addition, ten per centum on the amount thereof; and, until such duties with such addition shall be paid, they shall be and remain a lien upon the distillery where such liquors have been distilled, or the brewery where such liquors have been brewed, and upon the stills, boilers, vats, and all other implements thereto belonging, until the same shall have been paid; and in case of refusal or neglect to pay said duties, with the addition, within ten days after the same shall have become payable, the amount thereof may be recovered by distraint and sale of the goods, chattels, and effects of the delinquent; and in case of such distraint, it shall be the duty of the officer charged with the collection to make, or cause to be made, an account of the goods, chattels, or effects which may be distrained, a copy of which, signed by the officer making such distraint, shall be left with the owner or possessor of such goods, chattels, or effects, at his, her, or their dwelling, with a note of the sum demanded, and the time and place of sale; and said officer shall forthwith cause a notification to be published in some newspaper, if any there be, within the county, and publicly posted up at the post office nearest to the residence of the person whose property shall be distrained, or at the court-house of the same county, if not more than ten miles distant, which notice shall specify the articles distrained, and the time and place proposed for the sale thereof, which time shall not be less than ten days from the date of such notification, and the place proposed for sale not more than five miles distant from the place of making such distraint: *Provided,* That in every case of distraint for the payment of the duties aforesaid, the goods, chattels, or effects so distrained may and shall be restored to the owner or possessor if, prior to the sale thereof, payment or tender thereof shall be made to the proper officer charged with the collection, of the full amount demanded, together with such fee for levying and advertising, and such sum for the necessary and reasonable expenses of removing and keeping the goods, chattels, and effects so distrained as may be allowed in like cases by the laws or practice of the State or Territory wherein the distraint shall have been made; but in case of nonpayment or neglect to tender as aforesaid, the said officer shall proceed to sell the said goods, chattels, and effects at public auction, after due notice of the time and place of sale, and may and shall retain from the proceeds of such sale the amount demandable for the use of the United States, with the said necessary and reasonable expenses of said distraint and sale, as aforesaid, and a commission of five per centum thereon for his own use; rendering the overplus, if any there be, to the person whose goods, chattels, and effects shall have been destrained.

SEC. 56. *And be it further enacted,* That every person licensed as aforesaid to distil spirituous liquors, or licensed as a brewer, shall, once in each month, upon the request of the assessor or assistant assessor for the district in which his business as a distiller or brewer may be carried on, respectively, furnish the said assessor or assistant assessor with an abstract of the entries upon his books, herein provided to be made, showing the amount of spirituous liquor distilled and sold, or removed for consumption or sale, or of beer, lager beer, ale, porter, or other fermented liquor made and sold, or removed for consumption or sale, during the preceding month, respectively; the truth and correctness of which abstract shall be verified by the oath of the party so furnishing the same. And the said assessor or assistant assessor shall have the right to examine the books of such person for the purpose of ascertaining the correctness of such abstract. And for any neglect to furnish such abstract when requested, or refusal to furnish an examination of the books as aforesaid, the person so neglecting shall forfeit the sum of five hundred dollars. *Of what.*

Penalty

LICENSES.

SEC. 57. *And be it further enacted,* That from and after the first day of August, eighteen hundred and sixty-two, no person, association of persons, or corporation, shall be engaged in, prosecute, or carry on, either of the trades or occupations mentioned in section sixty-fourth of this act, until he or they shall have obtained a license therefor in the manner hereinafter provided. *Trades and occupations to be licensed after Aug. 1, 1862.*

SEC. 58. *And be it further enacted,* That every person, association of persons, partnership or corporation, desiring to obtain a license to engage in any of the trades or occupations named in the sixty-fourth section of this act, shall register with the assistant assessor of the assessment district in which he shall design to carry on such trade or occupation—first, his or their name or style; and in case of an association or partnership, the names of the several persons constituting such association or partnership and their places of residence; second, the trade or occupation for which a license is desired; third, the place where such trade or occupation is to be carried on; fourth, if a rectifier, the number of barrels he designs to rectify; if a peddler, whether he designs to travel on foot, or with one, two, or more horses; if an innkeeper, the yearly rental of the house and property to be occupied for said purpose; or, if not rented, the assistant assessor shall value the same. All of which facts shall be returned duly certified by such assistant assessor, both to the assessor and collector of the district; and thereupon, upon payment to the collector or deputy collector of the district the amount as hereinafter provided, such collector or deputy collector shall make out and deliver a license for such trade or occupation, which license shall continue in force for one year, at the place or premises described therein. *Requirements to obtain license.*

Title.

Occupation.

Place, &c.

Proceedings of assessor.

SEC. 59. *And be it further enacted,* That if any person or persons shall exercise or carry on any trade or business hereinafter mentioned for the exercising or carrying on of which trade or business a license is required by this act, without taking out such license as in that behalf required, he, she, or they shall, for every such offence, respectively, forfeit a penalty equal to three times the amount of the duty or sum of money imposed for such license, one moiety thereof to the use of the United States, the other moiety to the use of the person who, if a collector, shall first discover, and if other than a collector, shall first give information of the fact whereby said forfeiture was incurred. *Penalty for not taking out a license.*

Moiety to informer.

SEC. 60. *And be it further enacted,* That in every license to be taken out under or by authority of this act shall be contained and set forth the purpose, trade, or business for which such license is granted, and the true name and place of abode of the person *Details of the license.*

or persons taking out the same; if for a rectifier, the quantity of spirits authorized to be rectified; if by a peddler, whether authorized to travel on foot, or with one, or two, or more horses, the time for which such license is to run, and the true date or time of granting such license, and (except in the case of auctioneers and peddlers) the place at which the trade or business for which such license is granted shall be carried on: *Provided*, That a license granted under this act shall not authorize the person or persons, association or corporation mentioned therein to exercise or carry on the trade or business specified in such license in any other place than that mentioned therein, but nothing herein contained shall prohibit the storage of goods, wares, or merchandise in other places than the place of business.

Proviso.

License for each trade a person carries on.

SEC. 61. *And be it further enacted*, That in every case where more than one of the pursuits, employments, or occupations, hereinafter described, shall be pursued or carried on in the same place by the same person at the same time, except as therein mentioned, license must be taken out for each according to the rates severally prescribed.

Auctioneers not to sell at private sale.

SEC. 62. *And be it further enacted*, That no auctioneer shall be authorized by virtue of his license as such auctioneer to sell any goods or other property at private sale; and if any such person shall sell any such goods or commodities, as aforesaid, otherwise than by auction, without having taken out such license as aforesaid for that purpose, he or she shall be subject and liable to the penalty in that behalf imposed upon persons dealing in or retailing, trading, or selling any such goods or commodities without license, notwithstanding any license to him or her before granted, as aforesaid, for the purpose of exercising or carrying on the trade or business of an auctioneer, or selling any goods or chattels, lands, tenements, or hereditaments by auction, anything herein contained to the contrary notwithstanding: *Provided, always*, That where such goods or commodities as aforesaid are the property of any person or persons duly licensed to deal in or retail, or trade in, or sell the same, such person or persons having made lawful entry of his, her, or their house or premises for such purpose, it shall and may be lawful for any person exercising or carrying on the trade or business of an auctioneer, or selling any goods or chattels, lands, tenements, or hereditaments, by auction as aforesaid, being duly licensed for that purpose, to sell such goods or commodities as aforesaid, at auction, for and on behalf of such person or persons, and upon his, her, or their entered house or premises, without taking out a separate license for such sale. The provisions of this section shall not apply to judicial or executive officers making auction sales by virtue of any judgment or decree of any court, nor public sales made by executors and administrators.

Penalty.

May sell for a licensed trader.

Not to apply to sales by executive officers, &c.

Executors, &c., may carry on trade under license of deceased person.

SEC. 63. *And be it further enacted*, That upon the death of any person or persons licensed under or by virtue of this act, or upon the removal of any such person or persons from the house or premises at which he, she, or they were authorized by such license to exercise or carry on the trade or business mentioned in such license, it shall and may be lawful for the person or persons authorized to grant licenses to authorize and empower, by indorsement on such license, or otherwise, as the Commissioner of Internal Revenue shall direct, the executors or administrators, or the wife or child of such deceased person, or the assignee or assigns of

Endorsement of license required.

such person or persons so removing as aforesaid, who shall be possessed of and occupy the house or premises before used for such purpose as aforesaid, in like manner to exercise or carry on the same trade or business mentioned in such license, in or upon the same house or premises at which such person or persons as aforesaid deceased, or removing as before mentioned, by virtue of such license to him, her, or them, in that behalf granted, before exercised or carried on such trade or business for or during the residue of the term for which such license was originally granted, without taking out any fresh license or payment of any additional duty, or any fee thereupon for the residue of such term, and until expiration thereof: *Provided, always*, That a fresh entry of the premises at which such trade or business shall continue to be so exercised or carried on as aforesaid shall thereupon be made by and in the name or names of the person or persons to whom such authority as aforesaid shall be granted. New entry of premises to be made.

SEC. 64. *And be it further enacted*, That on and after the first day of August, eighteen hundred and sixty-two, for each license granted the sum herewith stated shall be respectively and annually paid. Any number of persons carrying on such business in copartnership may transact such business at such place under such license, and not otherwise. Cost of licenses after Aug. 1, 1862. Who may act under a license.

1. Bankers shall pay one hundred dollars for each license. Every person shall be deemed a banker within the meaning of this act who keeps a place of business where credits are opened in favor of any person, firm, or corporation, by the deposit or collection of money or currency, and the same, or any part thereof, shall be paid out or remitted upon the draft, check, or order of such creditor, but not to include incorporated banks or other banks legally authorized to issue notes as circulation, nor agents for the sale of merchandise for account of producers or manufacturers. Bankers, $100. Who are bankers.

2. Auctioneers shall pay twenty dollars for each license. Every person shall be deemed an auctioneer within the meaning of this act whose occupation it is to offer property for sale to the highest or best bidder. Auctioneers, $20. Who are auctioneers.

3. Wholesale dealers in liquors of any and every description, including distilled spirits, fermented liquors, and wines of all kinds, shall pay one hundred dollars for each license. Every person, other than the distiller or brewer, who shall sell or offer for sale any such liquors or wines in quantities of more than three gallons at one time, to the same purchaser, shall be regarded as a wholesale dealer in liquors within the meaning of this act. Wholesale dealers in liquors, &c., $100. Who are wholesale dealers.

4. Retail dealers in liquors, including distilled spirits, fermented liquors, and wines of every description, shall pay twenty dollars for each license. Every person who shall sell or offer for sale such liquors in less quantities than three gallons at one time, to the same purchaser, shall be regarded as a retail dealer in liquors under this act. But this shall not authorize any spirits, liquors, wines, or malt liquors, to be drank on the premises. Retail dealers in liquors, $20. Who are retail dealers. A license will not authorize liquor to be drank on the premises.

5. Retail dealers shall pay ten dollars for each license. Every person whose business or occupation is to sell, or offer to sell, groceries, or any goods, wares, or merchandise, of foreign or domestic production, in less quantities than a whole original piece or package at one time, to the same person, (not including wines, spirituous or malt liquors, but not excluding drugs, medicines, cigars, snuff, or tobacco,) shall be regarded as a retail dealer under this act. All retail dealers, $10. Who are retail dealers.

28   EXCISE TAX.

Wholesale dealers, $50.   6. Wholesale dealers shall pay fifty dollars for each license. Every person whose business or occupation is to sell, or offer to sell, groceries, or any goods, wares, or merchandise, of foreign or domestic production, by one or more original package or piece at one time, to the same purchaser, not including wines, spirituous or malt liquors, shall be deemed a wholesale dealer under this act; but having taken out a license as a wholesale dealer, such person may also sell, as aforesaid, as a retailer.

Who are wholesale dealers.

Do not require license to retail.

Pawnbrokers, $50.   7. Pawnbrokers shall pay fifty dollars for each license. Every person whose business or occupation is to take or receive, by way of pledge, pawn, or exchange, any goods, wares, or merchandise, or any kind of personal property whatever, for the repayment or security of money lent thereon, shall be deemed a pawnbroker under this act.

Who are such.

Rectifiers, under 500 barrels, $25.   8. Rectifiers shall pay twenty-five dollars for each license to rectify any quantity of spirituous liquors, not exceeding five hundred barrels or casks, containing not more than forty gallons to each barrel or cask of liquor so rectified; and twenty-five dollars additional for each additional five hundred such barrels, or any fractional part thereof. Every person who rectifies, purifies, or refines spirituous liquors or wines by any process, or mixes distilled spirits, whiskey, brandy, gin, or wine, with any other materials for sale under the name of whiskey, rum, brandy, gin, wine, or any other name or names, shall be regarded as a rectifier under this act.

Every additional 500 barrels, $25.

Who are rectifiers.

Distillers, $50.   9. Distillers shall pay fifty dollars for each license, and every person or copartnership who distils or manufactures spirituous liquors for sale shall be deemed a distiller under this act: *Provided*, That any person or copartnership distilling or manufacturing less than three hundred barrels per year shall pay twenty-five dollars for a license. *And provided, further*, That no license shall be required for any still, stills, or other apparatus used by druggists and chemists for the recovery of alcohol for pharmaceutical and chemical purposes which has been used in those processes. *And provided, further*, That distillers of apples and peaches, distilling or manufacturing less than one hundred and fifty barrels per year from the same, shall pay twelve and one-half dollars for a license for that purpose, and for a greater quantity as other distillers.

Who are such.

Under 300 barrels, $25.
Proviso.

Still of druggist and chemist excepted.

Distillers of apples and peaches, $12.50.

Brewers, $50.   10. Brewers shall pay fifty dollars for each license. Every person who manufactures fermented liquors of any name or description, for sale, from malt, wholly or in part, shall be deemed a brewer under this act: *Provided*, That any person who manufactures less than five hundred barrels per year shall pay the sum of twenty-five dollars for a license.

Who are brewers.

Under 500 barrels, $25.

Hotels, inns, and taverns, classified.   11. Hotels, inns, and taverns shall be classified and rated according to the yearly rental, or, if not rented, according to the estimated yearly rental of the house and property intended to be occupied for said purposes, as follows, to wit: All cases where the rent or the valuation of the yearly rental of said house and property shall be ten thousand dollars or more shall constitute the first class, and shall pay two hundred dollars for each license; where the rent or the valuation of the yearly rental shall be five thousand dollars and less than ten thousand dollars, the second class, and shall pay one hundred dollars for each license; where the rent or the valuation of the yearly rental shall be twenty-five hundred dollars and less than five thousand dollars, the third class, and

First class, $200.

Second class, $100.

Third class, $75.

shall pay seventy-five dollars for each license; where the rent or the valuation of the yearly rental shall be one thousand dollars and less than twenty-five hundred dollars, the fourth class, and shall pay fifty dollars for each license; where the rent or the valuation of the yearly rental shall be five hundred dollars and less than one thousand dollars, the fifth class, and shall pay twenty-five dollars for each license; where the rent or the valuation of the yearly rental shall be three hundred dollars and less than five hundred dollars, the sixth class, and shall pay fifteen dollars for each license; where the rent or the valuation of the yearly rental shall be one hundred dollars and less than three hundred dollars, the seventh class, and shall pay ten dollars for each license; where the rent or the valuation of the yearly rental shall be less than one hundred dollars, the eighth class, and shall pay five dollars for each license. Every place where food and lodging are provided for and furnished to travellers and sojourners, in view of payment therefor, shall be regarded as a hotel, inn, or tavern under this act. All steamers and vessels upon waters of the United States, on board of which passengers or travellers are provided with food or lodging, shall be required to take out a license of the fifth class, as aforesaid, under this act. The rental or estimated rental shall be fixed and established by the assessor of the proper district at its proper value, but at not less than the actual rent agreed on by the parties: *Provided*, That if there be any fraud or collusion in the return of actual rent to the assessor, there shall be a penalty equal to double the amount of licenses required by this section, to be collected as other penalties under this act are collected.

Fourth class, $50.

Fifth class, $25.

Sixth class, $15.

Seventh class, $10.

Eighth class. $5.

What is a hotel, inn, or tavern.

Steamers and vessels carrying passengers, $25.

Penalty.

12. Eating-houses shall pay ten dollars for each license. Every place where food or refreshments of any kind are provided for casual visitors and sold for consumption therein shall be regarded as an eating-house under this act. But the keeper of any eating-house having taken out a license therefor shall not be required to take out a license as a confectioner, anything in this act to the contrary notwithstanding.

Eating-houses, $10.

What are eating-houses.

No license as a confectioner needed.

13. Brokers shall pay fifty dollars for each license. Any person whose business is to purchase or sell stocks, coined money, bank notes, or other securities for themselves or others, or who deals in exchanges relating to money, shall be regarded a broker under this act.

Brokers, $50.

Who is a broker.

14. Commercial brokers shall pay fifty dollars for each license. Any person or firm, except one holding a license as wholesale dealer or banker, whose business it is, as the agent of others, to purchase or sell goods, or seek orders therefor, in original or unbroken packages, or produce, or to manage business matters for the owners of vessels, or for the shippers or consignors of freight carried by vessels, or whose business it is to purchase, rent, or sell real estate for others, shall be regarded a commercial broker under this act.

Commercial brokers, $50.

Who are commercial brokers.

Agents, &c.

15. Land warrant brokers shall pay twenty-five dollars for each license. Any person shall be regarded as a land warrant broker within the meaning of this act who makes a business of buying and selling land warrants, and of furnishing them to settlers or other persons under contracts to have liens upon the land procured by means of them according to the value agreed on for the warrants at the time they are furnished.

Land warrant brokers, $25.

Who is one.

16. Tobacconists shall pay ten dollars for each license. Any

Tobacconists, $10.

30 EXCISE TAX.

Who is a tobacconist. — person whose business it is to sell, at retail, cigars, snuff, or tobacco in any form, shall be regarded a tobacconist under this act. But *Wholesale and retail dealers and hotel keepers need no license to sell.* wholesale and retail dealers, and keepers of hotels, inns, taverns, having taken out a license therefor, shall not be required to take out a license as tobacconists, anything in this act to the contrary notwithstanding.

Theatres, $100. 17. Theatres shall pay one hundred dollars for each license. Every edifice erected for the purpose of dramatic or operatic representations, plays, or performances, and not including halls rented or used occasionally for concerts or theatrical representations, shall be regarded as a theatre under this act.

Circuses, $50. 18. Circuses shall pay fifty dollars for each license. Every building, tent, space, or area where feats of horsemanship or acrobatic sports are exhibited, shall be regarded as a circus under this act.

Jugglers, $20. 19. Jugglers shall pay for each license twenty dollars. Every person who performs by sleight of hand shall be regarded as a juggler under this act. The proprietors or agents of all other *Public exhibitions.* public exhibitions or shows for money, not enumerated in this section, shall pay for each license ten dollars: *Provided*, That *License for each State.* no license procured in one State shall be held to authorize exhibitions in another State; and but one license shall be required under this act to authorize exhibitions within any one State.

Bowling-alleys and billiard tables, $5 per table. 20. Bowling-alleys and billiard rooms shall pay according to the number of alleys or tables belonging to or used in the building or place to be licensed. When not exceeding one alley or table, five dollars for each license; and when exceeding one alley or table, five dollars for each additional alley or table. Every *What are bowling-alleys.* place or building where bowls are thrown or billiards played, and open to the public with or without price, shall be regarded as a bowling-alley or billiard room, respectively, under this act.

Confectioners, $10. 21. Confectioners shall pay ten dollars for each license. Every person who sells at retail confectionery, sweetmeats, comfits, or *Who are confectioners.* other confects, in any building, shall be regarded as a confectioner under this act. But wholesale and retail dealers, having taken out a license therefor, shall not be required to take out a license as confectioner, anything in this act to the contrary notwithstanding.

Horse-dealers, $10. 22. Horse-dealers shall pay for each license the sum of ten dollars. Any person whose business it is to buy and sell horses or mules shall be regarded a horse-dealer under this act. *Provided*, That if such horse-dealer shall have taken out a license as a livery stable keeper no new license shall be required.

Livery stable keepers, $10. 23. Livery stable keepers shall pay ten dollars for each license. Any person whose occupation or business is to keep horses for hire or to let shall be regarded as a livery stable keeper under this act.

Cattle brokers, $10. 24. Cattle brokers shall pay for each license the sum of ten dollars. Any person whose business it is to buy and sell and *Who is one.* deal in cattle, hogs, or sheep, shall be considered as a cattle broker.

Tallow-chandlers and soap-makers, $10. 25. Tallow-chandlers and soap-makers shall pay for each license the sum of ten dollars. Any person whose business it is to make or manufacture candles or soap shall be regarded a tallow-chandler and soap-maker under this act.

Coal-oil distillers, $50. 26. Coal-oil distillers shall pay for each license the sum of fifty dollars. Any person who shall refine, produce, or distil crude *Who is a distiller.* petroleum or rock oil, or crude coal oil, or crude oil made of asphaltum, shale, peat, or other bituminous substances, shall be regarded a coal-oil distiller under this act.

27. Peddlers shall be classified and rated as follows, to wit: when travelling with more than two horses, the first class, and shall pay twenty dollars for each license; when travelling with two horses, the second class, and shall pay fifteen dollars for each license; when travelling with one horse, the third class, and shall pay ten dollars for each license; when travelling on foot, the fourth class, and shall pay five dollars for each license. Any person, except persons peddling newspapers, Bibles, or religious tracts, who sells or offers to sell, at retail, goods, wares, or other commodities, travelling from place to place, in the street, or through different parts of the country, shall be regarded a peddler under this act: *Provided*, That any peddler who sells, or offers to sell, dry goods, foreign and domestic, by one or more original packages or pieces, at one time, to the same person or persons, as aforesaid, shall pay fifty dollars for each license. And any person who peddles jewelry shall pay twenty-five dollars for each license: *Provided*, That manufacturers and producers of agricultural tools and implements, garden seeds, stoves, and hollow ware, brooms, wooden ware, and powder, delivering and selling at wholesale any of said articles, by themselves or their authorized agents at places other than the place of manufacture, shall not be required, for any sale thus made, to take out any additional license therefor.

<small>Peddlers:
First class, $20.
Second class, $15.
Third class, $10.
Fourth class, $5.
Who are peddlers.
By piece or package, $50.
Jewelry, $25.
Proviso.</small>

28. Apothecaries shall pay ten dollars for each license. Every person who keeps a shop or building where medicines are compounded or prepared according to prescriptions of physicians, and sold, shall be regarded an apothecary under this act. But wholesale and retail dealers, who have taken out a license therefor, shall not be required to take out a license as apothecary, anything in this act to the contrary notwithstanding.

<small>Apothecaries, $10.
Who require a license.</small>

29. Manufacturers shall pay ten dollars for each license. Any person or persons, firms, companies, or corporations, who shall manufacture by hand or machinery, and offer for sale any goods, wares, or merchandise, exceeding annually the sum of one thousand dollars, shall be regarded a manufacturer under this act.

<small>Manufacturers, $10.
Who are manufacturers.</small>

30. Photographers shall pay ten dollars for each license when the receipts do not exceed five hundred dollars; when over five hundred dollars and under one thousand dollars, fifteen dollars; when over one thousand dollars, twenty-five dollars. Any person or persons who make for sale photographs, ambrotypes, daguerreotypes, or pictures on glass, metal, or paper, by the action of light, shall be regarded a photographer under this act.

<small>Photographers, $10 to 25.
Who require a license.</small>

31. Lawyers shall pay ten dollars for each license. Every person whose business it is, for fee or reward, to prosecute or defend causes in any court of record or other judicial tribunal of the United States or of any of the States, or give advice in relation to causes or matters pending therein, shall be deemed to be a lawyer within the meaning of this act.

<small>Lawyers, $10.</small>

32. Physicians, surgeons, and dentists shall pay ten dollars for each license. Every person (except apothecaries) whose business it is, for fee and reward, to prescribe remedies or perform surgical operations for the cure of any bodily disease or ailing, shall be deemed a physician, surgeon, or dentist, as the case may be, within the meaning of this act.

<small>Physicians, surgeons, and dentists, $10.
Who are physicians.</small>

33. Claim agents and agents for procuring patents shall pay ten dollars for each license. Every person whose business it is

<small>Claim and patent agents, $10.</small>

to prosecute claims in any of the executive departments of the federal government, or procure patents, shall be deemed a claim or patent agent, as the case may be, under this act.

License not required in certain cases of apothecaries, confectioners, eating-houses, and tobacconists.

SEC. 65. *And be it further enacted*, That where the annual gross receipts or sales of any apothecaries, confectioners, eating-houses, tobacconists, or retail dealers, shall not exceed the sum of one thousand dollars, such apothecaries, confectioners, eating-houses, and retail dealers shall not be required to take out or pay for license, anything in this act to the contrary notwithstanding; the amount or estimated amount of such annual sales to be ascertained or estimated in such manner as the Commissioner of Internal Revenue shall prescribe, and so of all other annual sales or receipts, where the rate of the license is graduated by the amount of sales or receipts.

License not required to sell goods at place of manufacture.

SEC. 66. *And be it further enacted*, That nothing contained in the preceding sections of this act, laying duties on licenses, shall be construed to require a license for the sale of goods, wares, and merchandise made or produced and sold by the manufacturer or producer at the manufactory or place where the same is made or produced; to vintners who sell, at the place where the same is made, wine of their own growth;

Nor of apothecaries.

nor to apothecaries, as to wines or spirituous liquors which they use exclusively in the preparation or making up of medicines for sick, lame, or diseased persons;

Nor physicians.

nor shall the provisions of paragraph number twenty-seven extend to physicians who keep on hand medicines solely for the purpose of making up their own prescriptions for their own patients.

License not to be against State laws.

SEC. 67. *And be it further enacted*, That no license hereinbefore provided for, if granted, shall be construed to authorize the commencement or continuation of any trade, business, occupation, or employment therein mentioned, within any State or Territory of the United States in which it is or shall be specially prohibited by the laws thereof, or in violation of the laws of any State or Territory: *Provided*, Nothing in this act shall be held or construed

State may tax for State purposes.

so as to prevent the several States, within the limits thereof, from placing a duty, tax, or license, for State purposes, on any business matter or thing on which a duty, tax, or license is required to be paid by this act.

Manufactures, &c.

MANUFACTURES, ARTICLES, AND PRODUCTS.

SPECIFIC AND AD VALOREM DUTY.

SEC. 68. *And be it further enacted*, That on and after the first day of August, eighteen hundred and sixty-two, every individual, partnership, firm, association, or corporation, (and any word or words in this act indicating or referring to person or persons shall be taken to mean and include partnerships, firms, associations, or corporations, when not otherwise designated or manifestly incompatible with the intent thereof,) shall comply with the following requirements, that is to say:

Manufacturer to furnish list in 80 days to assessor.

First. Before commencing, or, if already commenced, before continuing, any such manufacture for which he, she, or they may be liable to be assessed, under the provisions of this act, and which shall not be differently provided for elsewhere, within thirty days after the date when this act shall take effect, he, she, or they shall furnish to the assistant assessor a statement, subscribed and

EXCISE TAX. 33

sworn to, or affirmed, setting forth the place where the manufacture is to be carried on, name of the manufactured article, the proposed market for the same, whether foreign or domestic, and generally the kind and quality manufactured or proposed to be manufactured.

Second. He shall within ten days after the first day of each and every month, after the day on which this act takes effect, as hereinbefore mentioned, or on or before a day prescribed by the Commissioner of Internal Revenue, make return of the products and sales or delivery of such manufacture in form and detail as may be required, from time to time, by the Commissioner of Internal Revenue. *To make monthly return of products and sales.*

Third. All such returns, statements, descriptions, memoranda, oaths and affirmations, shall be in form, scope, and detail as may be prescribed, from time to time, by the Commissioner of Internal Revenue. *Returns made under oath.*

SEC. 69. *And be it further enacted,* That upon the amounts, quantities, and values of produce, goods, wares, merchandise, and articles manufactured and sold, or delivered, hereinafter enumerated, the manufacturer thereof, whether manufactured for himself or for others, shall pay to the collector of internal revenue within his district, monthly, or on or before a day to be prescribed by the Commissioner of Internal Revenue, the duties on such manufactures: *Provided,* That when thread is manufactured and sold or delivered exclusively for knitted fabrics, or for weaving or spooling, as provided for in the seventy-fifth section of this act, the duties shall be assessed on the articles finished and prepared for use or consumption to the party so finishing or preparing the same, and any party so finishing or preparing any cloth or other fabrics of cotton, wool, or other materials, whether imported or otherwise, shall be considered the manufacturer thereof for the purposes of this act; and for neglect to pay such duties within ten days after demand, either personal or written, left at his, her, or their house or place of business, or manufactory, the amount of such duties may be levied upon the real and personal property of any such manufacturer. And such duties, and whatever shall be the expenses of levy, shall be a lien from the day prescribed by the commissioner for their payment aforesaid, in favor of the United States, upon the said real and personal property of such manufacturer, and such lien may be enforced by distraint, as provided in the general provisions of this act: *And provided, further,* That in all cases of goods manufactured, in whole or in part, upon commission, or where the material is furnished by one party and manufactured by another, if the manufacturer shall be required to pay under this act the tax hereby imposed, such person or persons so paying the same shall be entitled to collect the amount thereof of the owner or owners, and shall have a lien for the amount thus paid upon the manufactured goods: *And provided, further,* That the taxes on all articles manufactured and sold, in pursuance of contracts bona fide made before the passage of this act, shall be paid by the purchasers thereof, under regulations to be established by the Commissioner of Internal Revenue. *Duties to be paid monthly. Knitting thread. How assessed. Who is the manufacturer. Duties to be paid in ten days. Penalty. Manufacturer paying the duty may have lien on goods.*

SEC. 70. *And be it further enacted,* That for neglect or refusal to pay the duties provided by this act on manufactured articles, as aforesaid, the goods, wares, and merchandise manufactured and *Proceedings for neglect or refusal to pay duties.*

34 EXCISE TAX.

Forfeit. unsold by such manufacturer shall be forfeited to the United States, and may be sold or disposed of for the benefit of the same, in manner as shall be prescribed by the Commissioner of Internal Revenue, under the direction of the Secretary of the Treasury. In such case the collector or deputy collector may take possession *Seizure.* of said articles, and may maintain such possession in the premises and buildings where they may have been manufactured, or deposited, or may be. He shall summon, giving notice of not less than two nor more than ten days, the parties in possession of said goods, enjoining them to appear before the assessor, or assistant assessor, at a day and hour in such summons fixed, then and there *Proceedings.* to show cause, if any there be, why, for such neglect or refusal, such articles should not be declared forfeited to the United States. Such persons or parties interested shall be deemed to be the manufacturers of the same, if the articles shall be at the time of taking such possession upon the premises where manufactured; if they shall at such time have been removed from the place of manufacture, the parties interested shall be deemed to be the person in whose custody or possession the articles shall then be. Such summons shall be served upon such parties in person, or by leaving a copy thereof at the place of abode or business of the party to whom the same may be directed. In case no such party or place can be found, which fact shall be determined by the collector's return on the summons, such notice, in the nature of a summons, shall be given by advertisement for the term of three weeks in one newspaper in the county nearest to the place of such sale. If at or before such hearing such duties shall not have been paid, and the assessor or assistant assessor shall adjudge the summons and notice, service and return of the same to be sufficient, the said articles shall be declared forfeit, and shall be sold, disposed of, or turned over to the use of any department of the government as may be directed by the Secretary of the Treasury, who may require of any officer of the government into whose possession the same may be turned over the proper voucher therefor: *Provided,* *Surplus, how* That the proceeds of the sale of said articles, if any there be after *used.* deducting the duties thereon, together with the expenses of summons, advertising, and sale, or the excess of the value of said articles, after deducting the duties and expenses accrued thereon when turned over to the use of any department of the government, shall be refunded and paid to the manufacturer, or to the person in whose custody or possession the articles were when seized. The Commissioner of Internal Revenue, with the approval of the Secretary of the Treasury, may review any such case of forfeiture and do justice in the premises. If the forfeiture shall have been wrongly declared, and sale made, the Secretary is hereby authorized, in case the specific articles cannot be restored to the party aggrieved in as good order and condition as when seized, to make up to such party in money his loss and damage from the contingent fund of his department. Immediate return of seizures so forfeited shall be made to the Commissioner of Internal Revenue by the collector or deputy collector who shall make any such seizure. Articles which the collector may adjudge perishable may be sold or disposed of before declaration of forfeiture. Said sales shall be made at public auction, and notice thereof shall be given in the same manner as is provided in this section in case of forfeiture.

SEC. 71. *And be it further enacted,* That any violation of, or refusal to comply with, the provisions of the sixty-eighth section of this act, shall be good cause for seizure and forfeiture, substantially in manner as detailed in the section next preceding this, of all manufactured articles liable to be assessed under the provisions of this act, and not otherwise provided for; and such violation or refusal to comply shall further make any party so violating or refusing to comply liable to a fine of five hundred dollars, to be recovered in manner and form as provided in this act. Penalty for violation of 68th section.

SEC. 72. *And be it further enacted,* That in case of the manufacture and sale or delivery of any goods, wares, merchandise, or articles as hereinafter mentioned, without compliance on the part of the party manufacturing the same with all or any of the requirements and regulations prescribed in this act in relation thereto, the assistant assessor may, upon such information as he may have, assume and estimate the amount and value of such manufactures, and upon such assumed amount assess the duties, and said duties shall be collected in like manner as in case the provisions of this act in relation thereto had been complied with, and to such articles all the foregoing provisions for liens, fines, penalties, and forfeitures, shall in like manner apply. Assistant assessors to assess duties in certain cases.

SEC. 73. *And be it further enacted,* That all goods, wares, and merchandise, or articles manufactured or made by any person or persons not for sale, but for his, her, or their own use or consumption, and all goods, wares, and merchandise, or articles manufactured or made and sold, except spirituous and malt liquors, and manufactured tobacco, where the annual product shall not exceed the sum of six hundred dollars, shall be and are exempt from duty: *Provided,* That this shall not apply to any business or transaction where one party furnishes the materials, or any part thereof, and employs another party to manufacture, make, or finish the goods, wares, and merchandise or articles, paying or promising to pay therefor, and receiving the goods, wares, and merchandise or articles. Manufactures for consumption not exceeding $600 exempt. Proviso.

SEC. 74. *And be it further enacted,* That the value and quantity of the goods, wares, and merchandise required to be stated, as aforesaid, and subject to an ad valorem duty, shall be estimated by the actual sales made by the manufacturer, or by his, her, or their agent, or person or persons acting in his, her, or their behalf; and where such goods, wares, and merchandise have been removed for consumption, or for delivery to others, or placed on shipboard, or are no longer within the custody and control of the manufacturer or manufacturers, or his or their agent, not being in his, her, or their factory, store or warehouse, the value shall be estimated by the average of the market value of the like goods, wares, and merchandise, during the time when the same would have become liable to and charged with duty. Value and quantity of goods estimated by actual sales. For consumption by market value.

SEC. 75. *And be it further enacted,* That from and after the said first day of August, eighteen hundred and sixty-two, upon the articles, goods, wares, and merchandise, hereinafter mentioned, which shall thereafter be produced and sold, or be manufactured or made and sold, or removed for consumption, or for delivery to others than agents of the manufacturer or producer within the United States or Territories thereof, there shall be levied, collected, and paid the following duties, to be paid by the producer or manufacturer thereof, that is to say: Duties on manufactures.

On candles, of whatever material made, three per centum ad valorem; Candles.

Mineral coals.	On all mineral coals, except such as are known in the trade as pea coal and dust coal, three and a half cents per ton: *Provided*, That for all contracts of lease of coal lands made before the first day of April, eighteen hundred and sixty-two, the lessee shall pay the tax.
Oils.	On lard oil, mustard-seed oil, linseed oil, and on all animal or vegetable oils not exempted nor provided for elsewhere, whether pure or adulterated, two cents per gallon: *Provided*, That red oil or oleic acid, produced in the manufacture of candles, and used as a material in the manufacture of soap, paraffine, whale and fish oil, shall be exempted from this duty;
Gas.	On gas, illuminating, made of coal, wholly or in part, or any other material, when the product shall be not above five hundred thousand cubic feet per month, five cents per one thousand cubic feet; when the product shall be above five hundred thousand, and not exceeding five millions of cubic feet per month, ten cents per one thousand cubic feet; when the product shall be above five millions, fifteen cents per one thousand cubic feet; and the general average of the monthly product for the year preceding the return required by this act shall regulate the rate of duty herein imposed; and where any gas company shall not have been in operation for the year next preceding the return as aforesaid, then the rate shall be regulated upon the estimated average of the monthly product: *Provided*, That the product required to be returned by this act shall be understood to be the product charged in the bills actually rendered by any gas company during
Companies to charge tax.	the month preceding the return, and all gas companies are hereby authorized to add the duty or tax imposed by this act to the price per thousand cubic feet on gas sold: *Provided, further*, That all gas furnished for lighting street lamps, and not measured, and all gas made for and used by any hotel, inn, tavern, and private dwelling-house, shall be subject to duty, and may be estimated; and if the returns in any case shall be understated or under estimated, it shall be the duty of the assistant assessor of the district to increase the same as he shall deem just and proper: *And provided, further*,
Coal tar exempt.	That coal tar produced in the manufacture of illuminating gas, and the products of the redistillation of coal tar thus produced, shall be exempt from duty: *And provided, further*, That gas companies so located as to compete with each other shall pay the rate imposed by this act upon the company having the largest production.
Coal oil.	On coal illuminating oil, refined, produced by the distillation of coal, asphaltum, shale, peat, petroleum, or rock oil, and all other bituminous substances used for like purposes, ten cents
Refined coal oil.	per gallon: *Provided*, That such oil refined and produced by the distillation of coal exclusively shall be subject to pay a duty of eight cents per gallon, anything in this act to the contrary notwithstanding: *And provided, further*, That distillers of coal oil shall be subject to all the provisions of this act hereinbefore set forth and specified applicable to distillers of spirituous liquors, with regard to licenses, bonds, returns, and all other provisions designed for the purpose of ascertaining the quantity distilled, and securing the payment of duties, so far as the same may, in the judgment of the

EXCISE TAX.

Commissioner of Internal Revenue, and under regulations prescribed by him, be necessary for that purpose.

On ground coffee, and all preparations of which coffee forms a part, or which is prepared for sale as a substitute for coffee, three mills per pound; — *Ground coffee.*

On ground pepper, ground mustard, ground pimento, ground cloves, ground cassia, and ground ginger, and all imitations of the same, one cent per pound; — *Ground spices.*

On sugar, refined, whether loaf, lump, granulated, or pulverized, two mills per pound; — *Refined sugar.*

On sugar, refined or made from molasses, sirup of molasses, melado or concentrated melado, two mills per pound;

On all brown, Muscovado, or clarified sugars produced directly from the sugar cane, and not from sorghum or imphee, other than those produced by the refiner, one cent per pound; — *Brown sugar, &c.*

On sugar candy and all confectionery, made wholly or in part of sugar, one cent per pound; — *Sugar candy.*

On chocolate, and cocoa prepared, one cent per pound; — *Chocolate.*

On saleratus and bicarbonate of soda, five mills per pound; — *Saleratus.*

On starch, made of potatoes, one mill per pound; made of corn or wheat, one and a half mills per pound; made of rice or any other material, four mills per pound; — *Starch.*

On tobacco, cavendish, plug, twist, fine cut, and manufactured of all descriptions, (not including snuff, cigars, and smoking tobacco prepared with all the stems in, or made exclusively of stems,) valued at more than thirty cents per pound, fifteen cents per pound; valued at any sum not exceeding thirty cents per pound, ten cents per pound; — *Tobacco.*

On smoking tobacco prepared with all the stems in, five cents per pound;

On smoking tobacco made exclusively of stems, two cents per pound;

On snuff manufactured of tobacco, ground dry or damp, of all descriptions, twenty cents per pound; — *Snuff.*

On cigars, valued at not over five dollars per thousand, one dollar and fifty cents per thousand; — *Cigars.*

On cigars, valued at over five and not over ten dollars per thousand, two dollars per thousand;

On cigars, valued at over ten and not over twenty dollars per thousand, two dollars and fifty cents per thousand;

On cigars, valued at over twenty dollars per thousand, three dollars and fifty cents per thousand;

On gunpowder, and all explosive substances used for mining, blasting, artillery, or sporting purposes, when valued at eighteen cents per pound or less, five mills per pound; when valued at above eighteen cents per pound, and not exceeding thirty cents per pound, one cent per pound; and when valued at above thirty cents per pound, six cents per pound; — *Gunpowder.*

On white lead, twenty-five cents per one hundred pounds; — *White lead.*

On oxide of zinc, twenty-five cents per one hundred pounds; — *Oxide of zinc.*

On sulphate of barytes, ten cents per one hundred pounds: *Provided*, That white lead, oxide of zinc, and sulphate of barytes, or any one of them, shall not be subject to any additional duty in consequence of being mixed or ground with linseed oil, when the duties upon all the materials so mixed or ground shall have been previously actually paid — *Sulphate of barytes.* *Lead, zinc, and barytes mixed with oil.*

Paints and colors. On all paints and painters' colors, dry or ground in oil, or in paste with water, not otherwise provided for, five per centum ad valorem;

Clock movements. On clock movements made to run one day, five cents each; made to run more than one day, ten cents each;

Pins. On pins, solid head or other, five per centum ad valorem;

Umbrellas and parasols. On umbrellas and parasols made of cotton, silk, or other material, five per centum ad valorem;

Screws. On screws, commonly called wood screws, one and a half cent per pound;

Iron. On railroad iron and all other iron advanced beyond slabs, blooms, or loops, and not advanced beyond bars or rods, and band, hoop, and sheet iron, not thinner than number eighteen wire-gauge, and plate iron not less than one-eighth of an inch in thickness, one dollar and fifty cents per ton; on railroad iron, re-rolled, seventy-five cents per ton; on band, hoop, and sheet iron thinner than number eighteen wire-gauge, plate iron less than one-eighth of an inch in thickness, and cut nails and spikes, two dollars per ton: *Provided,* That bars, rods, bands, hoops, sheets, plates, nails, and spikes, manufactured from iron upon which the duty of one dollar and fifty cents has been levied and paid, shall be subject only to a duty of fifty cents per ton in addition thereto, anything in this act to the contrary notwithstanding. On stoves and hollow ware, one dollar and fifty cents per ton of two thousand pounds; cast iron used for bridges, buildings, or other permanent structures, one dollar per ton: *Provided,* That bar iron used for like purposes shall be charged no additional duty beyond the specific duty imposed by this act. On steel in ingots, bars, sheets, or wire not less than one-fourth of an inch in thickness, valued at seven cents per pound or less, four dollars per ton; valued at above seven cents per pound, and not above eleven cents per pound, eight dollars per ton; valued above eleven cents per pound, ten dollars per ton;

Proviso.

Paper. On paper of all descriptions, including pasteboard and binders' boards, three per centum ad valorem;

Soap. On soap, castile, palm-oil, erasive, and soap of all other descriptions, white or colored, except soft soap and soap otherwise provided for, valued not above three and a half cents per pound, one mill per pound; valued at above three and a half cents per pound, five mills per pound;

Fancy soap. On soap, fancy, scented, honey, cream, transparent, and all descriptions of toilet and shaving soap, two cents per pound;

Salt. On salt, four cents per one hundred pounds;

Preserved fruits and meats. On pickles and preserved fruits, and on all preserved meats, fish, and shell-fish in cans or air-tight packages, five per centum ad valorem;

Glue and gelatine. On glue and gelatine of all descriptions, in the solid state, five mills per pound;

Glue and cement. On glue and cement, made wholly or in part of glue, to be sold in the liquid state, twenty-five cents per gallon;

Leather. On patent or enamelled leather, five mills per square foot;

On patent Japanned split, used for dasher leather, four mills per square foot;

On patent or enamelled skirting leather, one and a half cent per square foot;

On all sole and rough or harness leather, made from hides, imported east of the Cape of Good Hope, and all damaged leather, five mills per pound;
On all other sole or rough leather, hemlock tanned, and harness leather, seven mills per pound;
On all sole or rough leather, tanned in whole or in part with oak, one cent per pound;
On all finished or curried upper leather, made from leather tanned in the interest of the parties finishing or currying such leather not previously taxed in the rough, except calf skins, one cent per pound;
On bend and butt leather, one cent per pound;
On offal leather, five mills per pound;
On oil-dressed leather, and deer skins dressed or smoked, two cents per pound;
On tanned calf skins, six cents each; Calf skins.
On morocco, goat, kid, or sheep skins, curried, manufactured, or finished, four per centum ad valorem: *Provided*, That the price at which such skins are usually sold shall determine their value; Morocco, &c.
Value, how determined.
On horse and hog skins tanned and dressed, four per centum ad valorem;
On American patent calf skins, five per centum ad valorem; Calf skins.
On conducting hose of all kinds for conducting water or other fluids, a duty of three per centum ad valorem; Conducti'g hose.
On wine, made of grapes, five cents per gallon; Wine.
On varnish, made wholly or in part of gum copal or other gums or substances, five per centum ad valorem; Varnish.
On furs of all descriptions, when made up or manufactured, three per centum ad valorem; Furs.
On cloth and all textile or knitted or felted fabrics of cotton, wool, or other materials, before the same has been dyed, printed, bleached, or prepared in any other manner, a duty of three per centum ad valorem: *Provided*, That thread or yarn manufactured and sold or delivered exclusively for knitted fabrics, or for weaving, when the spinning and weaving for the manufacture of cloth of any kind is carried on separately, shall not be regarded as manufactures within the meaning of this act; but all fabrics of cotton, wool, or other material, whether woven, knit, or felted, shall be regarded as manufactures, and be subject to the duty, as above, of three per centum ad valorem; Cloth.
Thread and yarn.
On all diamonds, emeralds, and all other jewelry, a tax of three per centum ad valorem; Diamonds and jewelry.
On and after the first day of October, eighteen hundred and sixty-two, there shall be levied, collected, and paid, a tax of one-half of one cent per pound on all cotton held or owned by any person or persons, corporation, or association of persons; and such tax shall be a lien thereon in the possession of any person whomsoever. And further, if any person or persons, corporations, or association of persons, shall remove, carry, or transport the same from the place of its production before said tax shall have been paid, such person or persons, corporation, or association of persons, shall forfeit and pay to the United States double the amount of such tax, to be recovered in any court having jurisdiction thereof: *Provided, however*, That the Commissioner of Internal Revenue Cotton.
Tax a lien.
Proviso.

is hereby authorized to make such rules and regulations as he may deem proper for the payment of said tax at places different from that of the production of said cotton: *And provided, further,* That all cotton owned and held by any manufacturer of cotton fabrics on the first day [of] October, eighteen hundred and sixty-two, and prior thereto, shall be exempt from the tax hereby imposed;

Manufactures of cotton, silk, &c.

On all manufactures of cotton, wool, silk, worsted, flax, hemp, jute, India-rubber, gutta-percha, wood, willow, glass, pottery-ware, leather, paper, iron, steel, lead, tin, copper, zinc, brass, gold, silver, horn, ivory, bone, bristles, wholly or in part, or of other materials, not in this act otherwise provided for, a duty of three per centum ad valorem:

Cloths dyed, &c.

Provided, That on all cloths dyed, printed, bleached, manufactured into other fabrics, or otherwise prepared, on which a duty or tax shall have been paid before the same were so dyed, printed, bleached, manufactured, or prepared, the said duty or tax of three per centum shall be assessed only upon the increased value thereof:

Gloves, mittens, &c.

And provided, further, That on all oil-dressed leather, and deer skins dressed or smoked, manufactured into gloves, mittens, or other articles on which a duty or tax shall have been paid before the same were so manufactured, the said duty or tax of three per centum shall be assessed only upon the increased valuation thereof:

Duties, how to be estimated.

And provided, further, That in estimating the duties upon articles manufactured when removed and sold at any other place than the place of manufacture, there shall be deducted from the gross amount of sales the freight, commission, and expenses of sale actually paid, and the duty shall be assessed and paid upon the net amount after the deductions as aforesaid:

Articles not regarded as within the meaning of this section.

And provided, further, That printed books, magazines, pamphlets, newspapers, reviews, and all other similar printed publications; boards, shingles, and all other lumber and timber; staves, hoops, headings, and timber only partially wrought and unfinished for chairs, tubs, pails, snathes, lasts, shovel and fork handles; umbrella stretchers; pig iron, and iron not advanced beyond slabs, blooms, or loops; maps and charts; charcoal; alcohol made or manufactured of spirits or materials upon which the duties imposed by this act shall have been paid; plaster or gypsum; malt; burning fluid; printers' ink; flax prepared for textile or felting purposes, until actually woven or fitted into fabrics for consumption; all flour and meal made from grain; bread and breadstuffs; pearl barley and split peas; butter; cheese; concentrated milk; bullion, in the manufacture of silverware; brick; lime; Roman cement; draining tiles; marble; slate; building stone; copper, in ingots or pigs; and lead, in pigs or bars, shall not be regarded as manufactures within the meaning of this act: *Provided,* That whenever, by the provisions of this act, a duty is imposed upon any article removed for consumption or sale, it shall apply only to such articles as are manufactured on or after the first day of August, eighteen hundred and sixty-two, and to such as are manufactured and not removed from the place of manufacture prior to that date.

AUCTION SALES.

Sec. 76. *And be it further enacted*, That on and after the first day of August, eighteen hundred and sixty-two, there shall be levied, collected, and paid on all sales of real estate, goods, wares, merchandise, articles, or things at auction, including all sales of stocks, bonds, and other securities, a duty of one-tenth of one per centum on the gross amount of such sales, and every auctioneer making such sales, as aforesaid, shall at the end of each and every month, or within ten days thereafter, make a list or return to the assistant assessor of the district of the gross amount of such sales, made as aforesaid, with the amount of duty which has accrued, or should accrue thereon, which list shall have annexed thereto a declaration under oath or affirmation, in form and manner as may be prescribed by the Commissioner of Internal Revenue, that the same is true and correct, and shall at the same time, as aforesaid, pay to the collector or deputy collector the amount of duty or tax thereupon, as aforesaid, and in default thereof shall be subject to and pay a penalty of five hundred dollars. In all cases of delinquency in making said list or payment the assessment and collection shall be made in the manner prescribed in the general provisions of this act: *Provided*, That no duty shall be levied under the provisions of this section upon any sales by judicial or executive officers making auction sales by virtue of a judgment or decree of any court, nor to public sales made by executors or administrators.

Auction sales.

Make monthly returns of gross amount of sales.

Penalty.

No duty levied on sales by judicial officers, &c.

CARRIAGES, YACHTS, BILLIARD-TABLES, AND PLATE.

Sec. 77. *And be it further enacted*, That from and after the first day of May, eighteen hundred and sixty-two, there shall be levied, collected, and paid, by any person or persons owning, possessing, or keeping any carriage, yacht, and billiard-table, the several duties or sums of money set down in figures against the same respectively, or otherwise specified and set forth in schedule marked A.

SCHEDULE A.

CARRIAGES, YACHTS, BILLIARD-TABLES, AND PLATE.

	Duty. Dolls. cts.	
Carriage, gig, chaise, phæton, wagon, buggy-wagon, carryall, rockaway, or other like carriage, the body of which rests upon springs of any description, kept for use, and which shall not be exclusively employed in husbandry or for the transportation of merchandise, and valued at seventy-five dollars or over, including the harness used therewith, when drawn by one horse, one dollar, ...	1 00	Carriages, drawn by one horse.
Carriages of like description drawn by two horses, and any coach, hackney-coach, omnibus, or four-wheel carriage, the body of which rests upon springs of any description, which may be kept for use, for hire, or for passengers, and which shall not be exclusively employed in husbandry or for the transportation of		Carriages, &c., drawn by two horses or more.

	Duty.
	Dolls. cts.

merchandise, valued at seventy-five dollars, and not exceeding two hundred dollars, including the harness used therewith, drawn by two horses or more, two dollars, ... 2 00

Carriages of like description, when valued above two hundred dollars, and not exceeding six hundred dollars, five dollars, ... 5 00

Carriages of like description, valued above six hundred dollars, ten dollars, ... 10 00

Pleasure vessels. Pleasure or racing vessels, known as yachts, whether by sail or steam, under the value of six hundred dollars, five dollars, ... 5 00

Yachts. Yachts valued above six hundred dollars, and not exceeding one thousand dollars, ten dollars, . . . 10 00

And for each additional one thousand dollars in value of said yachts, ten dollars, ... 10 00

Billiard-tables. Billiard-tables, kept for use, ten dollars, ... 10 00

Plate. Plate of gold, kept for use, per ounce troy, fifty cents, . 50

Plate of silver, kept for use, per ounce troy, three cents, 3

Amount exempt from duty. Provided, That silver spoons or plate of silver, to an amount not exceeding forty ounces, as aforesaid, belonging to any one person, shall be exempt from duty.

Slaughtered cattle, hogs and sheep.

SLAUGHTERED CATTLE, HOGS, AND SHEEP.

SEC. 78. *And be it further enacted,* That on and after the first day of August, eighteen hundred and sixty-two, there shall be levied, collected, and paid by any person or persons, firms, companies, or agents or employees thereof, the following duties or taxes, that is to say:

Cattle. On all horned cattle exceeding eighteen months old, slaughtered for sale, thirty cents per head;

On all calves and cattle under eighteen months old, slaughtered for sale, five cents per head;

Hogs. On all hogs, exceeding six months old, slaughtered for sale, when the number thus slaughtered exceeds twenty in any one year, ten cents per head;

Sheep. On all sheep, slaughtered for sale, five cents per head: *Provided,* That all cattle, hogs, and sheep, slaughtered by any person for his or her own consumption, shall be exempt from duty.

SEC. 79. *And be it further enacted,* That on and after the date on which this act shall take effect, any person or persons, firms, or companies, or agents or employees thereof, whose business or occupation it is to slaughter for sale any cattle, calves, sheep, or *To make monthly statement.* hogs, shall be required to make and render a list at the end of each and every month to the assistant assessor of the district where the business is transacted, stating the number of cattle, calves, if any, the number of hogs, if any, and the number of sheep, if any, slaughtered, as aforesaid, with the several rates of duty as fixed therein in this act, together with the whole amount thereof, which list shall have annexed thereto a declaration of said person or persons, agents or employees thereof, as aforesaid, under oath or affirmations, in such manner and form as may be prescribed by the Commissioner of Internal Revenue, that the same is true and correct, and shall, at the time of rendering said list, pay the full amount of duties which have accrued or should accrue, as aforesaid, to the collector or deputy collector of the district, as aforesaid; and in case of default in making the return or payment of the duties, as aforesaid, the assessment and collection shall be made as in the general provisions of this act required, and in case of fraud or evasion the party offending shall forfeit and pay a penalty of ten dollars per head for any cattle, calves, hogs, or sheep so slaughtered upon which the duty is fraudulently withheld, evaded, or attempted to be evaded: *Provided,* That the Commissioner of Internal Revenue shall prescribe such further rules and regulations as he may deem necessary for ascertaining the correct number of cattle, calves, hogs, and sheep, liable to be taxed under the provisions of this act. Penalty.

RAILROADS, STEAMBOATS, AND FERRY-BOATS.

SEC. 80. *And be it further enacted,* That on and after the first day of August, eighteen hundred and sixty-two, any person or persons, firms, companies, or corporations, owning or possessing, or having the care or management of any railroad or railroads upon which steam is used as a propelling power, or of any steamboat or other vessel propelled by steam-power, shall be subject to and pay a duty of three per centum on the gross amount of all the receipts of such railroad or railroads or steam vessel for the transportation of passengers over and upon the same; and any person or persons, firms, companies, or corporations, owning or possessing, or having the care or management of any railroad or railroads using any other power than steam thereon, or owning, possessing, or having the care or management of any ferry-boat, or vessel used as a ferry-boat, propelled by steam or horse power, shall be subject to and pay a duty of one and a half per centum upon the gross receipts of such railroad or ferry-boat, respectively, for the transportation of passengers over and upon said railroads, steamboats, and ferry-boats, respectively; and any person or persons, firms, companies, or corporations, owning, possessing, or having the care or management of any bridge authorized by law to receive toll for the transit of passengers, beasts, carriages, teams, and freight of any description over such bridge, shall be subject to and pay a duty of three per centum on the gross amount of all their receipts of every description. And the owner, possessor, or person or persons having the care and management of any such railroad, steamboat, ferry-boat, or other vessel, or bridge, as aforesaid, shall, within five days after the end of each and every month, commencing as hereinbefore mentioned, make a list or return to the assistant assessor of the district within which such owner, possessor, company, or corporation may have his or its place of business, or where any such railroad, steamboat, ferry-boat, or bridge is located or belongs, respectively, stating the gross amount of such receipts for the month next preceding, which return shall be verified by the oath or affirmation of such owner, possessor, manager, agent, or other proper officer, in the manner and form to be prescribed from time to time by the Commissioner of Internal Revenue, and shall also, monthly, at the time of making such return, pay to the collector or deputy collector of the district the full amount of duties which have accrued on such receipts for the month aforesaid; and in case of neglect or refusal to make said lists or return for the space of five days after such return should be made as aforesaid, the assessor or assistant assessor shall proceed to estimate the amount received and the duties payable thereon, as hereinbefore provided in other cases of delinquency to make return for purposes of assessment; and for the purpose of making such assessment, or of ascertaining the correctness of any such return, the books of any such person, company, or corporation shall be subject to the inspection of the assessor or assistant assessor on his demand or request therefor; and in case of neglect or refusal to pay the duties as aforesaid when the same have been ascertained as aforesaid for the space of five days after the same shall have become payable, the owner, possessor, or person having the management as aforesaid, shall pay, in addition, five per centum on the amount of such duties; and for any attempt knowingly to evade the payment of such duties, the said owner, possessor, or person having the care or management as aforesaid, shall be liable to pay a penalty of one thousand dollars for every such attempt, to be recovered as provided in this act for the recovery of penalties; and all provisions of this act in relation to liens and collections by distraint not incompatible herewith shall apply to this section and the objects therein embraced: *Provided*, That all such persons, companies, and corporations shall have the right to add the duty or tax imposed hereby to their rates of fare whenever their liability thereto may commence, any limitations which may exist by law or by agreement with any person or company which may have paid or be liable to pay such fare to the contrary notwithstanding.

RAILROAD BONDS.

SEC. 81. *And be it further enacted*, That on and after the first day of July, eighteen hundred and sixty-two, any person or persons owning or possessing, or having the care or management of any railroad company or railroad corporation, being indebted for any sum or sums of money for which bonds or other evidences of indebtedness have been issued, payable in one or more years after date, upon which interest is, or shall be, stipulated to be paid, or coupons representing the interest shall be or shall have been issued to be paid, and all dividends in scrip or money or sums of money thereafter declared due or payable to stockholders of any railroad company, as part of the earnings, profits, or gains of said companies, shall be subject to and pay a duty of three per centum on the amount of all such interest or coupons or dividends whenever the same shall be paid; and said railroad companies or railroad corporations, or any person or persons owning, possessing, or having the care or management of any railroad company or railroad corporation, are hereby authorized and required to deduct and withhold from all payments made to any person, persons, or party, after the first day of July, as aforesaid, on account of any interest or coupons or dividends due and payable as aforesaid, the said duty or sum of three per centum; and the duties deducted as aforesaid, and certified by the president or other proper officer of said company or corporation, shall be a receipt and discharge, according to the amount thereof, of said railroad companies or railroad corporations, and the owners, possessors, and agents thereof, on dividends and on bonds or other evidences of their indebtedness, upon which interest or coupons are payable, holden by any person or party whatsoever, and a list or return shall be made and rendered within thirty days after the time fixed when said interest or coupons or dividends become due or payable, and as often as every six months, to the Commissioner of Internal Revenue, which shall contain a true and faithful account of the duties received and chargeable, as aforesaid, during the time when such duties have accrued or should accrue, and remaining unaccounted for; and there shall be annexed to every such list or return a declaration under oath or affirmation, in manner and form as may be prescribed by the Commissioner of Internal Revenue, of the president, treasurer, or some proper officer of said railroad company or railroad corporation, that the same contains a true and faithful account of the duties so withheld and received during the time when such duties have accrued or should accrue, and not accounted for, and for any default in the making or rendering of such list or return, with the declaration annexed, as aforesaid, the person or persons owning, possessing, or having the care or management of such railroad company or railroad corporation, making such default, shall forfeit, as a penalty, the sum of five hundred dollars; and in case of any default in making or rendering said list, or of any default in the payment of the duty, or any part thereof, accruing or which should accrue, the assessment and collection shall be made according to the general provisions of this act. Statement to be made every six months. Penalty.

BANKS, TRUST COMPANIES, SAVINGS INSTITUTIONS, AND INSURANCE COMPANIES.

SEC. 82. *And be it further enacted*, That on and after the first day of July, eighteen hundred and sixty-two, there shall be levied, collected, and paid by all banks, trust companies, and savings institutions, and by all fire, marine, life, inland, stock, and mutual insurance companies, under whatever style or name known or called, of the United States or Territories, specially incorporated or existing under general laws, or which may be hereafter incorporated or exist as aforesaid, on all dividends in scrip or money thereafter declared due or paid to stockholders, to policy holders, or to depositors, as part of the earnings, profits, or gains of said banks, trust companies, savings institutions, or insurance companies, and on all sums added to their surplus or contingent funds, a duty of three per centum: *Provided*, That the duties upon the dividends of life insurance companies shall not be deemed due, or to be collected until such dividends shall be payable by such companies. And said banks, trust companies, savings institutions, and insurance companies are hereby authorized and required to deduct and withhold from all payments made to any person, persons, or party, on account of any dividends or sums of money that may be due and payable, as aforesaid, after the first day of July, eighteen hundred and sixty-two, the said duty of three per centum. And a list or return shall be made and rendered within thirty days after the time fixed when such dividends or sums of money shall be declared due and payable, and as often as every six months, to the Commissioner of Internal Revenue, which shall contain a true and faithful account of the amount of duties accrued or which should accrue from time to time, as aforesaid, during the time when such duties remain unaccounted for, and there shall be annexed to every such list or return a declaration, under oath or affirmation, to be made in form and manner as shall be prescribed by the Commissioner of Internal Revenue, of the president, or some other proper officer of said bank, trust company, savings institution, or insurance company, respectively, that the same contains a true and faithful account of the duties which have accrued or should accrue, and not accounted for, and for any default in the delivery of such list or return, with such declaration annexed, the bank, trust company, savings institution, or insurance company making such default shall forfeit, as a penalty, the sum of five hundred dollars.

Penalty.

SEC. 83. *And be it further enacted*, That any person or persons owning or possessing, or having the care or management of any railroad company or railroad corporation, bank, trust company, savings institution, or insurance company, as heretofore mentioned, required under this act to make and render any list or return to the Commissioner of Internal Revenue, shall, upon rendering the same, pay to the said Commissioner of Internal Revenue the amount of the duties due on such list or return, and in default thereof shall forfeit as a penalty the sum of five hundred dollars; and in case of neglect or refusal to make such list or return as aforesaid, or to pay the duties as aforesaid, for the space of thirty days after the time when said list should have been made and rendered, or when said duties shall have become due and payable, the assessment and collection shall be made according to the general provisions heretofore prescribed in this act.

Pay duties upon rendering statement.

Penalty.

SEC. 84. *And be it further enacted*, That on the first day of October, anno Domini eighteen hundred and sixty-two, and on the first day of each quarter of a year thereafter, there shall be paid by each insurance company, whether inland or marine, and by each individual or association engaged in the business of insurance from loss or damage by fire, or by the perils of the sea, the duty of one per centum upon the gross receipts for premiums and assessments by such individual, association, or company during the quarter then preceding; and like duty shall be paid by the agent of any foreign insurance company having an office or doing business within the United States.

Insurance companies.

Duty.

SEC. 85. *And be it further enacted*, That on the first day of October next, and on the first day of each quarter thereafter, an account shall be made and rendered to the Commissioner of Internal Revenue by all insurance companies, or their agents, or associations or individuals making insurance, except life insurance, including agents of all foreign insurance companies, which shall contain a true and faithful account of the insurance made, renewed, or continued, or indorsed upon any open policy by said companies, or their agents, or associations, or individuals during the preceding quarter, setting forth the amount insured, and the gross amount received, and the duties accruing thereon under this act; and there shall be annexed to and delivered with every such quarterly account an affidavit, in the form to be prescribed by the Commissioner of Internal Revenue, made by one of the officers of said company or association, or individual, or by the agent in the case of a foreign company, that the statements in said accounts are in all respects just and true; and such quarterly accounts shall be rendered to the Commissioner of Internal Revenue within thirty days after the expiration of the quarter for which they shall be made up, and upon rendering such account, with such affidavit, as aforesaid, thereto annexed, the amount of the duties due by such

To make quarterly returns.

EXCISE TAX.

quarterly accounts shall be paid to the Commissioner of Internal Revenue; and for every default in the delivery of such quarterly account, with such affidavit annexed thereto, or in the payment of the amount of the duties due by such quarterly account, the company, or agent, or association, or individual making such default shall forfeit and pay, in addition to such duty, the sum of five thousand dollars. *Penalty.*

SALARIES AND PAY OF OFFICERS AND PERSONS IN THE SERVICE OF THE UNITED STATES, AND PASSPORTS.

SEC. 86. *And be it further enacted,* That on and after the first day of August, eighteen hundred and sixty-two, there shall be levied, collected, and paid on all salaries of officers, or payments to persons in the civil, military, naval, or other employment or service of the United States, including senators and representatives and delegates in Congress, when exceeding the rate of six hundred dollars per annum, a duty of three per centum on the excess above the said six hundred dollars; and it shall be the duty of all paymasters, and all disbursing officers, under the government of the United States, or in the employ thereof, when making any payments to officers and persons as aforesaid, or upon settling and adjusting the accounts of such officers and persons, to deduct and withhold the aforesaid duty of three per centum, and shall, at the same time, make a certificate stating the name of the officer or person from whom such deduction was made, and the amount thereof, which shall be transmitted to the office of the Commissioner of Internal Revenue, and entered as part of the internal duties; and the pay-roll, receipts, or account of officers or persons paying such duty, as aforesaid, shall be made to exhibit the fact of such payment. *Tax on salaries over $600.* *Duty.*

SEC. 87. *And be it further enacted,* That for every passport issued from the office of the Secretary of State, after the thirtieth day of June, eighteen hundred and sixty-two, there shall be paid the sum of three dollars; which amount may be paid to any collector appointed under this act, and his receipt therefor shall be forwarded with the application for such passport to the office of the Secretary of State, or any agent appointed by him. And the collectors shall account for all moneys received for passports in the manner hereinbefore provided, and a like amount shall be paid for every passport issued by any minister or consul of the United States, who shall account therefor to the treasury. *Tax on passports.*

ADVERTISEMENTS.

SEC. 88. *And be it further enacted,* That on and after the first day of August, eighteen hundred and sixty-two, there shall be levied, collected, and paid by any person or persons, firm, or company, publishing any newspaper, magazine, review, or other literary, scientific, or news publication, issued periodically, on the gross receipts for all advertisements, or all matters for the insertion of which in said newspaper or other publication, as aforesaid, or in extras, supplements, sheets, or fly-leaves accompanying the same, pay is required or received, a duty of three per centum; and the person or persons, firm or company, owning, possessing, or having the care or management of any and every such newspaper or other *Advertisements.* *Duty.*

publication, as aforesaid, shall make a list or return quarterly, commencing as heretofore mentioned, containing the gross amount of receipts as aforesaid, and the amount of duties which have accrued thereon, and render the same to the assistant assessor of the respective districts where such newspaper, magazine, review, or other literary or news publication is or may be published, which list or return shall have annexed a declaration, under oath or affirmation, to be made according to the manner and form which may be from time to time prescribed by the Commissioner of Internal Revenue, of the owner, possessor, or person having the care or management of such newspaper, magazine, review, or other publication, as aforesaid, that the same is true and correct, and *Make quarterly returns.* shall also, quarterly, and at the time of making said list or return, pay to the collector or deputy collector of the district, as aforesaid, the full amount of said duties; and in case of neglect or refusal to comply with any of the provisions contained in this section, or to make and render said list or return, as aforesaid, for the space of thirty days after the time when said list or return ought to have been made, as aforesaid, the assistant assessor of the respective districts shall proceed to estimate the duties, as heretofore provided in other cases of delinquency; and in case of neglect or refusal to pay the duties, as aforesaid, for the space of thirty days after said duties become due and payable, said owner, possessor, or person or persons having the care or management of said newspapers *Penalty.* or publications, as aforesaid, shall pay, in addition thereto, a penalty of five per centum on the amount due; and in case of fraud or evasion, whereby the revenue is attempted to be defrauded, or the duty withheld, said owners, possessors, or person or persons having the care or management of said newspapers or other publica- *Penalty for fraud.* tions, as aforesaid, shall forfeit and pay a penalty of five hundred dollars for each offence, or for any sum fraudulently unaccounted for; and all provisions in this act in relation to liens, assessments, and collection, not incompatible herewith, shall apply to this sec- *Proviso.* tion and the objects herein embraced: *Provided,* That in all cases where the rate or price of advertising is fixed by any law of the United States, State, or Territory, it shall be lawful for the company, person or persons, publishing said advertisements, to add the duty or tax imposed by this act to the price of said advertisements, any law, as aforesaid, to the contrary notwithstanding: *Receipts under $1,000 exempt. Provided, further,* That the receipts for advertisements to the amount of one thousand dollars, by any person or persons, firm, or company, publishing any newspaper, magazine, review, or other literary, scientific, news publication, issued periodically, shall be *Newspapers circulating under two thousand, exempt.* exempt from duty: *And provided, further,* That all newspapers whose circulation does not exceed two thousand copies shall be exempted from all taxes for advertisements.

INCOME DUTY.

SEC. 89. *And be it further enacted,* That for the purpose of modifying and re-enacting, as hereinafter provided, so much of an *Act Aug. 5, 1861, repealing sections 49, 50, 51.* act, entitled "An act to provide increased revenue from imports to pay interest on the public debt, and for other purposes," approved fifth of August, eighteen hundred and sixty-one, as relates to income tax; that is to say, sections forty-nine, fifty, (except so much thereof as relates to the selection and appointment of depositaries,) and fifty-one, be, and the same are hereby, repealed.

EXCISE TAX.

Sec. 90. *And be it further enacted,* That there shall be levied, collected, and paid annually, upon the annual gains, profits, or income of every person residing in the United States, whether derived from any kind of property, rents, interest, dividends, salaries, or from any profession, trade, employment, or vocation carried on in the United States or elsewhere, or from any other source whatever, except as in hereinafter mentioned, if such annual gains, profits, or income exceed the sum of six hundred dollars, and do not exceed the sum of ten thousand dollars, a duty of three per centum on the amount of such annual gains, profits, or income over and above the said sum of six hundred dollars; if said income exceeds the sum of ten thousand dollars, a duty of five per centum upon the amount thereof exceeding six hundred dollars; and upon the annual gains, profits, or income, rents, and dividends accruing upon any property, securities, and stocks owned in the United States by any citizen of the United States residing abroad, except as hereinafter mentioned, and not in the employment of the government of the United States, there shall be levied, collected, and paid a duty of five per centum. *[Income. Not exceeding $10,000. Duty. Exceed'g $10,000. Duty.]*

Sec. 91. *And be it further enacted,* That in estimating said annual gains, profits, or income, whether subject to a duty, as provided in this act, of three per centum, or of five per centum, all other national, State, and local taxes, lawfully assessed upon the property or other sources of income of any person as aforesaid, from which said annual gains, profits, or income of such person is or should be derived, shall be first deducted from the gains, profits, or income of the person or persons who actually pay the same, whether owner or tenant, and all gains, profits, or income derived from salaries of officers, or payments to persons in the civil, military, naval, or other service of the United States, including senators, representatives, and delegates in Congress, above six hundred dollars, or derived from interest or dividends on stock, capital, or deposits in any bank, trust company, or savings institution, insurance, gas, bridge, express, telegraph, steamboat, ferry-boat, or railroad company, or corporation, or on any bonds, or other evidences of indebtedness of any railroad company or other corporation, which shall have been assessed and paid by said banks, trust companies, savings institutions, insurance, gas, bridge, telegraph, steamboat, ferry-boat, express, or railroad companies, as aforesaid, or derived from advertisements, or on any articles manufactured, upon which specific, stamp or ad valorem duties shall have been directly assessed or paid, shall also be deducted; and the duty herein provided for shall be assessed and collected upon the income for the year ending the thirty-first day of December next preceding the time for levying and collecting said duty, that is to say, on the first day of May, eighteen hundred and sixty-three, and in each year thereafter: *Provided,* That upon such portion of said gains, profits, or income, whether subject to a duty as provided in this act of three per centum or five per centum, which shall be derived from interest upon notes, bonds, or other securities of the United States, there shall be levied, collected, and paid a duty not exceeding one and one-half of one per centum, anything in this act to the contrary notwithstanding. *[All other taxes to be deducted. When to be assessed. When to be collected. Proviso. U. S. securities.]*

Sec. 92. *And be it further enacted,* That the duties on incomes

50 EXCISE TAX.

Limitation to income tax.
Five per cent. added.
Penalty for non-payment.
Tax a lien.
Distraint.
Commissioner to levy after ten days' notice.
Certificate of collector to make valid title.
Persons to make return of income.
Guardians and trustees.

herein imposed shall be due and payable on or before the thirtieth day of June, in the year eighteen hundred and sixty-three, and in each year thereafter until and including the year eighteen hundred and sixty-six, and no longer; and to any sum or sums annually due and unpaid for thirty days after the thirtieth of June, as aforesaid, and for ten days after demand thereof by the collector, there shall be levied in addition thereto, the sum of five per centum on the amount of duties unpaid, as a penalty, except from the estates of deceased and insolvent persons; and if any person or persons, or party, liable to pay such duty, shall neglect or refuse to pay the same, the amount due shall be a lien in favor of the United States from the time it was so due until paid, with the interest, penalties, and costs that may accrue in addition thereto, upon all the property, and rights to property, stocks, securities, and debts of every description from which the income upon which said duty is assessed or levied shall have accrued or may or should accrue; and in default of the payment of said duty for the space of thirty days, after the same shall have become due, and be demanded, as aforesaid, said lien may be enforced by distraint upon such property, rights to property, stocks, securities, and evidences of debt, by whomsoever holden; and for this purpose the Commissioner of Internal Revenue, upon the certificate of the collector or deputy collector that said duty is due and unpaid for the space of ten days after notice duly given of the levy of such duty, shall issue a warrant, in form and manner to be prescribed by said Commissioner of Internal Revenue, under the directions of the Secretary of the Treasury, and by virtue of such warrant there may be levied on such property, rights to property, stocks, securities, and evidences of debt, a further sum, to be fixed and stated in such warrant, over and above the said annual duty, interest, and penalty for non-payment, sufficient for the fees and expenses of such levy. And in all cases of sale, as aforesaid, the certificate of such sale by the collector or deputy collector of the sale, shall give title to the purchaser, of all right, title, and interest of such delinquent in and to such property, whether the property be real or personal; and where the subject of sale shall be stocks, the certificate of said sale shall be lawful authority and notice to the proper corporation, company, or association, to record the same on the books or records, in the same manner as if transferred or assigned by the person or party holding the same, to issue new certificates of stock therefor in lieu of any original or prior certificates, which shall be void whether cancelled or not; and said certificates of sale of the collector or deputy collector, where the subject of sale shall be securities or other evidences of debt, shall be good and valid receipts to the person or party holding the same, as against any person or persons, or other party holding, or claiming to hold, possession of such securities or other evidences of debt.

SEC. 93. *And be it further enacted,* That it shall be the duty of all persons of lawful age, and all guardians and trustees, whether such trustees are so by virtue of their office as executors, administrators, or other fiduciary capacity, to make return in the list or schedule, as provided in this act, to the proper officer of internal revenue, of the amount of his or her income, or the income of such minors or persons as may be held in trust as aforesaid, according to the requirements hereinbefore stated, and in case of neglect or refusal to make such return, the assessor or assistant assessor shall assess the amount of his or her income, and proceed thereafter to collect the duty thereon in the same manner as is provided for in other cases of neglect and refusal to furnish lists or schedules in the general provisions of this act, where not otherwise incompatible, and the assistant assessor may increase the amount of the list or return, or of any party making such return, if he shall be satisfied that the same is understated : *Provided,* That any party, in his or her own behalf, or as guardian or trustee, as aforesaid, shall be permitted to declare, under oath or affirmation, the form and manner of which shall be prescribed by the Commissioner of Internal Revenue, that he or she was not possessed of an income of six hundred dollars, liable to be assessed according to the provisions of this act, or that he or she has been assessed elsewhere and the same year for an income duty, under authority of the United States, and shall thereupon be exempt from an income duty ; or, if the list or return of any party shall have been increased by the assistant assessor, in manner as aforesaid, he or she may be permitted to declare, as aforesaid, the amount of his or her annual income, or the amount held in trust, as aforesaid, liable to be assessed, as aforesaid, and the same so declared shall be received as the sum upon which duties are to be assessed and collected.

Assessors to make return in cases of neglect.

Proviso.

STAMP DUTIES.

SEC. 94. *And be it further enacted,* That on and after the first day of October, eighteen hundred and sixty-two, there shall be levied, collected, and paid, for and in respect of the several instruments, matters, and things mentioned, and described in the schedule (marked B) hereunto annexed, or for or in respect of the vellum, parchment, or paper upon which such instruments, matters, or things, or any of them, shall be written or printed, by any person or persons, or party who shall make, sign, or issue the same, or for whose use or benefit the same shall be made, signed, or issued, the several duties or sums of money set down in figures against the same, respectively, or otherwise specified or set forth in the said schedule.

Stamp duties.

Schedule B.

SEC. 95. *And be it further enacted,** That if any person or persons shall make, sign, or issue, or cause to be made, signed, or issued, any instrument, document, or paper of any kind or description whatsoever, without the same being duly stamped for denoting the duty hereby imposed thereon, or without having thereupon an adhesive stamp to denote said duty, such person or persons shall incur a penalty of fifty dollars, and such instrument, document, or paper, as aforesaid, shall be deemed invalid and of no effect.

Penalty for not using stamp.

SEC. 96. *And be it further enacted,* That no stamp appropriated to denote the duty charged on any particular instrument, and bearing the name of such instrument on the face thereof, shall be used for denoting any other duty of the same amount, or if so used the same shall be of no avail.

Stamp for a particular instrument not to be used for another.

SEC. 97. *And be it further enacted,* That no vellum, parchment, or paper, bearing a stamp appropriated by name to any particular instrument, shall be used for any other purpose, or if so used the same shall be of no avail.

SEC. 98. *And be it further enacted,* That if any person shall forge or counterfeit, or cause or procure to be forged or counter-

Forging, counterfeiting, or misusing stamps or dies.

* See amendment, p. 67.

52   EXCISE TAX.

feited, any stamp or die, or any part of any stamp or die, which shall have been provided, made, or used in pursuance of this act, or shall forge, counterfeit, or resemble, or cause or procure to be forged, counterfeited, or resembled, the impression, or any part of the impression of any such stamp or die, as aforesaid, upon any vellum, parchment, or paper, or shall stamp or mark, or cause or procure to be stamped or marked, any vellum, parchment, or paper, with any such forged or counterfeited stamp or die, or part of any stamp or die, as aforesaid, with intent to defraud the United States of any of the duties hereby imposed, or any part *Selling forged* thereof, or if any person shall utter, or sell, or expose to sale, any vellum, parchment, or paper, article, or thing, having thereupon the impression of any such counterfeited stamp or die, or any part of any stamp or die, or any such forged, counterfeited, or resembled impression, or part of impression, as aforesaid, knowing the same respectively to be forged, counterfeited, or resembled; or if any person shall knowingly use any stamp or die which shall have been so provided, made, or used, as aforesaid, with intent to defraud the United States; or if any person shall fraudulently *Or cut and deface.* cut, tear, or get off, or cause, or procure to be cut, torn, or got off, the impression of any stamp or die which shall have been provided, made, or used in pursuance of this act, from any vellum, parchment, or paper, or any instrument or writing charged or chargeable with any of the duties hereby imposed, then, and in every such case, every person so offending, and every person knowingly and wilfully aiding, abetting, or assisting in committing any such offence, as aforesaid, shall be deemed guilty of felony, and shall, on conviction thereof, forfeit the said counterfeit stamps and the articles upon which they are placed, and be punished by fine not ex-*Penalty.* ceeding one thousand dollars, and by imprisonment and confinement to hard labor not exceeding five years.

Mode of cancelling adhesive stamps.   SEC. 99. *And be it further enacted,* That in any and all cases where an adhesive stamp shall be used for denoting any duty imposed by this act, except as hereinafter provided, the person using or affixing the same shall write thereupon the initials of his name, and the date upon which the same shall be attached or used, so that the same may not again be used. And if any person shall fraudulently make use of an adhesive stamp to denote any duty imposed by this act without so effectually cancelling and obliterating such stamp, except as before mentioned, he, she, or *Penalty.* they shall forfeit the sum of fifty dollars: *Provided, nevertheless, Proviso.* That any proprietor or proprietors of proprietary articles, or arti-*Schedule C.* cles subject to stamp duty under schedule C of this act, shall have the privilege of furnishing, without expense to the United States, in suitable form, to be approved by the Commissioner of Internal Revenue, his or their own dies or designs for stamps to be used thereon, to be retained in the possession of the Commissioner of Internal Revenue, for his or their separate use, which shall not be duplicated to any other person. That in all cases *Private stamps.* where such stamp is used, instead of his or their writing his or their initials and the date thereon, the said stamp shall be so affixed on the box, bottle, or package, that in opening the same, or using the contents thereof, the said stamp shall be effectually destroyed; and in default thereof shall be liable to the same penalty imposed for neglect to affix said stamp as hereinbefore pre-*Penalty for forging or counterfeiting stamps.* scribed in this act. Any person who shall fraudulently obtain, or use any of the aforesaid stamps or designs therefor, and any person forging, or counterfeiting, or causing or procuring the forging or counterfeiting any representation, likeness, similitude, or colorable imitation of the said last-mentioned stamp, or any engraver or printer who shall sell or give away said stamps, or selling the same, or, being a merchant, broker, peddler, or person dealing, in whole or in part, in similar goods, wares, merchandise, manufactures, preparations, or articles, or those designed for similar objects or purposes, shall have knowingly or fraudulently in his, her, or their possession any such forged, counterfeited likeness, similitude, or colorable imitation of the said last-mentioned stamp, shall be deemed guilty of a misdemeanor, and, upon conviction thereof, shall be subject to all the penalties, fines, and forfeitures prescribed in section ninety-three of this act.

SEC. 100. *And be it further enacted*, That if any person or persons shall make, sign, or issue, or cause to be made, signed, or issued, or shall accept or pay, or cause to be accepted or paid, with design to evade the payment of any stamp duty, any bill of exchange, draft or order, or promissory note for the payment of money, liable to any of the duties imposed by this act, without the same being duly stamped, or having thereupon an adhesive stamp for denoting the duty hereby charged thereon, he, she, or they shall, for every such. bill, draft, order, or note, forfeit the sum of two hundred dollars. *Bills of exchange, notes, drafts, &c., to be stamped.*

Penalty for neglect.

SEC. 101. *And be it further enacted*, That the acceptor or acceptors of any bill of exchange or order for the payment of any sum of money drawn, or purporting to be drawn, in any foreign country, but payable in the United States, shall, before paying or accepting the same, place thereupon a stamp, indicating the duty upon the same, as the law requires for inland bills of exchange, or promissory notes; and no bill of exchange shall be paid or negotiated without such stamp; and if any person shall pay or negotiate, or offer in payment, or receive or take in payment, any such draft or order, the person or persons so offending shall forfeit the sum of one hundred dollars. *Foreign bills of exchange to pay same duty as inland.*

No bill negotiated without a stamp.
Penalty.

SEC. 102. *And be it further enacted*, That the Commissioner of Internal Revenue be, and is hereby, authorized to sell to and supply collectors, deputy collectors, postmasters, stationers, or any other persons, at his discretion, with adhesive stamps or stamped paper, vellum, or parchment, as herein provided for, upon the payment, at the time of delivery, of the amount of duties said stamps, stamped paper, vellum, or parchment, so sold or supplied, represent, and may thereupon allow and deduct from the aggregate amount of such stamps, as aforesaid, the sum of not exceeding five per centum as commission to the collectors, postmasters, stationers, or other purchasers; but the cost of any paper, vellum, or parchment shall be added to the amount, after deducting the allowance of per centum, as aforesaid: *Provided*, That no commission shall be allowed on any sum or sums so sold or supplied of less amount than fifty dollars : *And provided, further*, That any proprietor or proprietors of articles named in schedule C, who shall furnish his or their own die or design for stamps, to be used especially for his or their own proprietary articles, shall be allowed the following discount, namely: on amounts purchased at one time of not less than fifty nor more than five hundred dollars, five per centum ; on amounts over five hundred dollars, ten per centum. The Commissioner of Internal Revenue .may from time to time make regulations for the *Commissioner to furnish stamps.*

Commission to collectors, &c.

Private stamps
Discount on.

allowance of such of the stamps issued under the provisions of this act as may have been spoiled or rendered useless or unfit for the purpose intended, or for which the owner may have no use, or which through mistake may have been improperly or unnecessarily used, or where the rates or duties represented thereby have been paid in error, or remitted; and such allowance shall be made either by giving other stamps in lieu of the stamps so allowed for, or by repaying the amount or value, after deducting therefrom, in case of repayment, the sum of five per centum to the owner thereof.

Commissioner to stamp instruments exempt from duty. SEC. 103. *And be it further enacted*, That it shall be lawful for any person to present to the Commissioner of Internal Revenue any instrument, and inquire his opinion whether or not the same is chargeable with any duty; and if the said Commissioner shall be of opinion that such instrument is not chargeable with any stamp duty, it shall be lawful for him, and he is hereby required, to impress thereon a particular stamp, to be provided for that purpose, with such word or words or device thereon as he shall judge proper, which shall signify and denote that such instrument is not chargeable with any stamp duty; and every such instrument upon which the said stamp shall be impressed shall be deemed to be not so chargeable, and shall be received in evidence in all courts of law or equity, notwithstanding any objections made to the same, as being chargeable with stamp duty, and not stamped to denote the same.

Telegraph companies not to receive messages without stamp. SEC. 104. *And be it further enacted*, That on and after the date on which this act shall take effect, no telegraph company or its agent or employee shall receive from any person, or transmit to any person any despatch or message without an adhesive stamp denoting the duty imposed by this act being affixed to a copy thereof, or having the same stamped thereupon, and in default thereof shall incur a penalty of ten dollars: *Provided*, That only one stamp shall be required, whether sent through one or more companies.

Penalty.

Express companies not to receive packages without stamp. SEC. 105. *And be it further enacted*, That on and after the date on which this act shall take effect, no express company or its agent or employee shall receive for transportation from any person any bale, bundle, box, article, or package of any description, without either delivering to the consignor thereof a printed receipt, having stamped or affixed thereon a stamp denoting the duty imposed by this act, or without affixing thereto an adhesive stamp or stamps denoting such duty, and in default thereof shall incur a penalty of ten dollars: *Provided*, That but one stamped receipt or stamp shall be required for each shipment from one party to another party at the same time, whether such shipment consists of one or more packages: *And provided, also*, That no stamped receipts or stamp shall be required for any bale, bundle, box, article, or package transported for the government, nor for such bales, bundles, boxes, or packages as are transported by such companies without charge thereon.

Penalty. Proviso.

No stamps for government boxes.

Schedule C subject to stamp duties. SEC. 106. *And be it further enacted*, That all the provisions of this act relating to dies, stamps, adhesive stamps, and stamp duties shall extend to and include (except where manifestly inapplicable) all the articles or objects enumerated in schedule marked C, subject to stamp duties, and apply to the provisions in relation thereto.

EXCISE TAX. 55

SEC. 107. *And be it further enacted,* That on and after the first day of August, eighteen hundred and sixty-two, no person or persons, firms, companies, or corporations, shall make, prepare, and sell, or remove for consumption or sale, drugs, medicines, preparations, compositions, articles, or things, including perfumery, cosmetics, and playing cards, upon which a duty is imposed by this act, as enumerated and mentioned in schedule C, without affixing thereto an adhesive stamp or label denoting the duty before mentioned, and in default thereof shall incur a penalty of ten dollars: *Provided,* That nothing in this act contained shall apply to any uncompounded medicinal drug or chemical, nor to any medicine compounded according to the United States or other national pharmacopœia, nor of which the full and proper formula is published in either of the dispensatories, formularies, or text books in common use among physicians and apothecaries, including homœopathic and eclectic, or in any pharmaceutical journal now used by any incorporated college of pharmacy, and not sold or offered for sale, or advertised under any other name, form, or guise than that under which they may be severally denominated and laid down in said pharmacopœias, dispensatories, text books, or journals, as aforesaid, nor to medicines sold to or for the use of any person, which may be mixed and compounded specially for said persons, according to the written recipe or prescription of any physician or surgeon.

<small>Penalty for preparing drugs, &c., for consumption or sale without stamp.</small>

<small>Not to apply to prescriptions of college of pharmacy or physicians.</small>

SEC. 108. *And be it further enacted,* That every manufacturer or maker of any of the articles for sale mentioned in schedule C, after the same shall have been so made, and the particulars hereinbefore required as to stamps have been complied with, who shall take off, remove, or detach, or cause or permit, or suffer to be taken off, or removed or detached, any stamp, or who shall use any stamp, or any wrapper or cover to which any stamp is affixed, to cover any other article or commodity than that originally contained in such wrapper or cover, with such stamp when first used, with the intent to evade the stamp duties, shall for every such article, respectively, in respect of which any such offence shall be committed, be subject to a penalty of fifty dollars, to be recovered together with the costs thereupon accruing, and every such article or commodity as aforesaid shall also be forfeited.

<small>Penalty for removing stamps from articles named in schedule C.</small>

SEC. 109. *And be it further enacted,* That every maker or manufacturer of any of the articles or commodities mentioned in schedule C, as aforesaid, who shall sell, send out, remove, or deliver any article or commodity, manufactured as aforesaid, before the duty thereon shall have been fully paid, by affixing thereon the proper stamp, as in this act provided, or who shall hide or conceal, or cause to be hidden or concealed, or who shall remove or convey away, or deposit, or cause to be removed or conveyed away from or deposited in any place, any such article or commodity, to evade the duty chargeable thereon, or any part thereof, shall be subject to a penalty of one hundred dollars, together with the forfeiture of any such article or commodity: *Provided,* That medicines, preparations, compositions, perfumery, and cosmetics, upon which stamp duties are required by this act, may, when intended for exportation, be manufactured and sold, or removed without having stamps affixed thereto, and without being charged with duty, as aforesaid; and every manufacturer or maker of any article, as aforesaid, intended for exportation, shall give such bonds and be subject to such rules and regulations to protect the revenue

<small>Articles mentioned in schedule C not to be sold without stamp.</small>

<small>Penalty.</small>

<small>Unless for export.</small>

against fraud as may be from time to time prescribed by the Secretary of the Treasury.

<small>Manufacturers to make monthly statement of articles removed.</small>

SEC. 110. *And be it further enacted,* That every manufacturer or maker of any of the articles or commodities, as aforesaid, or his chief workman, agent, or superintendent, shall at the end of each and every month make and sign a declaration in writing that no such article or commodity, as aforesaid, has, during such preceding month, or time when the last declaration was made, been removed, carried, or sent, or caused, or suffered, or known to have been removed, carried, or sent from the premises of such manufacturer or maker, other than such as have been duly taken account of and charged with the stamp duty, on pain of such manufacturer or maker forfeiting for every refusal or neglect to make such declaration one hundred dollars; and if any such manufacturer or maker, or his chief workman, agent, or superintendent, shall make any false or untrue declaration, such manufacturer or maker, or chief workman, agent, or superintendent, making the same, shall forfeit five hundred dollars.

<small>Penalty</small>

<small>Penalty for false statement.</small>

SCHEDULE B.

STAMP DUTIES.

		Duty. Dolls. cts.
Agreement.	AGREEMENT OR CONTRACT, other than those specified in this schedule; any appraisement of value or damage, or for any other purpose; for every sheet or piece of paper upon which either of the same shall be written, five cents, . . .	5
Bank checks.	Bank check, draft, or order for the payment of any sum of money exceeding twenty dollars, drawn upon any bank, trust company, or any person or persons, companies, or corporations, at sight or on demand, two cents, ...	2
Bills of exchange (inland.)	Bill of exchange, (inland) draft, or order for the payment of any sum of money exceeding twenty and not exceeding one hundred dollars, otherwise than at sight or on demand, or any promissory note except bank notes issued for circulation, for a sum exceeding twenty and not exceeding one hundred dollars, five cents, ...	5
	Exceeding one hundred dollars and not exceeding two hundred dollars, ten cents, . . .	10
	Exceeding two hundred dollars and not exceeding three hundred and fifty dollars, fifteen cents, .	15
	Exceeding three hundred and fifty dollars and not exceeding five hundred dollars, twenty cents, . .	20
	Exceeding five hundred dollars and not exceeding seven hundred and fifty dollars, thirty cents, . .	30
	Exceeding seven hundred and fifty dollars and not exceeding one thousand dollars, forty cents, . .	40
	Exceeding one thousand dollars and not exceeding fifteen hundred dollars, sixty cents, . . .	60
	Exceeding fifteen hundred dollars and not exceeding twenty-five hundred dollars, one dollar, . .	1 00
	Exceeding twenty-five hundred dollars and not exceeding five thousand dollars, one dollar and fifty cents,	1 50

EXCISE TAX.

	Duty. Dolls. cts.	
And for every twenty-five hundred dollars, or part of twenty-five hundred dollars in excess of five thousand dollars, one dollar,	1 00	
Bill of exchange (foreign) or letter of credit, drawn in but payable out of the United States, if drawn singly, or otherwise than in a set of three or more, according to the custom of merchants and bankers, shall pay the same rates of duty as inland bills of exchange or promissory notes.		Bills of exchange, (foreign.)
If drawn in sets of three or more: For every bill of each set, where the sum made payable shall not exceed one hundred and fifty dollars, or the equivalent thereof, in any foreign currency in which such bills may be expressed, according to the standard of value fixed by the United States, three cents,	3	
Above one hundred and fifty dollars and not above two hundred and fifty dollars, five cents,	5	
Above two hundred and fifty dollars and not above five hundred dollars, ten cents,	10	
Above five hundred dollars and not above a thousand dollars, fifteen cents,	15	
Above one thousand dollars and not above one thousand five hundred dollars, twenty cents,	20	
Above one thousand five hundred dollars and not above two thousand two hundred and fifty dollars, thirty cents,	30	
Above two thousand two hundred and fifty dollars and not above three thousand five hundred dollars, fifty cents,	50	
Above three thousand five hundred dollars and not above five thousand dollars, seventy cents,	70	
Above five thousand dollars and not above seven thousand five hundred dollars, one dollar,	1 00	
And for every two thousand five hundred dollars, or part thereof, in excess of seven thousand five hundred dollars, thirty cents,	30	
BILL OF LADING or receipt, (other than charter-party,) for any goods, merchandise, or effects, to be exported from a port or place in the United States to any foreign port or place, ten cents,	10	Bills of lading.
EXPRESS.—For every receipt or stamp used, or issued by any express company, or carrier, or person whose occupation it is to act as such, for all boxes, bales, packages, articles, or bundles, for the transportation of which such company, carrier, or person, shall receive a compensation of not over twenty-five cents, one cent,	1	Express.
When such compensation exceeds the sum of twenty-five cents, and not over one dollar, two cents,	2	
When one or more packages are sent to the same address at the same time, and the compensation therefor exceeds one dollar, five cents,	5	
BOND.—For indemnifying any person who shall have become bound or engaged as surety for the payment of any sum of money, or for the due execution or		Bond.

EXCISE TAX.

		Duty. Dolls. cts
	performance of the duties of any office, and to account for money received by virtue thereof, fifty cents, ...	50
	BOND of any description other than such as may be required in legal proceedings, and such as are not otherwise charged in this schedule, twenty-five cents,	25
Certificate.	CERTIFICATE of stock in any incorporated company, twenty-five cents, ...	25
	CERTIFICATE of profits, or any certificate or memorandum showing an interest in the property or accumulations of any incorporated company, if for a sum not less than ten dollars and not exceeding fifty dollars, ten cents, ...	10
	For a sum exceeding fifty dollars, twenty-five cents, .	25
	CERTIFICATE.—Any certificate of damage, or otherwise, and all other certificates or documents issued by any port warden, marine surveyor, or other person acting as such, twenty-five cents, . . .	25
	CERTIFICATE of deposit of any sum of money in any bank or trust company, or with any banker or person acting as such—	
	If for a sum not exceeding one hundred dollars, two cents, ...	2
	For a sum exceeding one hundred dollars, five cents, .	5
	CERTIFICATE of any other description than those specified, ten cents, ...	10
Charter-party.	CHARTER-PARTY.—Contract or agreement for the charter of any ship or vessel, or steamer, or any letter, memorandum, or other writing between the captain, master, or owner, or person acting as agent of any ship or vessel, or steamer, and any other person or persons for or relating to the charter of such ship or vessel, or steamer, if the registered tonnage of such ship or vessel, or steamer, does not exceed three hundred tons, three dollars, . . .	3 00
	Exceeding three hundred tons, and not exceeding six hundred tons, five dollars, ...	5 00
	Exceeding six hundred tons, ten dollars, . .	10 00
Contract.	CONTRACT.—Broker's note, or memorandum of sale of any goods or merchandise, stocks, bonds, exchange, notes of hand, real estate, or property of any kind or description issued by brokers or persons acting as such, ten cents, ...	10
Conveyance.	CONVEYANCE.—Deed, instrument, or writing, whereby any lands, tenements, or other realty sold shall be granted, assigned, transferred, or otherwise conveyed to, or vested in, the purchaser or purchasers, or any other person or persons by his, her, or their direction, when the consideration or value exceeds one hundred dollars and does not exceed five hundred dollars, fifty cents, ...	50
	When the consideration exceeds five hundred dollars and does not exceed one thousand dollars, one dollar, .	1 00
	Exceeding one thousand dollars and not exceeding two thousand five hundred dollars, two dollars, .	2 00

	Duty.	
	Dolls. cts.	
Exceeding two thousand five *hundred* dollars, and not exceeding five thousand dollars, five dollars,	5 00	
Exceeding five thousand dollars and not exceeding ten thousand dollars, ten dollars,	10 00	
Exceeding ten thousand dollars and not exceeding twenty thousand dollars, twenty dollars,	20 00	
And for every additional ten thousand dollars, or fractional part thereof, in excess of twenty thousand dollars, twenty dollars,	20 00	
DESPATCH, TELEGRAPHIC.—Any despatch or message, the charge for which for the first ten words does not exceed twenty cents, one cent,	1	Despatch, (telegraphic.)
When the charge for the first ten words exceeds twenty cents, three cents,	3	
ENTRY of any goods, wares, or merchandise at any custom-house, either for consumption or warehousing, not exceeding one hundred dollars in value, twenty-five cents,	25	Entry of goods.
Exceeding one hundred dollars and not exceeding five hundred dollars in value, fifty cents,	50	
Exceeding five hundred dollars in value, one dollar,	1 00	
ENTRY for the withdrawal of any goods or merchandise from bonded warehouse, fifty cents,	50	
INSURANCE, (LIFE.)—Policy of insurance, or other instrument by whatever name the same shall be called, whereby any insurance shall be made upon any life or lives—		Insurance.
When the amount insured shall not exceed one thousand dollars, twenty-five cents,	25	
Exceeding one thousand and not exceeding five thousand dollars, fifty cents,	50	
Exceeding five thousand dollars, one dollar,	1 00	
INSURANCE, (MARINE, INLAND, AND FIRE.)—Each policy of insurance or other instrument, by whatever name the same shall be called, by which insurance shall be made or renewed upon property of any description, whether against perils by the sea or by fire, or other peril of any kind, made by any insurance company, or its agents, or by any other company or person, twenty-five cents,	25	
LEASE, agreement, memorandum, or contract for the hire, use, or rent of any land, tenement, or portion thereof—		Lease.
If for a period of time not exceeding three years, fifty cents,	50	
If for a period exceeding three years, one dollar,	1 00	
MANIFEST for custom-house entry or clearance of the cargo of any ship, vessel, or steamer for a foreign port—		Manifest.
If the registered tonnage of such ship, vessel, or steamer does not exceed three hundred tons, one dollar,	1 00	
Exceeding three hundred tons, and not exceeding six hundred tons, three dollars,	3 00	
Exceeding six hundred tons, five dollars,	5 00	
MORTGAGE of lands, estate, or property, real or personal, heritable or movable whatsoever, where the same shall be made as a security for the payment		Mortgage.

	Duty.
	Dolls. cts.

of any definite and certain sum of money lent at the time or previously due and owing or forborne to be paid, being payable; also any conveyance of any lands, estate, or property whatsoever, in trust to be sold or otherwise converted into money, which shall be intended only as security, and shall be redeemable before the sale or other disposal thereof, either by express stipulation or otherwise; or any personal bond given as security for the payment of any definite or certain sum of money exceeding one hundred dollars, and not exceeding five hundred dollars, fifty cents, ...	50
Exceeding five hundred dollars, and not exceeding one thousand dollars, one dollar, ...	1 00
Exceeding one thousand dollars, and not exceeding two thousand five hundred dollars, two dollars, . .	2 00
Exceeding two thousand five hundred dollars, and not exceeding five thousand dollars, five dollars, . .	5 00
Exceeding five thousand dollars, and not exceeding ten thousand dollars, ten dollars, ...	10 00
Exceeding ten thousand dollars, and not exceeding twenty thousand dollars, fifteen dollars, ...	15 00
And for every additional ten thousand dollars, or fractional part thereof, in excess of twenty thousand dollars, ten dollars, ...	10 00

Passage ticket. PASSAGE TICKET, by any vessel from a port in the United States to a foreign port, if less than thirty dollars, fifty cents, ... 50
Exceeding thirty dollars, one dollar, ... 1 00

Power of attorney. POWER OF ATTORNEY for the sale or transfer of any stock, bonds, or scrip, or for the collection of any dividends or interest thereon, twenty-five cents, . 25
POWER OF ATTORNEY OR PROXY for voting at any election for officers of any incorporated company or society, except religious, charitable, or literary societies, or public cemeteries, ten cents, ... 10
POWER OF ATTORNEY to receive or collect rent, twenty-five cents, ... 25
POWER OF ATTORNEY to sell and convey real estate, or to rent or lease the same, or to perform any and all other acts not hereinbefore specified, one dollar, . 1 00

Probate of will. PROBATE OF WILL, or letters of administration: Where the estate and effects for or in respect of which such probate or letters of administration applied for shall be sworn or declared not to exceed the value of two thousand five hundred dollars, fifty cents, . . 50
To exceed two thousand five hundred dollars and not exceeding five thousand dollars, one dollar, . . 1 00
To exceed five thousand dollars, and not exceeding twenty thousand dollars, two dollars, ... 2 00
To exceed twenty thousand dollars, and not exceeding fifty thousand dollars, five dollars, ... 5 00
To exceed fifty thousand dollars, and not exceeding one hundred thousand dollars, ten dollars, . . . 10 00

EXCISE TAX. 61

	Duty. Dolls. cts.	
Exceeding one hundred thousand dollars, and not exceeding one hundred and fifty thousand dollars, twenty dollars, ...	20 00	
And for every additional fifty thousand dollars, or fractional part thereof, ten dollars, ...	10 00	
PROTEST.—Upon the protest of every note, bill of exchange, acceptance, check or draft, or any marine protest, whether protested by a notary public or by any other officer who may be authorized by the law of any State or States to make such protest, twenty-five cents, ...	25	Protest.
WAREHOUSE RECEIPT for any goods, merchandise, or property of any kind held on storage in any public or private warehouse or yard, twenty-five cents, .	25	Warehouse receipt.
LEGAL DOCUMENTS: Writ, or other original process by which any suit is commenced in any court of record, either law or equity, fifty cents, ...	50	Legal documents.
Provided, That no writ, summons, or other process issued by a justice of the peace, or issued in any criminal or other suits commenced by the United States or any State, shall be subject to the payment of stamp duties: And provided, further, That the stamp duties imposed by the foregoing schedule B on manifests, bills of lading, and passage tickets, shall not apply to steamboats or other vessels plying between ports of the United States and ports in British North America.		Proviso.

SCHEDULE C.

MEDICINES OR PREPARATIONS.—For and upon every packet, box, bottle, pot, phial, or other enclosure, containing any pills, powders, tinctures, troches or lozenges, syrups, cordials, bitters, anodynes, tonics, plasters, liniments, salves, ointments, pastes, drops, waters, essences, spirits, oils, or other preparations or compositions whatsoever, made and sold, or removed for consumption and sale, by any person or persons whatever, wherein the person making or preparing the same has, or claims to have, any private formula or occult secret or art for the making or preparing the same, or has, or claims to have, any exclusive right or title to the making or preparing the same, or which are prepared, uttered, vended, or exposed for sale under any letters patent, or held out or recommended to the public by the makers, venders, or proprietors thereof as proprietary medicines, or as remedies or specifics for any disease, diseases, or affections whatever affecting the human or animal body, as follows: where such packet, box, bottle, pot, phial, or other enclosure, with its contents, shall not exceed, at the retail price or value, the sum of twenty-five cents, one cent, ...

Medicines or preparations.

	Duty. Dolls. cts.

Where such packet, box, bottle, pot, phial, or other enclosure, with its contents, shall exceed the retail price or value of twenty-five cents, and not exceed the retail price or value of fifty cents, two cents, .   2

Where such packet, box, bottle, pot, phial, or other enclosure, with its contents, shall exceed the retail price or value of fifty cents, and shall not exceed the retail price or value of seventy-five cents, three cents, ...   3

When such packet, box, bottle, pot, phial, or other enclosure, with its contents, shall exceed the retail price or value of seventy-five cents, and shall not exceed the retail price or value of one dollar, four cents, ...   4

When such packet, box, bottle, pot, phial, or other enclosure, with its contents, shall exceed the retail price or value of one dollar, for each and every fifty cents or fractional part thereof over and above the one dollar, as before mentioned, an additional two cents, ...   2

Perfumery and cosmetics. PERFUMERY AND COSMETICS.—For and upon every packet, box, bottle, pot, phial, or other enclosure, containing any essence, extract, toilet, water, cosmetic, hair oil, pomade, hairdressing, hair restorative, hair dye, toothwash, dentifrice, tooth paste, aromatic cachous, or any similar articles, by whatsoever name the same heretofore have been, now are, or may hereafter be called, known, or distinguished, used or applied, or to be used or applied as perfumes or applications to the hair, mouth, or skin, made, prepared, and sold or removed for consumption and sale in the United States, where such packet, box, bottle, pot, phial, or other enclosure, with its contents, shall not exceed at the retail price or value the sum of twenty-five cents, one cent, . . .   1

Where such packet, box, bottle, pot, phial, or other enclosure, with its contents, shall exceed the retail price or value of twenty-five cents, and shall not exceed the retail price or value of fifty cents, two cents,   2

Where such packet, box, bottle, pot, phial, or other enclosure, with its contents, shall exceed the retail price or value of fifty cents, and shall not exceed the retail price or value of seventy-five cents, three cents, ...   3

Where such packet, box, bottle, pot, phial, or other enclosure, with its contents, shall exceed the retail price or value of seventy-five cents, and shall not exceed the retail price or value of one dollar, four cents, .   4

Where such packet, box, bottle, pot, phial, or other enclosure, with its contents, shall exceed the retail price or value of one dollar, for each and every fifty cents or fractional part thereof over and above the one dollar, as before mentioned, an additional two cents, ...   2

EXCISE TAX. 63

	Duty. Dolls. cts.	
PLAYING CARDS.—For and upon every pack of whatever number, when the price per pack does not exceed eighteen cents, one cent, ...	1	Playing cards.
Over eighteen cents and not exceeding twenty-five cents per pack, two cents, ...	2	
Over twenty-five and not exceeding thirty cents per pack, three cents, ...	3	
Over thirty and not exceeding thirty-six cents per pack, four cents, ...	4	
Over thirty-six cents per pack, five cents, . . .	5	

LEGACIES AND DISTRIBUTIVE SHARES OF PERSONAL PROPERTY.

Legacies.

SEC. 111. *And be it further enacted,* That any person or persons having in charge or trust, as administrators, executors, or trustees of any legacies or distributive shares arising from personal property, of any kind whatsoever, where the whole amount of such personal property, as aforesaid, shall exceed the sum of one thousand dollars in actual value, passing from any person who may die after the passage of this act possessed of such property, either by will or by the intestate laws of any State or Territory, or any part of such property or interest therein, transferred by deed, grant, bargain, sale, or gift, made or intended to take effect in possession or enjoyment after the death of the grantor or bargainor, to any person or persons, or to any body or bodies politic or corporate, in trust or otherwise, shall be, and hereby are, made subject to a duty or tax, to be paid to the United States, as follows, that is to say : *Legacies exceeding $1,000.*

First. Where the person or persons entitled to any beneficial interest in such property shall be the lineal issue or lineal ancestor, brother or sister, to the person who died possessed of such property, as aforesaid, at and after the rate of seventy-five cents for each and every hundred dollars of the clear value of such interest in such property. *Lineal descendants.*

Second. Where the person or persons entitled to any beneficial interest in such property shall be a descendant of a brother or sister of the person who died possessed, as aforesaid, at and after the rate of one dollar and fifty cents for each and every hundred dollars of the clear value of such interest. *Descendant of brother or sister.*

Third. Where the person or persons entitled to any beneficial interest in such property shall be a brother or sister of the father or mother, or a descendant of a brother or sister of the father or mother of the person who died possessed, as aforesaid, at and after the rate of three dollars for each and every hundred dollars of the clear value of such interest. *Brother or sister of father or mother.*

Fourth. Where the person or persons entitled to any beneficial interest in such property shall be a brother or sister of the grandfather or grandmother, or a descendant of the brother or sister of the grandfather or grandmother of the person who died possessed, as aforesaid, at and after the rate of four dollars for each and every hundred dollars of the clear value of such interest. *Brother or sister of grandfather or grandmother.*

Fifth. Where the person or persons entitled to any beneficial interest in such property shall be in any other degree of collateral consanguinity than is hereinbefore stated, or shall be a stranger in blood to the person who died possessed, as aforesaid, or shall be a *Any other degree of consanguinity.*

body politic or corporate, at and after the rate of five dollars for each and every hundred dollars of the clear value of such interest: *Provided*, That all legacies or property passing by will, or by the laws of any State or Territory, to husband or wife of the person who died possessed, as aforesaid, shall be exempt from tax or duty.

Tax a lien upon property of deceased.

SEC. 112. *And be it further enacted*, That the tax or duty aforesaid shall be a lien and charge upon the property of every person who may die as aforesaid, until the same shall be fully paid to and discharged by the United States; and every executor, administrator, or other person who may take the burden or trust of administration upon such property shall, after taking such bur-

Pay tax before distribution.

den or trust, and before paying and distributing any portion thereof to the legatees or any parties entitled to beneficial interest therein, pay to the collector or deputy collector of the district the amount of the duty or tax, as aforesaid, and shall also

Executor, &c., to make list of property and amount of tax.

make and render to the assistant assessor of the district a schedule, list, or statement of the amount of such property, together with the amount of duty which has accrued or should accrue thereon, verified by his oath or affirmation, to be administered and certified thereon by some magistrate or officer having lawful power to administer such oaths, in such form and manner as may be prescribed by the Commissioner of Internal Revenue, which schedule, list, or statement shall contain the names of each and every person entitled to any beneficial interest therein, together with the clear value of such interest, which schedule,

List to contain names of legatees and value of interest.

list, or statement shall be by him delivered to such collector; and upon such payment and delivery of such schedule, list, or statement, said collector or deputy collector, shall grant to such person paying such duty or tax a receipt or receipts for the same in duplicate, which shall be prepared as is hereinafter provided; such receipt or receipts, duly signed and delivered by such collector or deputy collector, shall be sufficient evidence to entitle the person who paid such duty or tax as having taken the burden or trust of administering such property or personal estate to be allowed for such payment by the person or persons entitled to the beneficial interest in respect to which such tax or duty was paid; and such person administering such property or personal estate shall be credited and allowed such payment by every tribunal which, by the laws of any State or Territory, is or may be empowered to decide upon and settle the accounts of executors and administrators; and in case such person who has taken the burden or trust of administering upon any such property or personal estate shall refuse or neglect to pay the aforesaid duty or tax to the collector or deputy collector, as aforesaid, within the time hereinbefore provided, or shall neglect or refuse to deliver to said collector or deputy collector the schedule, list, or statement of such legacies, property, or personal estate under oath, as aforesaid, or shall deliver to said collector or deputy collector a false schedule or statement of such legacies, property, or personal estate, or give the names and relationship of the persons entitled to beneficial interests therein untruly, or shall not truly and correctly set forth and state therein the clear value of such beneficial interest, or where no administration upon such prop-

Penalty for neglect or false return; proper officer to proceed in court.

erty or personal estate shall have been granted or allowed under existing laws, the proper officer of the United States shall commence such proceedings in law or equity before any court of

EXCISE TAX.

the United States as may be proper and necessary to enforce and realize the lien or charge upon such property or personal estate, or any part thereof, for which such tax or duty has not been truly and justly paid. Under such proceedings the rate of duty or tax enforced shall be the highest rate imposed or assessed by this act, and shall be in the name of the United States against such person or persons as may have the actual or constructive custody or possession of such property or personal estate, or any part thereof, and shall subject such property or personal estate, or any portion of the same, to be sold upon the judgment or decree of such court, and from the proceeds of such sale, the amount of such tax or duty, together with all costs and expenses of every description to be allowed by such court, shall be first paid, and the balance, if any, deposited according to the order of such court, to be paid under its direction to such person or persons as shall establish their lawful title to the same. The deed or deeds, or any proper conveyance of such property or personal estate, or any portion thereof, so sold under such judgment or decree, executed by the officer lawfully charged with carrying the same into effect, shall vest in the purchaser thereof all the title of the delinquent to the property or personal estate sold under and by virtue of such judgment or decree, and shall release every other portion of such property or personal estate from the lien or charge thereon created by this act. And every person or persons who shall have in his possession, charge, or custody, any record, file, or paper, containing or supposed to contain any information concerning such property or personal estate, as aforesaid, passing from any person who may die, as aforesaid, shall exhibit the same at the request of the collector of the revenue, his deputy, or agent, and to any law officer of the United States, in the performance of his duty under this act, his deputy or agent, who may desire to examine the same; and if any such person, having in his possession, charge, or custody, any such records, files, or papers, shall refuse or neglect to exhibit the same on request, as aforesaid, he shall forfeit and pay the sum of five hundred dollars; and in case of any delinquency in making the schedule, list, or statement, or in the payment of the duty or tax accruing, or which should accrue thereon, the assessment and collection shall be made as provided for in the general provisions of this act: *Provided*, In all legal controversies where such deed or title shall be the subject of judicial investigation the recital in said deed shall be presumed to be true, and that the requirements of the law had been complied with by the officers of the government. *Penalty for refusing to exhibit records, files, &c.*

Proviso.

SEC. 113. *And be it further enacted*, That whenever by this act any license, duty, or tax of any description has been imposed on any corporate body, or property of any incorporated company, it shall be lawful for the Commissioner of Internal Revenue to prescribe and determine in what district such tax shall be assessed and collected, and to what officer thereof the official notices required in that behalf shall be given, and of whom payment of such tax shall be demanded. *Commissioner to determine the district where corporations shall pay tax.*

SEC. 114. *And be it further enacted*, That all articles upon which duties are imposed by the provisions of this act, which shall be found in the possession of any person or persons for the purpose of being sold by such person or persons in fraud thereof *Proceedings in case of fraud to be in United States' courts.*

and with the design to avoid payment of said duties, may be seized by any collector or deputy collector who shall have reason to believe that the same are possessed for the purpose aforesaid, and the same shall be forfeited to the United States. And the proceedings to enforce said forfeiture shall be in the nature of a proceeding in rem in the circuit or district court of the United States for the district where such seizure is made, or in any other court of competent jurisdiction. And any person who shall have in his possession any such articles for the purpose of selling the same, with the design of avoiding payment of the duties imposed thereon by this act, shall be liable to a penalty of one hundred dollars, to be recovered as hereinbefore provided.

Penalty.

APPROPRIATION.

Payment of salaries of assessors and collectors.

SEC. 115. *And be it further enacted*, That the pay of the assessors, assistant assessors, collectors, and deputy collectors, shall be paid out of the accruing internal duties or taxes before the same is paid into the treasury, according to such regulations as the Commissioner of Internal Revenue, under the direction of the Secretary of the Treasury, shall prescribe; and for the purpose of paying the Commissioner of Internal Revenue and clerks, procuring dies, stamps, adhesive stamps, paper, printing forms and regulations, advertising, and any other expenses of carrying this act into effect, the sum of five hundred thousand dollars be, and hereby is, appropriated, or so much thereof as may be necessary.

Appropriation of $500,000.

ALLOWANCE AND DRAWBACK.

Allowance of drawback on manufactures exported.

SEC. 116. *And be it further enacted*, That from and after the date on which this act takes effect there shall be an allowance or drawback on all articles on which any internal duty or tax shall have been paid, except raw or unmanufactured cotton, equal in amount to the duty or tax paid thereon, and no more, when exported, the evidence that any such duty or tax has been paid to be furnished to the satisfaction of the Commissioner of Internal Revenue by such person or persons as shall claim the allowance or drawback, and the amount to be ascertained under such regulations as shall, from time to time, be prescribed by the Commissioner of Internal Revenue, under the direction of the Secretary of the Treasury, and the same shall be paid by the warrant of the Secretary of the Treasury on the Treasurer of the United States, out of any money arising from internal duties not otherwise appropriated: *Provided*, That no allowance or drawback shall be made or had for any amount claimed or due less than twenty dollars, anything in this act to the contrary notwithstanding: *And provided, further*, That any certificate of drawback for goods exported, issued in pursuance of the provisions of this act, may, under such regulations as may be prescribed by the Secretary of the Treasury, be received by the collector or his deputy in payment of duties under this act. And the Secretary of the Treasury may make such regulations with regard to the form of said certificates and the issuing thereof as, in his judgment, may be necessary: *And provided, further*, That in computing the allowance or drawback upon articles manufactured exclusively of cotton when exported, there shall be allowed, in addition to the three per centum duty which shall have been paid on such articles, a draw-

Appropriation.
Drawback not less than $20.

Certificates of drawback receivable for duties.

EXCISE TAX. 67

back of five mills per pound upon such articles, in all cases where the duty imposed by this act upon the cotton used in the manufacture thereof has been previously paid; the amount of said allowance to be ascertained in such manner as may be prescribed by the Commissioner of Internal Revenue, under the direction of the Secretary of the Treasury. *Additional drawback on cotton goods.*

SEC. 117. *And be it further enacted,* That if any person or persons shall fraudulently claim or seek to obtain an allowance or drawback on goods, wares, or merchandise, on which no internal duty shall have been paid, or shall fraudulently claim any greater allowance or drawback than the duty actually paid, as aforesaid, such person or persons shall forfeit triple the amount wrongfully or fraudulently claimed or sought to be obtained, or the sum of five hundred dollars, at the election of the Secretary of the Treasury, to be recovered as in other cases of forfeiture provided for in the general provisions of this act. *Penalty for fraudulent claim for drawback.*

SEC. 118. *And be it further enacted,* That the sum of sixty thousand dollars appropriated to complete the capitol in New Mexico, by the second section of an act of Congress, approved June twenty-five, eighteen hundred and sixty, and the sum of fifty thousand dollars, appropriated for military roads in New Mexico, by act of Congress approved March two, eighteen hundred and sixty-one, be, and the same are hereby, credited to the Territory of New Mexico in payment of the direct annual tax of sixty-two thousand six hundred and forty-eight dollars levied upon said Territory under the eighth section of an act of Congress, approved August five, eighteen hundred and sixty-one, to be taken up on account of said direct tax under said [act] as the same may fall due to the United States from said Territory. *Direct tax of New Mexico credited.*

SEC. 119. *And be it further enacted,* That so much of an act entitled "An act to provide increased revenue from imports to pay interest on the public debt, and for other purposes," approved August fifth, eighteen hundred and sixty-one, as imposes a direct tax of twenty millions of dollars on the United States, shall be held to authorize the levy and collection of one tax to that amount; and no other tax shall be levied under and by virtue thereof, until the first day of April, eighteen hundred and sixty-five, when the same shall be in full force and effect. *Direct tax limited to one year.*

GALUSHA A. GROW,
Speaker of the House of Representatives.
SOLOMON FOOT,
President of the Senate pro tempore.

Approved July 1, 1862.
ABRAHAM LINCOLN.

THE following sections of the "Act increasing, temporarily, the duties on imports, and for other purposes," approved July 14, 1862, are amendatory of the foregoing internal revenue or tax bill:

SEC. 25. *And be it further enacted,* That the 95th section of the act entitled "An act to provide internal revenue to support the government and pay interest on the public debt," approved July 1, 1862, be so amended that no instrument, document, or paper, made, signed, or issued, prior to the 1st day of January, 1863, without being duly stamped, or having thereon an adhesive stamp to denote the duty imposed thereon, shall for that cause be deemed invalid and of no effect:

Provided, however, that no such instrument, document, or paper, shall be admitted or used as evidence in any court until the same shall have been duly stamped, nor until the holder thereof shall have proved to the satisfaction of the court that he has paid to the collector or deputy collector of the district within which such court may be held, the sum of five dollars for the use of the United States.

SEC. 26. *And be it further enacted,* That no part of the act aforesaid, in relation to stamp duties, shall be held to take effect before the 1st day of September, 1862. And all of said act, except so much thereof as relates to the appointment of a Commissioner of Internal Revenue, shall be held to take effect on the 21st day of July, 1862, instead of from and after its approval by the President.

INDEX TO EXCISE TAX.

A

		TAX.	PAGE
Absent persons, to present list to assessor within ten days after notice is given or sent by mail, and penalty for neglect,			4
Advertisements inserted in newspapers, magazines, reviews, or any other publication, on gross receipts for,		3 per ct.	47
Do.,	in newspapers denied the use of the mails,	10 per ct.	
Do.,	all receipts for, to the amount of $1,000,	exempt.	48
Do.,	in papers whose circulation does not exceed 2,000 copies,	exempt.	48
Agents to purchase or sell goods, cost of license,		$50 00.	29
Do.,	to seek wholesale orders for goods, cost of license,	50 00.	29
Do.,	for ship owners, cost of license,	56 00.	29
Do.,	Real Estate, cost of license,	50 00.	29
Do.,	Claim, cost of license,	10 00.	31
Do.,	Patent, cost of license,	10 00.	31
Agreements, for each sheet or piece of paper, on which written, stamp duty,		5 cents.	56
Do.,	for the hire, use, or rent of any land, tenement, or portion thereof, if for a period of time not exceeding three years, stamp duty,	50 cents.	59
Do.,	if for a period of time exceeding three years, stamp duty,	$1 00.	59
Ale, per barrel of thirty-one gallons, fractional parts of a barrel to pay proportionately,		1 00.	21
Alteratives, on each package of, the retail price or value of which does not exceed 25 cents, stamp duty,		1 cent.	61
Do.,	on each package of, the retail price or value of which exceeds 25 cents and does not exceed 50 cents, stamp duty,	2 cents.	62
Do.,	on each package of, the retail price or value of which exceeds 50 cents and does not exceed 75 cents, stamp duty,	3 cents.	62
Do.,	on each package of, the retail price or value of which exceeds 75 cents and does not exceed one dollar,	4 cents.	62
Do.,	on each package of, the retail price or value of which exceeds one dollar, for each and every 50 cents, or fractional part thereof, over and above one dollar, an additional stamp duty of	2 cents.	62
Animal oils, per gallon,		2 cents.	36
Anodynes, on each package of, the retail price or value of which does not exceed 25 cents, stamp duty,		1 cent.	61
Do.,	on each package of, the retail price or value of which exceeds 25 cents and does not exceed 50 cents, stamp duty,	2 cents.	62
Do.,	on each package of, the retail price or value of which exceeds 50 cents and does not exceed 75 cents, stamp duty,	3 cents.	62
Do.,	on each package of, the retail price or value of which exceeds 75 cents and does not exceed one dollar,	4 cents.	62
Do.,	on each package of, the retail price or value of which exceeds one dollar, for each and every 50 cents or fractional part thereof, over and above one dollar, an additional stamp duty of	2 cents.	62
Apothecaries' license not required in certain cases,			32

	TAX.	PAGE

Apothecaries, when a license as wholesale or retail dealer has not been taken out, and where the annual gross receipts on sales exceed one thousand dollars, for license, . . $10 00. 81
    Do., whose gross annual sales are less than one thousand dollars, require no license, ... 81
Appeal not allowed in cases of fraudulent lists or under-valuation, . 4
    Do., notice of time and place for hearing, . . . 6
    Do., before whom made, and question at issue, . . . 6
    Do., to be in writing, ... 6
Appraisements of value or damage, on each, a stamp duty of . 5 cents. 56
Aromatic Snuff, on each package of, the retail price or value of which does not exceed 25 cents, a stamp duty of . . 1 cent. 61
    Do., on each package of, the retail price or value of which exceeds 25 cents and does not exceed 50 cents, a stamp duty of . . . . . . 2 cents. 62
    Do., on each package of, the retail price or value of which exceeds 50 cents and does not exceed 75 cents, a stamp duty of . . . . . . 3 cents. 62
    Do., on each package of, the retail price or value of which exceeds 75 cents and does not exceed one dollar, . 4 cents. 62
    Do., on each package of, the retail price or value of which exceeds one dollar, for each and every 50 cents, or fractional part thereof, over and above one dollar, an additional stamp duty of . . . . . . 2 cents. 62
Articles not to be considered as manufactures, ... 40
Assessors for each district, ... 1
    Do., how appointed, ... 1
    Do., subdivide his district and appoint assistants, . . 2
    Do., to take an oath, ... 2
    Do., certificate of, to be delivered to collector, . . 2
    Do., penalty for not taking oath, ... 2
    Do., when assessments are to be made, . . . 3
    Do., how taxable persons and property may be found out, . 3
    Do., duty when persons fail to make out a list, . . 4
    Do., penalty on persons making fraudulent lists, . 4
    Do., duty in case of fraudulent lists or under-valuation, . 4
    Do., duty when persons notified fail or neglect to make out lists, 4
    Do., duty in case of non-residents, . . . 5
    Do., duty relative to lists of property owned in other districts, 5
    Do., two general lists to be made of persons liable to pay tax, and amount, ... 5
    Do., lists to be sent to the principal assessor within thirty days, 6
    Do., to advertise when list may be examined, . . 6
    Do., to keep lists open fifteen days, . . . 6
    Do., to advertise time and place of hearing appeals, . 6
    Do., to submit lists to the inspection of all persons, . 6
    Do., to determine appeals in a summary way, . . 6
    Do., question to be decided by assessors on an appeal, . 6
    Do., to re-examine and equalize valuations, . . 6
    Do., to give notice of an increase of valuation, . . 6
    Do., to make lists of persons liable to taxation, and amount payable, ... 7
    Do., to make separate lists of non-residents, . . 7
    Do., to send lists to collectors, and penalty for neglect, . 7
    Do., penalty may be remitted by commissioner, . . 7
    Do., compensation of assessors, ... 7
    Do., in Oregon and California, and the territories, . 8
    Do., other cases of compensation, . . . 8
    Do., other duties under act of 1861, . . . 16
    Do., to receive abstract of books of distillers and brewers monthly, if desired, ... 24
    Do., right to examine said books, . . . 25
    Do., proceedings when persons apply for a license, . 25
    Do., to receive lists from manufacturers, . . . 33

		TAX.	PAGE
Assessors	how to assess knitting thread,		33
Do.,	to assess duties in certain cases,		35
Do.,	to estimate gas,		36
Do.,	to receive monthly report of auctioneers,		41
Do.,	do. do. butchers,		42
Do.,	do. do. railroad companies,		43
Do.,	do. do. steamboat captains,		43
Do.,	do. do. ferry boat owners,		43
Do.,	do. do. bridge keepers,		43
Do.,	to receive list of advertisements from publishers,		48
Do.,	to make return of neglect to report income,		51
Assessors assisting, how appointed,			2
Do.,	to take an oath,		2
Do.,	duties when they commence,		3
Do.,	to notify absent persons,		4
Do.,	duty when persons notified fail to make out lists,		4
Do.,	penalty for neglect to send lists to assessors,		6
Do.,	to send lists to districts where persons reside,		7
Do.,	compensation of,		7
Associations to make a list, &c.,			3
Auctioneers, for license,		$20 00.	27
Auctioneers not to sell at private sale,			26
Do.,	may sell for a licensed trader,		26
Do.,	who are auctioneers?		27
Do.,	to make monthly returns to the assessors, and penalty for neglect,		41
Auction sales of goods, merchandise, articles, and stocks, on gross amount of sales,		$\frac{1}{10}$ of 1 per ct.	41

B

		TAX.	PAGE
Band Iron. See "Iron."			
Banks, on all dividends,		3 per ct.	45
Banks, to make semi-annual statement,			45
Do.,	authorized to deduct the amount of tax from the dividend,		45
Bankers, every person who keeps a place of business where credits are opened in favor of any person, firm, or corporation, by the deposit or collection of money or currency, and the same, or any part thereof, shall be paid or remitted upon the draft, check, or order, of such creditor, but which does not include incorporated banks, or other banks legally authorized to issue notes as circulation, for license,		$100 00.	27
Bar Iron. See "Iron."			
Barytes, sulphate of, per 100 pounds,		10 cents.	37
Beer, per barrel of 31 gallons, fractional parts of a barrel to pay proportionately,		$1 00.	21
Bend Leather, per pound,		1 cent.	39
Benzine, or Benzole, per gallon,		10 cents.	36
Bicarbonate of soda, per pound,		5 mills.	37
Billiard Tables, for private use,		$10 00.	42
Do.,	for public use, each table, for license,	5 00.	30
Bills of Exchange (inland) for the payment of any sum of money exceeding $20 and not exceeding $100, otherwise than at sight or demand, stamp duty of		5 cents.	56
Do.,	exceeding $100 and not exceeding $200,	10 cents.	56
Do.,	exceeding $200 and not exceeding $350,	15 cents.	56
Do.,	exceeding $350 and not exceeding $500,	20 cents.	56
Do.,	exceeding $500 and not exceeding $750,	30 cents.	56
Do.,	exceeding $750 and not exceeding $1,000,	40 cents.	56
Do.,	exceeding $1,000 and not exceeding $1,500,	60 cents.	56
Do.,	exceeding $1,500 and not exceeding $2,500,	$1 00.	56
Do.,	exceeding $2,500 and not exceeding $5,000,	1 50.	56
Do.,	for every $2,500, or part of $2,500, in excess of $5,000,	1 00.	57

INDEX TO EXCISE TAX.

	TAX.	PAGE
Bills of Exchange (foreign) drawn in, but payable out of the United States, if drawn singly, or otherwise than in sets of three or more, according to the custom of merchants and bankers, same as bill of exchange (inland).		
Do., if drawn in sets of three or more, for every bill of each set, where the sum made payable shall not exceed $150, or the equivalent thereof in any foreign currency,	3 cents.	57
Do., above $150 and not above $250,	5 cents.	57
Do., above $250 and not above $500,	10 cents.	57
Do., above $500 and not above $1,000,	15 cents.	57
Do., above $1,000 and not above $1,500,	20 cents.	57
Do., above $1,500 and not above $2,250,	30 cents.	57
Do., above $2,250 and not above $3,500,	50 cents.	57
Do., above $3,500 and not above $5,000,	70 cents.	57
Do., above $5,000 and not above $7,500,	$1 00.	57
Bills of Exchange (foreign), &c., for every $2,500 or part thereof, in excess of $7,500,	30 cents.	57
Bills of Lading for any goods, merchandise, or effects, to be exported from a port or place in the United States to any foreign port or place, excepting the ports of British North America, a stamp duty of	10 cents.	57
Bitters: See "Preparations."		
Boards are not to be considered as a manufacture,		40
Bonds, auction sales of, on gross amounts of sales,	$\frac{1}{10}$ of 1 per ct.	
Bonds, for indemnifying any person who shall have become bound or engaged as surety for the payment of any sum of money, or for the due execution or performance of the duties of any office, and to account for money received by virtue thereof, a stamp duty of	50 cents.	57
Do., of any description other than such as are required in legal proceedings not otherwise charged, a stamp duty of	25 cents.	58
Bone, manufactures of, wholly or in part, if not otherwise specified, ad valorem,	3 per ct.	40
Books are not to be regarded as a manufacture,		40
Bottles, containing medicines, of which the maker claims to have some secret formula, or exclusive right for preparing the same, the retail price or value of which, contents included, does not exceed 25 cents, a stamp duty of	1 cent.	61
Do., containing medicines, &c., the retail price or value of which, contents included, exceeds 25 cents, and does not exceed 50 cents, a stamp duty of	2 cents.	62
Do., containing medicines, &c., the retail price or value of which, contents included, exceeds 50 cents, but does not exceed 75 cents,	3 cents.	62
Do., containing medicines, &c., the value of which, contents included, shall exceed 75 cents, and shall not exceed one dollar,	4 cents.	62
Do., containing medicines, &c., the value of which, contents included, exceeds one dollar, for each and every 50 cents or fractional part thereof over and above one dollar, an additional stamp duty of	2 cents.	62
Bowling alleys, for each alley, duty for license,	$5 00.	30
Boxes, containing medicines, &c., same as "Bottles."		
Brass, manufactures of, if not otherwise specified,	3 per ct.	40
Breweries and distilleries may be inspected by the collector in the day time,		14
Do., penalty for refusal to admit him,		14
Brewers, every person who manufactures fermented liquors of any name or description for sale, from malt, wholly or in part, who manufactures less than 500 bbls. per year, for license,	$25 00.	28
Do., who manufactures 500 bbls. and upward, per year, for license,	50 00.	28
Brewers, to pay duty on ale, beer, lager beer, and porter,		22
Do., to keep a record of grain used, and quantity of fermented liquors made and sold,		22

INDEX TO EXCISE TAX. 73

	TAX.	PAGE
Brewer's record open to inspection,		22
Do., render monthly accounts to the collector,		22
Do., verified by oath,		22
Do., pay duties,		22
Do., removal for storage, how authorized,		22
Do., original entries verified by oath,		23
Do., entries made by other persons verified,		23
Do., penalty for neglect to make true reports,		23
Do., fine, seizure to be made within thirty days,		23
Do., ten per cent. for neglect to pay duties, added,		24
Do., duties a lien,		24
Do., may be collected by distraint,		24
Do., restored on payment of duties,		24
Do., furnish abstract of entries on books to assessors monthly, if requested,		24
Bricks are not to be considered as a manufacture,		40
Bridges, toll, on gross receipts,	3 per ct.	43
Bridge keeper, to make monthly statement,		43
Bristles, manufactures of, not otherwise specified,	3 per ct.	40
Brokers, auction sales by, of goods, wares, merchandise, articles, or things, on gross amount of sale,	$\frac{1}{10}$ of 1 per ct.	41
Brokers, for license,	$50 00.	29
Brokers, commercial, for license,	50 00.	29
Brokers, land warrants (see Land Warrant Brokers),	25 00.	29
Brokers, who require a broker's license,		29
Do., cattle, cost of license,	10 00.	30
Do., commercial, who require such a license,		29
Bullion, in the manufacture of silverware, is not to be considered a manufacture,		40
Burning Fluid is not to be considered a manufacture,		40
Butchers, to report monthly to assessors,		42

C

Calfskins, tanned, each,	6 cents.	39
Do., American patent,	5 per ct.	39
Candles, of whatever material made,	3 per ct.	35
Cards, playing, per pack of whatever number, when the price per pack does not exceed 18 cents,	1 cent.	63
Do., over 18 and not over 25 cents per pack,	2 cents.	63
Do., over 25 and not over 30 cents per pack,	3 cents.	63
Do., over 30 and not over 36 cents per pack,	4 cents.	63
Do., over 36 cents per pack,	5 cents.	63
Calves, slaughtered, per head,	5 cents.	42
Carriages, &c., valued at $75 or over, including the harness, drawn by one horse,	$1 00.	41
Do., drawn by two horses, valued at $75, and not exceeding $200,	2 00.	42
Do., exceeding in value $200, and not exceeding $600,	5 00.	42
Do., exceeding $600 in value,	10 00.	42
Cassia, ground, and all imitations of, per pound,	1 cent.	37
Castile Soap, valued not above 3½ cents per pound, per pound,	1 mill.	38
Do., valued above 3½ cents per pound, per pound,	5 mills.	38
Catarrh Snuff, each package of, the retail price or value of which does not exceed 25 cents, a stamp duty of	1 cent.	61
Do., each package of, the retail price or value of which exceeds 25 cents, and does not exceed 50 cents, a stamp duty of	2 cents.	62
Do., each package of, the retail price or value of which exceeds 50 cents, and does not exceed 75 cents, a stamp duty of	3 cents.	62
Do., each package of, the value of which exceeds 75 cents, and does not exceed one dollar, a stamp duty of	4 cents.	62
Do., each package of, the retail price or value of which exceeds one dollar, for each and every additional 50 cents, or frac-		

INDEX TO EXCISE TAX.

	TAX.	PAGE
tional part thereof, over and above one dollar, an additional stamp duty of	2 cents.	62
Cattle Brokers, cost of license,	$10 00	30
Do., who is one,		30
Cattle, horned, exceeding eighteen months old, slaughtered for sale, each,	30 cents.	42
Do., under eighteen months old, per head,	5 cents.	42
Do., slaughtered by any person for his own consumption,	exempt.	42
Cattle brokers, for license,	$10 00.	30
Cavendish tobacco, valued at more than 30 cents per pound, per pound,	15 cents.	37
Do., valued at any sum not exceeding 30 cents per pound, per pound,	10 cents.	37
Cement, made wholly or in part of glue, to be sold in a liquid state, per gallon,	25 cents.	38
Certificate of stock in any incorporated company, stamp duty on each,	25 cents.	58
Certificate of profits, or any certificate or memorandum showing an interest in the property or accumulations of any incorporated company, if for not less than $10, and not exceeding $50, stamp duty,	10 cents.	58
Certificate of profits, &c., for sum exceeding fifty dollars,	25 cents.	58
Certificate—Any certificate of damage, and all other certificates or documents issued by any port warden, marine surveyor, or other person acting as such, stamp duty,	25 cents.	58
Certificate of deposit of any sum of money in any bank or trust company, or with any banker or person acting as such, if for a sum not exceeding one hundred dollars, a stamp duty,	2 cents.	58
Do., for a sum exceeding one hundred dollars. stamp duty,	5 cents.	58
Certificate of any other description than those specified, a stamp duty of	10 cents.	58
Charter Party—Contract of agreement for the charter of any ship or vessel, or steamer, or any letter, or memorandum, or other writing, between the captain, master, or owner, or person acting as agent of any ship or vessel, or steamer, and any other person or persons, for or relating to the charter of such ship or vessel, or steamer, if the registered tonnage of such ship or vessel, or steamer, does not exceed three hundred tons, stamp duty,	$3 00.	58
Do., exceeding three hundred tons, and not exceeding six hundred tons, stamp duty,	5 00.	58
Do.. exceeding six hundred tons, stamp duty,	10 00.	58
Checks drawn upon any bank, trust company, or any person or persons, companies or corporations, for the payment of money at sight or on demand,	2 cents.	50
Cheese is not to be considered a manufacture.		
Chemical preparations, same as "Medicines."		
Chocolate, prepared, per pound,	1 cent.	37
Circuses, every building, tent, space, or area, where feats of horsemanship or acrobatic sports are exhibited, for license,	$50 00.	30
Citizens, to make a list, &c.,		3
Claim agents, whose business it is to prosecute claims in any of the executive departments of the Federal Government, or procure patents, for each license,	10 00.	31
Clock movements, made to run one day, each,	5 cents.	38
Do., made to run over one day, each,	10 cents.	38
Cloth, before it has been dyed, printed, bleached, or prepared in any other manner,	3 per ct.	39
Do., after it has been dyed, duty assessed on increased value,	3 per ct.	40
Cloves, ground, and all imitations of, per pound,	1 cent.	37
Coal, all mineral, except pea coal and dust coal, per ton,	3½ cents.	36
Coal oil, refined, per gallon,	8 and 10 cents.	36
Coal oil distillers, each license,	$50 00.	30
Coal oil may be removed for export, or re-distillation,		20
Do., bonds to be given,		20
Do., oath, amount of duties to exceed $300,		21
Do., duties to be paid when not exported,		21
Do., illuminating, refined, and all other bituminous substances used for like purpose,	10 cents.	36

		TAX.	PAGE
Coal oil, refined by the distillation of coal alone,		8 cents.	36
Do., distillers subject to same provisions as distillers of spirituous liquors,			36
Coal tar, produced in the manufacture of gas,		exempt.	36
Cocoa, prepared, per pound,		1 cent.	37
Coffee, ground, per pound,		3 mills.	37
Collection districts to be designated,			1
Do., number of,			2
Collectors, how appointed,			1
Do.. number of,			2
Do., bonds of, and powers of,			2
Do., number of sureties,			2
Do., responsible for deputies,			3
Do., may collect all the taxes in his district,			3
Do., duty on receiving lists from assistant assessors, give receipts, &c.,			8
Do., to advertise when and where tax payable,			8
Do., to demand payment personally within twenty days after neglect,			8
Do., to collect by distraint,			9
Do., notice to owner or agent,			9
Do., make list of property distrained,			9
Do., to advertise,			9
Do., to restore property on payment of taxes and fees,			9
Do., sale, and disposition of surplus,			9
Do., give notice of time and place of sale of real estate to the owner,			10
Do., advertise and sell,			10
Do., may adjourn sale five days,			10
Do., how to give deeds of real estate,			10
Do., may sell lands in other districts,			11
Do., to keep a record of sales of land,			11
Do., record, how to be kept,			11
Do., duty in cases of redemption,			11
Do., proceedings with property of persons not residents of United States,			11
Do., to transmit monthly statements of collections,			12
Do., to complete collections in six months,			12
Do., charged with the amount of taxes receipted for,			12
Do., how credited,			12
Do., penalty for failure to account for taxes,			13
Do., proceedings against, by United States marshal,			13
Do., penalty for extortion or oppression,			13
Do., may inspect breweries and distilleries in the day time,			14
Do., penalty when refused an abstract,			14
Do., duties, how performed in case of sickness,			14
Do., sureties still held,			14
Do., duty to collect all duties and taxes imposed,			15
Do., to sue for fines,			15
Do., separate accounts to be kept,			15
Do., compensation of,			15
Do., other duties of collectors under act of 1861,			16
Do., shall grant licenses to distillers,			17
Do., may grant permits for the removal of spirits after inspection,			20
Do., may distrain for duties on fermented liquors,			24
Do., proceedings,			24
Collectors, Deputy, how appointed,			2
Do., number and bonds of,			2
Do., powers,			3
Do., to certify their proceedings to the Collector,			11
Do., oldest Deputy to act on disability of Collector,			14
Do., bond of Deputy available to heirs of Collectors,			14
Commercial Brokers. See "Brokers, Commercial."			
Commissioner of Revenue, office of,			1

INDEX TO EXCISE TAX.

	TAX.	PAGE
Commissioner, where located,		1
Do., salary, duties and powers,		1
Do., clerks, how appointed,		1
Confectioners, who are confectioners,		30
Do., license not required in certain cases,		32
Do., corporations to make a list, &c.,		3
Do., commissioner to determine which district shall pay tax,		65
Confectioners, whose gross annual sales exceed one thousand dollars (confectioners who have taken out a license as wholesale or retail dealers are not required to take a separate license), for each license,	$10 00.	30
Confectioners, whose gross annual sales do not exceed one thousand dollars, are not required to take out or pay for license,		30
Confectionery, made wholly or in part of sugar, per lb.	1 cent.	37
Consumption entry, at any custom house, not exceeding $100 in value, stamp duty,	25 cents.	59
Do., exceeding $100 in value and not exceeding $500,	50 cents.	59
Do., exceeding $500 in value,	$1 00.	59
Contracts, for each piece or sheet of paper on which written, stamp duty,	5 cents.	56
Do., for the hire, use or rent of any land, tenement, or portion thereof, if for a period of time not exceeding three years, stamp duty,	50 cents.	59
Do., for a period of time exceeding three years	$1 00.	59
Contracts, brokers' note, or memorandum of sale of any goods or merchandise, stocks, bonds, exchange, notes of hand, real estate, or property of any kind or description issued by persons acting as such, stamp duty,	10 cents.	58
Conveyance, deed, instrument, or writing, whereby any lands, tenements, or other realty, sold, shall be granted, leased, assigned, transferred, or otherwise conveyed to or vested in the purchaser or purchasers, or any other person or persons, by his, her, or their direction, when the consideration exceeds $100, and does not exceed $500, stamp duty,	50 cents.	58
Do., when the consideration exceeds $500, and does not exceed $1,000,	$1 00.	58
Do., when the consideration exceeds $1,000, and does not exceed $2,500,	2 00.	58
Do., exceeding $2,500, and not exceeding $5,000,	5 00.	59
Do., exceeding $5,000 and not exceeding $10,000	10 00.	59
Do., exceeding $10,000, and not exceeding $20,000,	20 00.	59
Do., for every additional $10,000, or fractional part, in excess of $20,000,	20 00.	59
Copper, manufactures of, not otherwise provided for, ad valorem,	3 per ct.	40
Cordials, medicinal, same as "Catarrh Snuff."		
Cosmetics, same as "Dentifrice."		
Cotton, raw, per lb.	½ cent.	39
Cotton, manufactures of, wholly or in part, not otherwise provided for,	3 per ct.	40
Cotton umbrellas,	5 per ct.	38
Coupons, railroad,	3 per ct.	44

D

	TAX.	PAGE
Deeds. See "Conveyances."		
Deerskins, dressed or smoked, per pound,	2 cents.	39
Do., manufactured,	3 per ct.	40
Dentifrice, each package of, the retail price or value of which does not exceed 25 cents, stamp duty,	1 cent.	62
Do., exceeding 25 cents, but not exceeding 50 cents, stamp duty,	2 cents.	62
Do., exceeding 50 cents, but not exceeding 75 cents, stamp duty,	3 cents.	62
Do. each package of, the value of which shall exceed 75 cents, and shall not exceed one dollar, stamp duty,	4 cents.	62
Do., exceeding one dollar, for each and every 50 cents, or frac-		

	TAX.	PAGE
tional part thereof, over and above one dollar, an additional stamp duty of	2 cents.	62
Dentists, for license,	$10 00.	31
Depositories of taxes collected,		12
Deputy Collectors. See "Collectors, Deputy."		
Despatch, telegraphic, when the charge for the first ten words does not exceed 20 cents, stamp duty,	1 cent.	59
Do., when it exceeds 20 cents,	3 cents.	59
Diamonds,	3 per ct.	39
Direct tax act, limited to one year,		67
Distilled spirits, first proof, per gallon,	20 cents.	
Distilled spirits, duty on first proof,	20 cts. per gal.	18
Do., increased for greater strength,		18
Do., standard for first proof,		18
Do., duty when payable,		18
Do., all to be inspected before used or removed,		18
Do., penalty for fraudulent attempt to evade payment of duties,		19
Do., may be removed after inspection,		20
Do., who to be shipper and consignee, and pay duties,		20
Do., stored till duties are paid and costs,		20
Do., not less than fifty barrels permitted,		20
Do., may be removed for export or redistillation,		20
Do., bonds, oath,		20
Do., amount of duties to exceed $300,		21
Do., duties to be paid when not exported,		21
Distillers.—Every person or copartnership which distils or manufactures spirituous liquors or sale, when manufacturing 300 bbls. or more per year, for license,	$50 00.	28
Do., making less than 300 bbls. per year,	25 00.	28
Do., of apples and peaches, making less than 150 bbls. per year,	12 50.	28
Distillers must have a license and give bond to report each additional still,		17
Do., keep record of gallons distilled and quantity of grain used open to inspection,		17
Do., render tri-monthly accounts of amount distilled, amount removed, and grain used,		17
Do., not to sell or remove until inspected,		17
Do., must pay duties when account is rendered,		18
Do., bond may be renewed or changed,		18
Do., must state place and capacity of still,		18
Do., penalty for false statement,		18
Do., may erect fire-proof warehouses,		19
Do., regarded as bonded warehouses,		19
Do., pay duty when spirits are sold,		19
Do., daily record of spirits made and sold to be kept,		19
Do., record open to inspection of the Collector,		19
Do., render tri-monthly accounts from record,		19
Do., record of grain, &c., used to be kept,		19
Do., to be verified by oath,		20
Do., pay duties when account is rendered,		20
Do., may remove spirits after inspection,		20
Do., how shipped and duties paid,		20
Do., not less than fifty barrels to be permitted,		20
Do., may remove for export or re-distillation,		20
Do., bond, oath,		20
Do., amount of duties to exceed $300,		21
Do., entries of books to be verified by oath,		21
Do., entries made by other persons to be verified,		21
Do., to furnish abstract of entries on books to assessors monthly, if required,		24
Distraining for taxes, proceedings by Collector,		9
Do., rights of parties aggrieved by,		16
Do., proceeding to have tax refunded,		16
Dividends, annual income from, when exceeding $600, and not exceeding $10,000, on the excess over $600,	3 per ct.	49

		TAX.	PAGE
Dividends, exceeding $10,000, on excess over $600,		5 per ct.	49
Do., annual income from, when realized by any citizen of the United States residing abroad, and not in the employment of the United States, not otherwise provided for,		5 per ct.	49
Draft, drawn upon any bank, trust company, or any person or persons, companies or corporations, for the payment of any sum exceeding $20, at sight or on demand, stamp duty,		2 cents.	56
Draining tiles are not to be considered a manufacture,			46
Drawback allowed on manufactures exported,			65
Do., certificate of receivable for taxes,			66
Do., on cotton goods,			67
Do., penalty for fraudulent claim,			67
Duties to be estimated on the net value,			40

E

Eating-houses, when gross annual receipts exceed $1,000,	$10 00.	29
Do., when gross annual receipts do not exceed $1,000, no license is required; nor, when a license has been taken out for the sale of confectionery, is an additional one required,		29
Eating-houses,		29
Do., do not require license as confectioners,		29
Do., what are eating-houses,		29
Do., license not required in certain cases,		32
Emeralds,	3 per ct.	39
Enamelled leather, per square foot,	5 mills.	38
Enamelled skirting leather, per square foot,	1½ cents.	38
Entry of any goods, wares, or merchandise, at any custom house, for consumption or warehousing, less than $100 in value,	25 cents.	59
Do., exceeding $100 in value, and not $500,	50 cents.	50
Do., exceeding $500 in value,	$1 00.	59
Entry for the withdrawal of any goods, wares, or merchandise, from bonded warehouse, stamp duty,	50 cents.	59
Epileptic pills, same as "Dentifrice."		
"Essence of Life," same as "Dentifrice."		
Executors may carry on trade under license of deceased persons,		26
Do., indorsement required, &c.,		26
Express.—For every receipt issued by an express company or carrier, or person whose occupation it is to act as such, for all boxes, bales, packages, articles, or bundles, when the fee for transportation does not exceed 25 cents,	1 cent.	57
Do., when it exceeds 25 cents, but does not exceed one dollar,	2 cents.	57
Do., when one or more packages are sent to the same address, at the same time, and the compensation exceeds one dollar,	5 cents.	57
Express Companies, not to receive packages unless stamped or a stamped receipt given,		54

F

False swearing, penalty of,		15
Ferry-boat owner to make monthly statement,		43
Ferry boats, propelled by steam or horse power, on gross receipts,	1½ per ct.	43
Fire Insurance Companies, on all dividends,	3 per ct.	45
Firms in business, to make a list, &c.,		3
Fish, preserved, ad valorem,	5 per ct.	38
Fish oil,	exempt.	36
Flax, manufactures of, not otherwise specified,	3 per ct.	40
Flax, prepared for textile or felting purposes, is not to be considered a manufacture until actually woven, knit, or felted into fabric for consumption.		40
Flour, made from grain, is not to be considered a manufacture.		40

INDEX TO EXCISE TAX. 79

	TAX.	PAGE
Fraud, proceedings in case of, to be in U. S. Courts,		65
Fruits, preserved,	5 per ct.	38
Fans made up,	3 per ct.	39

G

	TAX.	PAGE
Gains, annual, of every person, when exceeding $600, and not exceeding $10,000, on the excess of gain over $600,	3 per ct.	49
Do., exceeding $10,000, on the excess of gain over $600,	5 per ct.	49
Gains, annual, from property of any kind in the United States, realized by any citizen of the United States, residing abroad, and in employment of the United States, not otherwise provided for,	5 per ct.	49
Gas, coal, when the product shall be not above 500,000 cubic feet per month, per 1,000 cubic feet,	5 per ct.	36
Do., when the product shall be above 500,000 and not exceeding 5,000,000 cubic feet per month, per 1,000 cubic feet,	10 cents.	36
Do., when the product shall be above 5,000,000 cubic feet per month, per 1,000 cubic feet,	15 cents.	36
Gas Companies competing pay the rates of the highest,		36
Do., if furnished to streeet lamps, hotels, and private dwellings, may be estimated,		36
Gas, all illuminating, same as coal gas,		36
Gelatine, of all descriptions, in solid state, per pound,	5 mills.	38
Ginger, ground, and all imitations of, per pound,	1 cent.	37
Glass, manufactures of, not otherwise specified,	3 per ct.	40
Gloves, deer skin or oil leather,	3 per ct.	40
Glue, in a liquid form, per gallon,	25 cents.	38
Do., in a solid state, per pound,	5 mills.	38
Glycerine lotion, same as "Dentifrice."		
Goat-skins, curried, manufactured, or finished,	4 per ct.	39
Gold, manufactures of, not otherwise provided for,	3 per ct.	40
Goods, all, except spirituous and malt liquors, and leaf, stem, or manufactured tobacco, where the annual product does not exceed $600, provided that this shall not apply to any business or transaction where one party furnishes the materials, or any part thereof, and employs another party to manufacture, make, or finish the goods, wares, or merchandise, or articles, paying, or promising to pay therefor, and receiving the goods, wares, and merchandise, or articles; but, in all such cases, the party furnishing the materials and receiving the goods, wares, and merchandise, or articles, shall be liable to and charged with all accruing duties thereon,	Free.	35
Gunpowder, and all explosive substances used for mining, blasting, artillery, or sporting purposes, when valued at 18 cents per pound, or less, per pound,	5 mills.	37
Do., when valued above 18 cents per pound, and not exceeding 30 cents per pound,	1 cent.	37
Do., when valued above 30 cents per pound, per pound,	6 cents.	37
Gutta-percha, manufactures of, not otherwise provided for,	3 per ct.	40
Gypsum is not to be considered a manufacture,		40

H

	TAX.	PAGE
Harness leather, per pound,	7 mills.	39
Harness leather, made of hides imported east of the Cape of Good Hope, per pound,	5 mills.	39
Headings are not to be considered a manufacture,		40
Hemp, manufactures of, when not otherwise specified,	3 per ct.	40
Hog-skins, tanned or dressed,	4 per ct.	39
Hogs, exceeding six months old, slaughtered, when the number thus slaughtered exceeds twenty in any one year, for sale, per head,	10 cents.	42
Do., slaughtered by any person for his own consumption,	Exempt.	42

	TAX.	PAGE
Hollow ware, iron, per ton of 2,000 pounds,	$1 50.	38
Hoops not considered a manufacture,		40
Horn, manufactures of, not otherwise provided for,	3 per ct.	40
Horned cattle, exceeding eighteen months old, slaughtered for sale, each,	30 cents.	42
Do., under 18 months old, per head,	5 cents.	42
Horse-skins, tanned and dressed,	4 per ct.	39
Horse-dealers, every person whose business it is to buy and sell horses and mules, for each license,	$10 00.	30
Hose, conducting, all kinds, ad valorem,	3 per ct.	39
Hotels, Inns, Taverns, what is a hotel, inn, or tavern,		29
Do., do not require a license as a tobacconist,		30
Hotels, where the rent or the valuation of the yearly rental of the house and property occupied shall be $10,000 or more, for each yearly license,	$200 00.	28
Do., where the rent or the valuation of the yearly rental shall be $5,000, and less than $10,000 for each yearly license,	100 00.	28
Do., where the rent or the valuation of the yearly rental shall be $2,500 and less than $5,000 for each yearly license,	75 00.	28
Do., where the rent or the valuation of the rental shall be $1,000, and less than $2,500, for each yearly license,	50 00.	29
Do., where the rent or the valuation of the yearly rental shall be $500, and less than $1,000, for each yearly license,	25 00.	29
Do., where the rent or the valuation of the yearly rental shall be $300, and less than $500, for each yearly license,	15 00.	29
Do., where the rent or the valuation of the yearly rental shall be $100, and less than $300, for each yearly license,	10 00.	29
Do., where the rent or the valuation of the yearly rental shall be less than $100, for each yearly license,	5 00.	29

I

	TAX.	PAGE
Income, annual, of every person, when exceeding $600, and not exceeding $10,000, on the excess over $600,	3 per ct.	49
Do., exceeding $10,000, on excess over $600,	5 per ct.	49
Do., annual, from property of any kind in the United States, realized by any citizen of the United States residing abroad, and not in the employment of the United States Government, not otherwise provided for,	5 per ct.	49
Do., from United States securities,	1½ per ct.	49
Incomes, how estimated,		49
Do., when tax is due and penalty for non-payment,		50
Do., all persons to make return of income,		50
Do., rate of tax,		49
Do., limitation of,		50
Do., relating to Act of August 5th, 1861, repealed,		48
Do., assessors to make returns in cases of neglect,		51
India-rubber, manufactures of, not otherwise specified,	3 per ct.	40
Informers have a moiety of fines,		15
Inns. See "Hotels."		
Inspector's fees, paid by owners,		19
Do., penalty for fraudulent marking,		19
Do., of spirits, appointed by Collectors,		18
Do., oath, fees, duties,		18
Insurance Companies, all, on dividends,	3 per ct.	45
Insurance Companies, fire, inland or marine, upon gross receipts for premiums and assessments, quarterly,	1 per ct.	46
Insurance Companies, foreign, doing business in the United States, upon gross receipts for premiums and assessments, quarterly,	1 per ct.	46
Insurance Companies to make a quarterly statement,		46
Do., pay duty at the same time,		46
Insurance, Life, on each policy of insurance, or other instrument, by whatever name the same shall be called, whereby any insurance shall be made upon any life or lives, when the amount shall not exceed $1,000, a stamp duty of	25 cents.	59

INDEX TO EXCISE TAX.

	TAX.	PAGE
Insurance, Life, exceeding $1,000, and not exceeding $5,000,	50 cents.	59
Do., exceeding $5,000,	$1 00.	59
Insurance, Marine, Inland, or Fire, on each policy of insurance, or other instrument, by whatever name the same shall be called, whereby any insurance shall be made or renewed, marine or inland, upon property of any description, whether against perils by the sea or by fire, or other peril of any kind, made by any insurance company or its agents, or by any other company or person, stamp duty,	25 cents.	59
Interest, annual income from, when exceeding the sum of $600 per annum, and not exceeding $10,000, on the excess of income over $600,	3 per ct.	49
Do., exceeding $10,000, on the excess over $600,	5 per ct.	49
Do., annual income from, when realized by any citizen of the United States, residing abroad, and not in the employment of the United States Government, not otherwise provided for,	5 per ct.	49
Iron, manufactures of, if not otherwise specified,	3 per ct.	40
Do., railroad, advanced beyond slabs, blooms, or loops, and not advanced beyond bars or rods, per ton,	$1 50.	38
Do., band, hoop, and sheet, not thinner than No. 18 wire gauge, per ton,	1 50.	38
Do., plate, not less than one-eighth of an inch in thickness, per ton,	1 50.	38
Do., railroad, re-rolled, per ton,	75 cents.	38
Do., band, hoop, or sheet, thinner than No. 18 wire gauge, per ton,	$2 00.	38
Do., plate, less than one-eighth of an inch in thickness, per ton,	2 00.	38
Do., cut nails and spikes, per ton,	2 00.	38
Do., bars, rods, bands, hoops, sheets, plates, nails and spikes, manufactured from iron, upon which the duty of $1 50 has been levied and paid, are only subject to an additional duty of, per ton,	50 cents.	38
Do., cast, used for bridges, buildings, or other permanent structures, per ton,	$1 00.	38
Do., pig, and other, not advanced beyond slabs, blooms, or hoops, are not to be considered as manufactures,		40
Ivory, manufactures of, if not otherwise specified,	3 per ct.	40

J

Jewelry,	3 per ct.	39
Jute, manufactures of, if not otherwise specified,	3 per ct.	40
Jugglers, including every person who performs by sleight of hand, for each license,	$20 00.	30

K

Kid-skins, curried, manufactured, or finished,	4 per ct.	39
Knitting-thread, how to be assessed,		33

L

Lager beer, per barrel, containing 31 gallons, fractional parts of a barrel to pay proportionately,	$1, 00.	21
Land warrant brokers—every person who makes a business of buying and selling land warrants, and furnishing them to settlers or other persons, under contracts that the lands procured by means of them shall be bound for the prices agreed on for the warrants, for each license,	25 00.	29
Lard oil, per gallon,	2 cents.	36
Lawyers, for each license,	$10 00.	31

		TAX.	PAGE
Lead, manufactures of, if not otherwise specified,		3 per ct.	40
Lead, white, per hundred,		25 cents.	37
Lease, for the hire, use, or rent of any land, tenement, or portion thereof, if for a period of time not exceeding three years, stamp duty,		50 cents.	59
Do.,	for a period of time exceeding three years, stamp duty,	$1 00.	50
Leather, bend, per pound,		1 cent.	39
Do.,	butt, per pound,	1 cent.	39
Do.,	damaged, per pound,	5 mills.	39
Do.,	enamelled, per square foot,	5 mills.	38
Do.,	enamelled skirting, per square foot,	1½ cents.	38
Do.,	harness, per pound,	7 mills.	39
Do.,	harness, made from hides imported east of the Cape of Good Hope, per pound,	5 mills.	39
Do.,	offal, per pound,	5 mills.	39
Do.,	oil-dressed, per pound,	2 cents.	39
Do.,	oil-dressed, manufactured,	3 per ct.	4
Do.,	patent, per square foot,	5 mills.	38
Do.,	patent japanned split, used for dasher leather, per square foot,	4 mills.	38
Do.,	rough, made from hides imported east of the Cape of Good Hope, per pound,	5 mills.	39
Do.,	rough, all other, hemlock-tanned, per pound,	7 mills.	39
Do.,	rough, tanned in whole or in part with oak, per pound,	1 cent.	39
Leather, sole, made from hides imported east of the Cape of Good Hope, per pound,		5 mills.	39
Do.,	sole, all other, hemlock-tanned, per pound,	7 mills.	39
Do.,	sole, tanned in whole or in part with oak, per pound,	1 cent.	39
Do.,	tanned calf-skins, each,	6 cents.	39
Do.,	upper finished or curried, except calf-skins, made from leather tanned in the interest of parties furnishing or currying such leather, not previously taxed in the rough, per pound,	1 cent.	39
Do.,	manufactures of, when not otherwise specified,	3 per ct.	40
Legacies, exceeding $1,000 to parent or child, or brother or sister, for each and every hundred dollars of the clear value of such interest in such property,		75 cents.	63
Do.,	to nephew or niece, for each and every hundred dollars of the clear value of such interest,	$1 50.	63
Do.,	to an uncle, aunt, or cousin, for each and every hundred dollars of the clear value of such interest,	$3 00.	63
Do.,	to a great uncle or aunt, or second cousin, for each and every hundred dollars of the clear value of such interest,	4 00.	63
Do.,	where the person or persons entitled to any beneficial interest in such property shall be in any other degree of collateral consanguinity than is stated above, or shall be a stranger in blood to the person who died possessed, as aforesaid, or shall be a body politic or corporate, for each and every hundred dollars of the clear value of such interest,	5 00.	63
Do.	passing by will or by the laws of any State or Territory, to husband or wife of the person who died possessed of the property,	exempt.	64
Legacies—Tax on to be a lien on property of deceased,			64
Do.,	must be paid before distribution,		64
Do.,	executor must furnish assessor with a list of legatees and value of legacies,		64
Do.,	penalty for neglect or false return		64
Do.,	penalty for refusing to exhibit records, files, &c.,		65
Legal documents—Writ, or other original process commenced in any court of record, either of law or equity, stamp duty,		50 cents.	61
Do.,	issued by a justice of the peace, or in any criminal or other suits commenced by the United States, or any State, are not subject to the payment of stamp duties,		61
Letters of credit. See "Bills of Exchange, foreign."			

INDEX TO EXCISE TAX. 83

		TAX.	PAGE
Letters of administration—where the estate and effects for, or in respect of which such letters of administration applied for shall be sworn or declared not to exceed the value of $2,500, stamp duty,		50 cents.	60
Do.,	to exceed $2,500 and not exceeding $5,000,	$1 00.	60
Do.,	to exceed $5,000 and not exceeding $20,000,	2 00.	60
Do.,	to exceed $20,000 and not exceeding $50,000,	5 00.	60
Do.,	to exceed $50,000 and not exceeding $100,000,	10 00.	60
Do.,	to exceed $100,000 and not exceeding $150,000,	20 00.	61
Do.,	for every additional $50,000, or fractional part thereof,	10 00.	61
Licenses must be taken out each year by the following named persons:			
	Apothecaries,	10 00.	31
	Auctioneers,	20 00.	27
	Bankers,	100 00.	27
	Billiard tables, each, for public use,	5 00.	30
	Do., for private use,	10 00.	40
	Brewers. See "Brewers."		
	Brokers,	50 00.	29
	Bowling alleys, for each alley,	5 00.	30
	Cattle brokers,	10 00.	30
	Claim agents,	10 00.	31
	Coal oil distillers,	50 00.	30
	Commercial brokers,	50 00.	29
	Confectioners,	10 00.	30
	Circuses,	50 00.	30
	Dentists,	10 00.	31
	Eating-houses,	10 00.	29
	Horse-dealers,	10 00.	30
	Hotels,	from $5 to 200 00.	28
	Jugglers,	20 00.	30
	Land-warrant brokers,	25 00.	29
	Lawyers,	10 00.	31
	Livery-stable keepers,	10 00.	30
	Manufacturers,	10 00.	31
	Peddlers,	from $5 to 20 00.	31
	Photographers,	10 00.	31
	Pawnbrokers,	50 00.	28
	Physicians,	10 00.	31
	Retail dealers,	10 00.	27
	Retail dealers in liquors,	20 00.	27
	Rectifiers,	25 00.	28
	Soap-makers,	10 00.	30
	Surgeons,	10 00.	31
	Tobacconists,	10 00.	20
	Theatres,	100 00.	30
	Tallow chandlers,	10 00.	30
	Wholesale dealers,	50 00.	28
	Wholesale dealers in liquors,	100 00.	27
License, to whom granted, proceedings, tax,			17
Do.,	who shall obtain one,		25
Do.,	requirements to obtain one,		25
Do.,	penalty for neglect to take out,		25
Do.,	moiety to the informer,		25
Do.,	details of a license,		25
Do.,	one required for each trade a person carries on,		26
Do.,	do not expire on the death of the trader,		26
Do.,	cost of,		27
Do.,	who may act under a license,		27
Do.,	will not authorize liquor to be drunk on the premises where sold,		27
Do.,	not required on druggists' and chemists' still to recover alcohol, &c.,		28
Do.,	not required of apothecaries, confectioners, eating-houses and tobacconists, in certain cases,		32

INDEX TO EXCISE TAX.

	TAX.	PAGE
License not to be against the State laws,		32
Lime is not to be regarded as a manufacture,		40
Linseed oil, per gallon,	2 cents.	36
Lists to be made by persons, partners, firms, associations or corporations,		3
Do., fraudulent, penalty for making,		4
Do., of non-residents,		5
Do., how operate,		5
Do., of persons must include property owned in other districts.		5
Do., to be open for inspection fifteen days,		6
Livery-stable keepers—Every person whose occupation is to keep horses for hire or to let, for license,	$10 00.	30
Livery stable keepers, not require license to sell horses,		30
Lumber is not to be considered a manufacture,		40

M

	TAX.	PAGE
Magazines are not to be regarded as a manufacture of paper or submitted to a rate of duty as a manufacture,		40
Do., for all advertisements, on annual gross receipts, when more than one thousand dollars,	3 per ct.	47
Malt is not to be considered a manufacture,		40
Manifest of the cargo of any ship, vessel, or steamer, for a foreign port, if the registered tonnage of such ship, vessel, or steamer, does not exceed three hundred tons, stamp duty,	$1 00.	59
Do., exceeding three hundred tons, and not exceeding six hundred tons,	3 00.	59
Do., exceeding six hundred tons,	5 00.	59
Manufacturers, for license,	10 00.	31
Manufacturers' sales must exceed $1,000,		31
Do., who are manufacturers,		31
Do., license not required in certain cases,		32
Do., of agricultural tools, stoves, hollow ware, brooms, wooden ware, powder, and producers of garden seeds, require no additional license for sales in other places,		31
Do., to furnish list to assessors within thirty days,		32
Do., to make monthly returns of products and sales,		33
Do., verified by oath,		33
Do., must pay duties monthly,		33
Do., finishers of fabrics of cotton, wool, or other materials, to pay the tax,		33
Do., penalty for neglect ten days,		33
Do., on paying the duty on goods made on commission, manufacturers may have lien,		33
Do., proceedings on refusal to pay duties,		33
Do., goods forfeited,		34
Do., seizure and other proceedings,		34
Do., surplus after sale, how disposed of,		34
Do., penalty on failing to make lists and monthly returns to the assessor		35
Do., exempt from tax in certain cases,		37
Do., if one party furnishes the raw material, and another makes it up, no exemption,		35
Do., value and quantity of goods estimated by actual sales,		35
Do., scale of duties,		35
Manufactures, not otherwise specified:—		
Do., of bone,	3 per ct.	40
Do., of brass,	3 per ct.	40
Do., of bristles,	3 per ct.	40
Do., of copper,	3 per ct.	40
Do., of cotton,	3 per ct.	40
Do., of flax,	3 per ct.	40
Do., of glass,	3 per ct.	40
Do., of gold,	3 per ct.	40

INDEX TO EXCISE TAX. 85

	TAX.	PAGE
Manufactures of gutta-percha,	3 per ct.	40
Do., of hemp,	3 per ct.	40
Do., of horn,	3 per ct.	40
Do., of India-rubber,	3 per ct.	40
Do., of iron,	3 per ct.	40
Do., of ivory,	3 per ct.	40
Do., of jute,	3 per ct.	40
Do., of lead,	3 per ct.	40
Do., of leather,	3 per ct.	40
Do., of paper,	3 per ct.	40
Do., of pottery,	3 per ct.	40
Do., of silk,	3 per ct.	40
Do., of silver,	3 per ct.	40
Do., of steel,	3 per ct.	40
Do., of tin,	3 per ct.	40
Do.. of willow,	3 per ct.	40
Do., of wood,	3 per ct.	40
Do., of wool,	3 per ct.	40
Do., of worsted,	3 per ct.	40
Do., of zinc,	3 per ct.	40
Do., of other materials,	3 per ct.	40
Maps are not to be considered a manufacture,		40
Marine protest,	25 cents.	
Marshal, The U. S., his duty to levy on property of defaulting collector and sureties,		13
Meats, preserved,	5 per ct.	38
Medicines. See schedule C, p. 61.		
Merchandise. See "Goods."		
Mineral coal, except pea coal, per ton,	3½ cents.	36
Mittens, deer skin, or oil dressed leather,	3 per ct.	40
Morocco skins, cured, manufactured, or finished,	4 per ct.	39
Mortgage of lands, estate, or property, real or personal, or any personal bond given as security for the payment of any definite or certain sum of money exceeding $100 and not exceeding $500,	50 cents.	59
Do., exceeding five hundred dollars and not exceeding one thousand dollars,	$1 00.	60
Do., exceeding one thousand dollars and not exceeding two thousand five hundred dollars,	2 00.	60
Do., exceeding two thousand five hundred dollars and not exceeding five thousand dollars,	5 00.	60
Do., exceeding five thousand dollars and not exceeding ten thousand dollars,	10 00.	60
Do., exceeding ten thousand dollars and not exceeding twenty thousand dollars,	15 00.	60
Do., for every additional $10,000, or fractional part thereof, in excess of $20,000,	10 00.	60
Movements, clock, made to run one day, each	5 cents.	38
Do., made to run over one day, each	10 cents.	38
Mustard, ground, per pound,	1 cent.	37
Mustard seed oil, per gallon,	2 cents.	36
Mutual insurance companies. See "Insurance."		

N

Nails, cut, per ton,	$2 00.	38
Naphtha, per gallon,	10 cents.	36
New Mexico, direct tax of credited,		67
Newspapers are not to be regarded as a manufacture or submitted to a rate of duty as a manufacture,		40
Newspapers, for all advertisements, see "Advertisements."		
Non-residents, duty of assessors in case of,		8
Notarial act. See "Protest."		

INDEX TO EXCISE TAX.

		TAX.	PAGE
Note, promissory,	for the payment of any sum of money at sight or on demand, stamp duty	2 cents.	56
Do.,	for the payment in any other manner than at sight or on demand, of any sum of money exceeding twenty dollars and not exceeding one hundred dollars,	5 cents.	56
Do.,	exceeding one hundred dollars and not exceeding two hundred dollars,	10 cents.	56
Do.,	exceeding two hundred dollars and not exceeding three hundred and fifty dollars,	15 cents.	56
Do.,	exceeding three hundred and fifty dollars and not exceeding five hundred dollars,	20 cents.	56
Do.,	exceeding five hundred dollars and not exceeding seven hundred and fifty dollars	30 cents.	56
Do..	exceeding seven hundred and fifty dollars and not exceeding one thousand dollars,	40 cents.	56
Do.,	exceeding one thousand dollars and not exceeding one thousand five hundred dollars,	60 cents.	56
Do.,	exceeding one thousand five hundred dollars and not exceeding two thousand five hundred dollars,	$1 00.	56
Do.,	exceeding two thousand five hundred dollars and not exceeding five thousand dollars,	1 50.	56
Do.,	for every two thousand five hundred dollars in excess of five thousand dollars,	1 00.	57

O

Oath of Assessors and Assistants,			2
Oils, animal, pure or adulterated, if not otherwise provided for, per gallon,		2 cents.	36
Do.,	illuminating, refined, produced by the distillation of coal, asphaltum, shale, peat, petroleum or rock, and all other bituminous substances used for like purposes, per gallon,	10 cents.	36
Do.,	lard, pure or adulterated, if not otherwise provided for, per gallon,	2 cents.	36
Do.,	linseed, per gallon,	2 cents.	36
Do.,	mustard seed, per gallon,	2 cents.	36
Do.,	all vegetable, per gallon,	2 cents.	36
Do.,	refined, produced by distillation of coal exclusively, per gallon,	8 cents.	36
Oleic acid, produced in the manufacture of candles and used in the manufacture of soap,		exempt.	36
Order for the payment of any sum of money drawn upon any bank, trust company, or any person or persons, companies or corporations, at sight or on demand, stamp duty,		2 cents.	56
Oxide of zinc, per 100 lbs.		25 cents.	87

P

Packet, containing medicines, &c. See "Bottles."			
Paints, dry or ground in oil, or in paste with water, not otherwise provided for,		5 per ct.	38
Painters' colors, do.,		5 per ct.	38
Pamphlets are not to be regarded as a manufacture or submitted to a rate of duty as a manufacture,			40
Paper, manufactures of, if not otherwise specified,		3 per ct.	40
Do.,	account book,	3 per ct.	40
Do.,	bank-note,	3 per ct.	40
Do.,	binders' board,	3 per ct.	40
Do.,	card,	3 per ct.	40
Do.,	hanging,	3 per ct.	40
Do.,	letter,	3 per ct.	40
Do.,	map,	3 per ct.	40

INDEX TO EXCISE TAX.

	TAX.	PAGE
Paper, manufactures of, note,	3 per ct.	40
Do., printing, sized and colored,	3 per ct.	40
Do., printing, unsized,	3 per ct.	40
Do., pasteboard,	3 per ct.	40
Do., plate,	3 per ct.	40
Do., uncolored, calendered,	3 per ct.	40
Do., wrapping, made of manilla hemp, or made in imitation thereof,	3 per ct.	40
Do., writing,	3 per ct.	40
Do., all other descriptions of,	3 per ct.	4
Paraffine oil,	exempt.	36
Parasols of any material,	5 per ct.	38
Partnerships, to make a list, &c.,		3
Passport, on each issued from the office of the Secretary of State,	$3 00.	47
Do., on each issued by any ministers or consuls of the United States,	3 00.	47
Passage ticket, by any vessel from a port in the United States to a foreign port, if less than $30,	50 cents.	60
Do., exceeding $30,	$1 00.	60
Pasteboard, made of junk, straw, or other material,	3 per ct.	40
Patent leather, per square foot,	5 mills.	38
Pawnbrokers.—Every person whose business or occupation is to take or receive by way of pledge, pawn, or exchange, any goods, wares, or merchandise, or any kind of personal property whatever, for the repayment or security of money lent thereon, for license,	$50 00.	28
Paymaster U. S. to withhold tax in adjusting accounts,		47
Pearl barley is not to be considered a manufacture,		40
Peddlers.—Every person who sells, or offers to sell, at retail, goods, wares, or other commodities, travelling from place to place, in the street, or through different parts of the country, when travelling with more than two horses, for each license,	$20 00.	31
Do., when travelling with two horses, for each license,	15 00.	31
Do., when travelling with one horse, for each license,	10 00.	31
Do., when travelling on foot, for each license,	5 00.	31
Do., who sell newspapers, Bibles, or religious tracts,	exempt.	31
Do., who sell, or offer to sell, dry goods, foreign or domestic, by one or more original packages or pieces at one time to the same person, for each license,	$50 00.	31
Do., who peddles jewelry, for each license,	25 00.	31
Pepper, ground, and all imitations of, per pound,	1 cent.	37
Perfumery, same as "Dentifrice."		
Petroleum, refined, per gallon,	10 cents.	36
Phial, containing medicine, &c., same as "Bottles."		
Photographers, who require a license,		31
Photographers, for each license, when the receipts do not exceed $500,	$10 00.	31
Do., when the receipts are over $500 and under $1,000, for license,	15 30.	31
Do., when the receipts are over $1,000, for license,	25 00.	31
Physicians, whose business it is, for fee or reward, to prescribe remedies or perform surgical operations for the cure of any bodily disease or ailing, dentists included, for each license,	10 00.	31
Physicians, license not required in certain cases,		32
Pickles,	5 per ct.	38
Pig iron is not to be considered a manufacture.		
Pills, same as "Dentifrice."		
Pimento, ground, and all imitations of, per pound,	1 cent.	37
Pins, solid head or other, in boxes, packets, bundles or other form,	5 per ct.	38
Plaster, or gypsum is not to be considered a manufacture,		40
Plasters, same as "Dentifrice."		
Plate, gold, kept for use, per oz. troy,	50 cents.	42
Plate, silver, do., per oz. troy,	3 cents.	42
Plate, silver, as above, to the extent of 40 oz.	free.	42
Plate iron. See "Iron."		

	TAX.	PAGE
Playing cards. * See "Cards."		
Policy of insurance. See "Insurance."		
Porter, per barrel of 31 gallons, fractional parts in proportion,	$1 00.	21
Pot, containing medicines, &c., same as "Bottles."		
Pottery ware, if not otherwise specified,	3 per ct.	40
Powders, medicinal, same as "Dentifrice."		
Power of attorney, for the sale or transfer of any stock, bonds, or scrip, or for the collection of any dividends, or interest thereon, stamp duty	25 cents.	60
Power of attorney, or proxy for voting at any election for officers of any incorporated company or society, except charitable, religious, literary, and cemetery societies, stamp duty	10 cents.	60
Power of attorney to sell and convey real estate, or to rent or lease the same, or to perform any or all other acts not otherwise specified, stamp duty	$1 00.	60
Power of attorney to receive or collect rent, stamp duty	25 cents.	60
Preparations, medical. See schedule C, page 61.		
Preparations, of which coffee forms a part, or which are prepared for sale as a substitute for coffee, per pound,	3 mills.	37
Preserved fish	5 per ct.	38
Preserved fruit,	5 per ct.	38
Preserved meats,	5 per ct.	38
Printed books are not to be regarded as a manufacture, or submitted to a rate of duty as a manufacture.		40
Printers' ink is not to be considered a manufacture.		40
Probate of will, where the estate and effects for or in respect of which such probate applied for shall be sworn or declared not to exceed the value of $2,500, stamp duty,	50 cents.	60
Do., to exceed $2,500 and not exceeding $5,000,	$1 00.	60
Do., to exceed $5,000 and not exceeding $20,000,	2 00.	60
Do., to exceed $20,000 and not exceeding $50,000,	5 00.	60
Do., to exceed $50,000 and not exceeding $100,000,	10 00.	60
Do., exceeding $100,000 and not exceeding $150,000,	20 00.	61
Do., for every additional $50,000, or fractional part thereof,	10 00.	61
Profits, annual, of every person, when exceeding $600, and not exceeding $10,000, on the excess over $600,	3 per ct.	49
Do., exceeding $10,000, on the excess over $600,	5 per ct.	49
Do., annual, when realized by any citizen of the United States residing abroad, and not in the employment of the United States, not otherwise provided for,	5 per ct.	49
Promissory notes,	5 cents.	56
Property under distraint, when not divisible, all to be sold,		9
Do., when not sold to be purchased for the U. S.,		10
Do., annual income from, see "Income."		
Do., left by legacy. See "Legacies."		
Protest of every note, bill of exchange, acceptance, check, or draft,	25 cents.	61
Publications are not to be regarded as a manufacture.		
Public exhibitions, cost of license,	$10	10
Do., a license for each State required,		30
Pulmonary balsam, same as "Dentifrice."		
Do., syrup, same as "Dentifrice."		
Pulmonic syrup, same as "Dentifrice."		
Do., wafers, same as "Dentifrice."		

R

Railroad Company, to make monthly statement,		43
Railroads—On gross receipts from carrying passengers,	3 per ct.	43
the motive power of which is not steam, on gross receipts for carrying passengers,	1¼ per ct.	43
on bonds or other evidences of indebtedness upon which interest is stipulated to be paid, on the amount of interest,	3 per ct.	44
Railroad iron, per ton,	$1 50.	38

INDEX TO EXCISE TAX. 89

		TAX.	PAGE
Railroad iron, re-rolled, per ton,		75 cents.	
Railroad Pills, same as "Dentifrice."			
Ready Relief, same as "Dentifrice."			
Real estate, sale of for taxes, and proceedings,			10
Do., deed, how given, and contents, and validity,			10
Do., rights of third persons not affected by sales of the Collector,			11
Do., owner may tender amount of tax and costs,			11
Do., may be redeemed within one year,			11
Receipt, warehouse, stamp duty,		25 cents.	61
Do., (other than charter party) for any goods, merchandise, or effects, to be exported from a port or place in the United States to any foreign port or place, stamp duty		10 cents.	57
Rectifiers.—Every person who rectifies, purifies, or refines, spirituous liquors or wines by any process, or mixes distilled spirits, whiskey, brandy, gin, or wine, with any other materials, for sale, under the name of rum, whiskey, brandy, gin, wine, or any other name or names, for each license to rectify any quantity of spirituous liquors not exceeding 500 barrels, containing not more than 40 gallons to each,		$25 00.	28
Do., for each additional 500 barrels, or any fraction thereof,		25 00.	28
Red oil,		free.	36
Rents, annual income from, when exceeding $600, and not exceeding $10,000, on excess over $600,		3 per ct.	49
Do., exceeding $10,000, on excess over $600,		5 per ct.	49
Do., annual income from, when realized by a citizen of the United States residing in a foreign country and not in the employment of the United States,		5 per ct.	49
Retail dealers, whose gross annual sales or receipts exceed one thousand dollars, for each license,		$10 00.	27
Do., whose gross annual receipts are less than one thousand dollars, require no license,			27
Retail dealers in liquors. Every person who shall sell or offer for sale distilled spirits, fermented liquors or wines of every description, in less quantities than three gallons at one time, to the same purchaser, for each license		$20 00.	27
Retail dealers—who are regarded as retail dealers,			27
Do., do not require a license as tobacconists,			30
Do., need no license as a confectioner,			31
Do., nor as an apothecary,			31
Reviews are not to be considered as a manufacture			40
Roman cement is not to be regarded as a manufacture			40

S

		TAX.	PAGE
Salaries, annual income from, when exceeding $600, on the excess over $600,		3 per ct.	49
Do., all, of persons in the employ of the United States, when exceeding the rate of $600 per year, on the excess above $600,		3 per ct.	47
Salaries of officers, how paid,			66
Saleratus, per pound,		5 mills.	37
Sales at auction, on gross amount of sales,		1/10 of 1 per ct.	41
Sales at auction made by public officers, &c.,		exempt.	41
Salt, per one hundred pounds,		4 cents.	38
Salves, same as "Dentifrice."			
Savings institutions, on all dividends,		3 per ct.	45
Screws, called wood screws, per pound,		1½ cents.	38
Segars, (see "cigars,") valued at not over five dollars per thousand, per 1,000,		$1 50.	37
Do., valued at over five dollars and not over ten dollars per thousand, per 1,000,		2 00.	37
Do., valued at over ten and not over twenty dollars per thousand, per 1,000,		2 50.	37
Do., valued at over twenty dollars per thousand, per 1,000,		3 50.	37

	TAX.	PAGE
Shell fish, in cans or air-tight packages,	5 per ct.	38
Sheep, slaughtered for sale, per head,	5 cents.	42
Do., slaughtered by any person for his own consumption,	free.	42
Sheepskins, tanned, curried, or finished,	4 per ct.	39
Sheet iron. See "Iron."		
Shingles are not to be considered as a manufacture,		40
Silk parasols,	5 per ct.	38
Silk umbrellas,	5 per ct.	38
Silk, manufactures of, not otherwise specified,	3 per ct.	40
Silver, manufactures of, when not otherwise specified,	3 per ct.	40
Skins, calf, tanned, each,	6 cents.	39
Do., American patent,	5 per ct.	39
Do., goat, curried, manufactured, or finished,	4 per ct.	39
Do., kid, do.,	4 per ct.	39
Do., morocco, do.,	4 per ct.	39
Do., sheep, tanned, curried, or finished,	4 per ct.	39
Do., deer, dressed or smoked, per pound,	2 cents.	
Do., hog, tanned and dressed,	4 per ct.	39
Do., horse, do.,	4 per ct.	39
Slates are not to be considered a manufacture,		40
Snuff, manufactured of tobacco, ground, dry, or damp, of all descriptions, per pound,	20 cents.	37
Do., aromatic. See "Aromatic Snuff."		
Do., catarrh. See "Catarrh Snuff."		
Soap, castile, valued not above 3½ cents per pound, per pound,	1 mill.	38
Do., valued above 3½ cents per pound, per pound,	5 mills.	38
Do., cream, per pound,	2 cents.	38
Do., erasive, valued not above 3½ cents per pound, per pound,	1 mill.	38
Do., erasive valued above 3½ cents per pound, per pound,	5 mills.	38
Do., palm-oil, valued not above 3½ cents per pound, per pound,	1 mill.	38
Do., palm-oil, valued above 3½ cents per pound, per pound,	5 mills.	38
Do., fancy, scented, honey, toilet, and shaving, of all descriptions, per pound,	2 cents.	38
Do., transparent, per pound,	2 cents.	38
Do., of all other descriptions, white or colored, except soft soap, and soap otherwise provided for, valued not above 3½ cents per pound, per pound,	1 mill.	38
Do., do., valued above 3½ cents per pound, per pound,	5 mills.	38
Soap-makers, for each license,	$10 00.	20
Soda, bi-carbonate of, per pound,	5 mills.	37
Sole leather. See "Leather."		
Spikes, per ton,	$2 00.	38
Spirits, Distilled. See "Distilled Spirits."		
Spirits, distilled, per gallon,	20 cents.	
Split peas are not to be considered a manufacture,		40
Stamps, duties when to commence,		51
Do., penalty for not using stamps,		51
Do., stamps for one instrument not to be used for another,		51
Do., forging, counterfeiting, or misusing stamps prohibited,		51
Do., or selling the same, or defacing stamps, penalty,		52
Do., mode of cancelling adhesive stamps,		52
Do., certain persons allowed to furnish their own dies,		52
Do., penalty for forging or counterfeiting,		52
Do., what paper stamped,		53
Do., discount to purchasers of stamps,		53
Do., instruments exempt from duty may be stamped,		54
Do., telegraph messages and packages for express companies,		54
Do., penalty for preparing drugs for consumption or sale without stamp,		55
Do., prescriptions of the College of Pharmacy or of Physicians do not require a stamp,		55
Do., penalty for removing stamps from certain articles,		55
Do., certain articles not to be sold without a stamp, unless for export,		55
Do., manufacturers of such articles to make monthly returns, &c.		56

	TAX.	PAGE
Starch, made of corn, per pound,	1¼ mills.	37
Do., made of potatoes, per pound,	1 mill.	37
Do., made of rice, per pound,	4 mills.	37
Do., made of wheat, per pound,	1½ mills.	37
Do., made of any other material, per pound,	4 mills.	37
States may tax without regard to the U. S. law,		32
States and Territories where the Act cannot be executed, proceedings,		16
Stationery, allowed to Assessors, &c.,		7
Do., to Collectors,		15
Staves are not to be considered a manufacture,		40
Steamboat captain, to make monthly statement,		43
Steamboats, except ferry boats, on gross receipts,	3 per ct.	43
Steamers, passenger, cost of license,	$25	29
Do., taxes, who must pay,		3
Do., to be paid within the district where persons reside,		7
Do., when payable, and penalty for neglect,		8
Do., when wrongful, how to be refunded,		16
Steel manufactures of, when not otherwise specified,	3 per ct.	40
Do., in ingots, bars, sheets, or wire, not less than one fourth of an inch in thickness, valued at seven cents per pound or less, per ton,	$4 00.	38
Do. do., valued above seven cents per pound and not above eleven cents per pound, per ton,	8 00.	38
Do. do., valued above eleven cents per pound, per ton,	10 00.	38
Stills, used in distilling spirituous liquors, where the annual product exceeds three hundred barrels, for each yearly license,	50 00.	38
Do., where the annual product is three hundred barrels or less, each license,	25 00.	
Do., used by distillers of apples and peaches, where the annual product is less than one hundred and fifty barrels, each license,	12 50.	
Stock of insurance companies. See "Insurance."		
Stoves, per ton of 2,000 pounds,	1 50.	38
Sugar, refined, whether loaf, lump, granulated, or pulverized, per pound,	2 mills.	37
Do., refined, or made from molasses, syrup of molasses, melado, or concentrated melado, per pound,	2 mills.	37
Do., brown, muscovado, or clarified, produced directly from the sugar-cane, and not from sorghum or imphee, other than that produced by the refiner, per pound,	1 cent.	37
Sugar candy, made wholly or in part of sugar, per pound,	1 cent.	37
Sugar-coated pills, same as "Dentifrice."		
Sulphate of barytes, per 100 pounds,	10 cents.	37

T

Tallow chandlers, for each license,	$10 00.	30
Tar, coal, produced in the manufacture of gas,	exempt.	36
Taverns. See "Hotels."		
Telegraph despatches. See "Despatch."		
Telegraph operators, not to receive a message unless it is stamped,		54
Theatres, what are regarded as theatres,		30
Theatres, for each license,	$100 00.	30
Ticket, passage, by any vessel from a port in the United States to a foreign port, if less than $30,	50 cents.	
Do., exceeding $30,	$1 00.	
Timber is not to be considered a manufacture,		40
Tin, manufactures of, when not otherwise specified,	3 per ct.	40
Tinctures, same as "Dentifrice."		
Tobacconists, for each license,	$10 00.	29
Do., whose gross annual sales do not exceed one thousand dollars, are not required to take out a license.		

	TAX.	PAGE
Tobacconists, who require such a license,		29
Do., license not required in certain cases,		32
Tobacco, Cavendish, valued at more than 30 cents per pound, per pound,	15 cents.	37
Do., valued at any sum not exceeding 30 cents per pound, per pound,	10 cents.	87
Do., fine cut, same as "Tobacco, Cavendish."		
Do., plug, same as "Tobacco, Cavendish."		
Do., twist, same as "Tobacco, Cavendish."		
Do., manufactured, of all kinds, not including snuff or segars, or smoking, prepared with stems in, valued at over 30 cents per pound,	15 cents.	37
Do., valued at less than 30 cents per pound,	10 cents.	37
Do., smoking, prepared with stems in, per pound,	5 cents.	37
Do., smoking, made exclusively of stems, per pound,	2 cents.	37
Tonic mixture, same as "Dentifrice."		
Tooth powder, same as "Dentifrice."		
Trust companies, on dividends, &c.,	3 per ct.	45

U

Umbrellas, made of cotton, silk, or other material,	5 per ct.	38
Umbrella stretchers are not to be considered a manufacture.		
Unguents, same as "Dentifrice."		
U. S. securities, tax on interest of,	1½ per ct.	49

V

Varnish, made wholly or in part of gum copal,	5 per ct.	39
Do., made of other gums or substances,	5 per ct.	89
Vegetable oils, not otherwise specified, per gallon,	2 cents.	36
Vegetable pulmonary balsam, same as "Dentifrice."		
Vermifuge, same as "Dentifrice."		
Vessels, passenger, cost of license,	$25	29
Vintners, license not required in certain cases,		32

W

Warehouse entry, at custom houses, not exceeding $1 in value, stamp duty,	25 cents.	59
Do., exceeding $1 and not exceeding $5,	50 cents.	59
Do., exceeding $5 in value,	$1 00.	59
Warehouse receipts, stamp duty,	25 cents.	61
Whale oil,	exempt.	36
Whiskey, per gallon,	20 cents.	
Do., rectified, is not to pay an additional duty.		
White lead, per 100 pounds,	25 cents.	37
Wholesale dealers.—Every person whose business or occupation is to sell, or offer to sell, groceries, or any goods, wares, or merchandise, of foreign or domestic production, by one or more original packages or piece, at one time, to the same purchaser, not including wines, spirituous or malt liquors, for each license,	$50 00.	28
Wholesale dealers in liquors of every description, including distilled spirits, fermented liquors and wines of all kinds (persons other than distillers, who sell or offer for sale any such liquors or wines in quantities of more than three gallons at one time to the same purchaser are included), for each license,	100 00.	27
Wholesale dealers need no license to retail,		28
Do., do not require a license as a tobacconist,		30
Do., need no license as a confectioner,		30
Do., nor as an apothecary,		31

	TAX.	PAGE
Willow, manufactures of,	3 per ct.	40
Wines, made of grapes, per gallon,	5 cents.	39
Withdrawal entry, at custom-house, stamp duty,	50 cents.	
Wood, manufactures of, if not otherwise provided for,	3 per ct.	40
Wood screws,	1½ cents.	
Wool, manufactures of, not otherwise specified,	3 per ct.	40
Worsted, manufactures of, not otherwise specified,	3 per ct.	40
Worm lozenges, same as "Dentifrice."		
Writ, stamp duty, see "Legal Documents,"	50 cents.	61

Y

Yachts, over six and under ten hundred dollars in value,	$10 00.	42
Do., each additional thousand dollars in value,	10 00.	42

Z

Zinc, manufactures of, not otherwise specified,	3 per ct.	40
Do., oxide of, per 100 pounds,	25 cents.	37

THE DIRECT TAX LAW,

(Passed August 5th, 1861.)

AND

THE ACT FOR THE COLLECTION OF TAXES IN INSURRECTIONARY DISTRICTS, ETC.

.This Act took effect Aug. 5, 1861; and so much as imposes a direct tax of twenty millions of dollars was suspended July 1, 1862, until April 1, 1865. (See page 67 of the preceding Act.).

DIRECT TAX.

AN ACT

To provide increased revenue from imports to pay interest on the public debt, and for other purposes.

Be it enacted by the Senate and House of Representatives of the United States of America in Congress assembled, That, from and after the date of the passage of this act, in lieu of the duties heretofore imposed by law on the articles hereinafter mentioned, and on such as may now be exempt from duty, there shall be levied, collected, and paid, on the goods, wares, and merchandise herein enumerated and provided for, imported from foreign countries, the following duties and rates of duty, that is to say: First, On raw sugar, commonly called muscovado or brown sugar, and on sugars not advanced above number twelve, Dutch standard, by claying, boiling, clarifying, or other process, and on sirup of sugar or of sugarcane and concentrated molasses, or concentrated melado, two cents per pound; and on white and clayed sugar, when advanced beyond the raw state, above number twelve, Dutch standard, by clarifying or other process, and not yet refined, two and a half cents per pound; on refined sugars, whether loaf, lump, crushed, or pulverized, four cents per pound; on sugars after being refined, when they are tinctured, colored, or in any way adulterated, and on sugar-candy, six cents per pound; on molasses, five cents per gallon: *Provided,* That all sirups of sugar or of sugar-cane, concentrated molasses or melado, entered under the name of molasses, or any other name than sirup of sugar or of sugar-cane, concentrated molasses, or concentrated melado, shall be liable to forfeiture to the United States. On all teas, fifteen cents per pound; on almonds, four cents per pound; shelled almonds, six cents per pound; on brimstone, crude, three dollars per ton; on brimstone, in rolls, six dollars per ton; on coffee, of all kinds, four cents per pound; on cocoa, three cents per pound; on cocoa leaves and cocoa shells, two cents per pound; on cocoa, prepared or manufactured, eight cents per pound; on chickory root, one cent per pound; and on chickory, ground, two cents per pound; on chocolate, six cents per pound; on cassia, ten cents per pound; cassia buds, fifteen cents per pound; on cinnamon, twenty cents per pound; on cloves, eight cents per pound; on cayenne pepper, six cents per pound; on cayenne pepper, ground, eight cents per pound; on currants, five cents per pound; on argol, three cents per pound; on cream tartar, six cents per pound; on tartaric acid, tartar emetic, and rochelle salts, ten cents per pound; on dates, two cents per pound; on figs, five cents per pound; on ginger root, three cents per pound; on ginger, ground, five cents per pound; on licorice paste and juice, five cents per pound; licorice root, one cent per pound; on mace and nutmegs, twenty-five cents per pound; on nuts of all kinds, not otherwise

[margin notes: Specific duties on certain imports. Sugar. Sirups of sugar, &c., entered as molasses, to be forfeited. Teas. Almonds, &c.]

provided for, two cents per pound; on pepper, six cents per pound; on pimento, six cents per pound; on plums, five cents per pound; on prunes, five cents per pound; on raisins, five cents per pound; on unmanufactured Russia hemp, forty dollars per ton; on manilla and other hemps of India, twenty-five dollars per ton; on lead, in pigs or bars, one dollar and fifty cents per one hundred pounds; in sheets, two dollars and twenty-five cents per one hundred pounds; on white lead, dry or ground in oil, and red lead, two dollars and twenty-five cents per one hundred pounds; on salt, in sacks, eighteen cents per one hundred pounds, and in bulk, twelve cents per one hundred pounds; on soda ash, one-half cent per pound; on bicarbonate of soda, one cent per pound; on sal soda, one-half cent per pound; on caustic soda, one cent per pound; on chloride of lime, thirty cents per one hundred pounds; on saltpetre, crude, one cent per pound; refined, or partially refined, two cents per pound; spirits of turpentine, ten cents per gallon; on oil of cloves, seventy cents per pound; on brandy, one dollar and twenty-five cents per gallon; on spirits distilled from grain or other materials, fifty cents per gallon; on gum copal, and other gums or resinous substances used for the same or similar purposes as gum copal, ten cents per pound.

Ad valorem duties on certain imports.

SEC. 2. *And be it further enacted,* That, from and after the day and year aforesaid, there shall be levied, collected, and paid, on the importation of the articles hereinafter mentioned, the following duties, that is to say: On arrow-root, twenty per centum ad valorem; on ginger, preserved or pickled, thirty per centum ad valorem; on limes, lemons, oranges, bananas, and plantains, twenty per centum ad valorem; on Peruvian bark, fifteen per centum ad valorem; on quinine, thirty per centum ad valorem; on rags, of whatever material, ten per centum ad valorem; on gunpowder, thirty per centum ad valorem; on feathers and downs, thirty per centum ad valorem; on hides, ten per centum ad valorem; on sole and bend leather, thirty per centum ad valorem; on India-rubber, raw or unmanufactured, ten per centum ad valorem; on India-rubber shoes and boots, thirty per centum ad valorem; on ivory, unmanufactured, and on vegetable ivory, ten per centum ad valorem; on wines of all kinds, fifty per centum ad valorem; on silk in the gum, not more advanced in the manufacture than single, tram, and thrown, or organzine, twenty-five per centum ad valorem; on all silks valued at not over one dollar per square yard, thirty per centum ad valorem; on all silks valued over one dollar per square yard, forty per centum ad valorem; on all silk velvets, or velvets of which silk is the component material of chief value, valued at three dollars per square yard, or under, thirty per centum ad valorem; valued at over three dollars per square yard, forty per centum ad valorem; on floss silks, thirty per centum ad valorem; on silk ribbons, galloons, braids, fringes, laces, tassels, buttons, button-cloths, trimmings, and on silk twist, twist composed of mohair and silk, sewing silk in gum or purified, and all other manufactures of silk, or of which silk shall be the component material of chief value, not otherwise provided for, forty per centum ad valorem.

Certain articles imported in foreign vessels to pay certain additional duty.

SEC. 3. *And be it further enacted,* That all articles, goods, wares, and merchandise, imported from beyond the Cape of Good Hope in foreign vessels, not entitled by reciprocal treaties to be exempt from discriminating duties, tonnage, and other charges, and all other articles, goods, wares, and merchandise not imported direct from the place of their growth or production, or in foreign vessels, entitled by reciprocal treaties to be exempt from discriminating duties, tonnage, and other charges, shall be subject to pay, in addition to the duties imposed by this act, ten per centum ad valorem: *Provided,* That this rule shall not apply to goods, wares, and merchandise imported from beyond the Cape of Good Hope in American vessels. Proviso.

SEC. 4. *And be it further enacted,* That, from and after the passage of this act, there shall be allowed, on all articles wholly manufactured of materials imported, on which duties have been paid when exported, a drawback, equal in amount to the duty paid on such materials, and no more, to be ascertained under such regulations as shall be prescribed by the Secretary of the Treasury: *Provided,* That ten per centum on the amount of all drawbacks, so allowed, shall be retained for the use of the United States by the collectors paying such drawbacks, respectively. Drawback on certain articles. Rules.

10 per cent. to be retained.

SEC. 5. *And be it further enacted,* That all goods, wares, and merchandise, actually on shipboard and bound to the United States, and all goods, wares, and merchandise, on deposit in warehouses or public stores at the date of the passage of this act, shall be subject to pay such duties as provided by law before and at the time of the passage of this act: *Provided,* That all goods deposited in public store or bonded warehouse after this act takes effect and goes into operation, if designed for consumption in the United States, must be withdrawn therefrom, or the duties thereon paid in three months after the same are deposited; and goods designed for exportation and consumption in foreign countries may be withdrawn by the owner at any time before the expiration of three years after the same are deposited, such goods, if not withdrawn in three years, to be regarded as abandoned to the Government, and sold under such regulations as the Secretary of the Treasury may prescribe, and the proceeds paid into the Treasury: *Provided,* That merchandise upon which the owner may have neglected to pay duties within three months from the time of its deposit may be withdrawn and entered for consumption at any time within two years of the time of its deposit upon the payment of the legal duties, with an addition of twenty-five per centum thereto: *Provided, also,* That merchandise upon which duties have been paid, if exported to a foreign country, within three years, shall be entitled to return duties, proper evidence of such merchandise having been landed abroad to be furnished to the collector by the importer, one per centum of said duties to be retained by the Government. Certain goods on shipboard and all goods in warehouses, &c., to pay former rate of duties.

Duties on bonded goods to be paid in three months, if, &c.

Proviso.

Further proviso.

SEC. 6. *And be it further enacted,* That the act entitled "An act to provide for the payment of outstanding treasury notes, to authorize a loan, to regulate and fix the duties on imports, and for other purposes," approved March two, eighteen hundred and sixty-one, be, and the same is hereby, amended, as follows—that is to say: First, in section six, article first, after the words "in cordials and," strike out "liquors," and insert "liqueurs;" Second, in the same section, after the word "represent," insert "*Provided, also,* That no lower rate or amount of duty shall be levied, collected, and paid on brandy, spirits, and all other spirituous beverages, than that now fixed by law for the description of first proof, but shall be increased in proportion for any greater strength than Amendments of act 1861, ch. 68, §§ 6, 7, 12, 13, 14, 15, 19, 22, 23.

the strength of first proof;" Third, in section seven, clause fifth, the words "on screws, washed or plated, and all other screws, of iron or any other metal," shall be stricken out, and the words "on screws, of any other metal than iron," shall be inserted; Fourth, section twelve, article first, after the words "eighteen cents," where they first occur, insert "or less;" Fifth, section thirteen, article second, after the word "manufacturer," insert "except hosiery;" Sixth, in the same section, article third, strike out "wool;" wherever it occurs, and insert in each place "worsted;" Seventh, in section fourteen, article first, after the words "ten per centum," insert "ad valorem;" Eighth, in section fifteen, before the word "yarns" insert "hemp;" in the same section, after the word "sheetings," insert "of flax or hemp;" and strike out "jute goods," and in lieu thereof insert "jute yarns;" Ninth, in section twenty-two, strike out the words "unwrought clay, three dollars per ton;" Tenth, in section nineteen, strike out "compositions of glass or paste, not set, intended for use by jewellers;" Eleventh, in section twenty-two, strike out "compositions of glass or paste, when set;" Twelfth, in section twenty-three, article sheathing metal, strike out "yard," and insert "foot."

Repealing clause. SEC. 7. *And be it further enacted*, That all acts and parts of acts repugnant to the provisions of this act be, and the same are
Saving as to laws for collection, &c. hereby, repealed: *Provided*, That the existing laws shall extend to, and be in force for, the collection of the duties imposed by this act, for the prosecution and punishment of all offences, and for the recovery, collection, distribution, and remission of all fines, penalties, and forfeitures, as fully and effectually as if every regulation, penalty, forfeiture, provision, clause, matter, and thing to that effect in the existing laws contained, had been inserted in and re-enacted by this act.

Direct tax of $20,000,000, how apportioned. SEC. 8. *And be it further enacted*, That a direct tax of twenty millions of dollars be, and is hereby, annually laid upon the United States, and the same shall be and is hereby apportioned to the States, respectively, in manner following:

Maine. To the State of Maine, four hundred and twenty thousand eight hundred and twenty-six dollars.
New Hampshire. To the State of New Hampshire, two hundred and eighteen thousand four hundred and six and two-third dollars.
Vermont. To the State of Vermont, two hundred and eleven thousand and sixty-eight dollars.
Massachusetts. To the State of Massachusetts, eight hundred and twenty-four thousand five hundred and eighty-one and one-third dollars.
Rhode Island. To the State of Rhode Island, one hundred and sixteen thousand nine hundred and sixty-three and two-third dollars.
Connecticut. To the State of Connecticut, three hundred and eight thousand two hundred and fourteen dollars.
New York. To the State of New York, two million six hundred and three thousand nine hundred and eighteen and two-third dollars.
New Jersey. To the State of New Jersey, four hundred and fifty thousand one hundred and thirty-four dollars.
Pennsylvania. To the State of Pennsylvania, one million nine hundred and forty-six thousand seven hundred and nineteen and one-third dollars.
Delaware. To the State of Delaware, seventy-four thousand six hundred and eighty-three and one-third dollars.

DIRECT TAX. 7

To the State of Maryland, four hundred and thirty-six thousand eight hundred and twenty-three and one-third dollars. — Maryland.

To the State of Virginia, nine hundred and thirty-seven thousand five hundred and fifty and two-third dollars. — Virginia.

To the State of North Carolina, five hundred and seventy-six thousand one hundred and ninety-four and two-third dollars. — North Carolina.

To the State of South Carolina, three hundred and sixty-three thousand five hundred and seventy and two-third dollars. — South Carolina.

To the State of Georgia, five hundred and eighty-four thousand three hundred and sixty-seven and one-third dollars. — Georgia.

To the State of Alabama, five hundred and twenty-nine thousand three hundred and thirteen and one-third dollars. — Alabama.

To the State of Mississippi, four hundred and thirteen thousand eighty-four and two-third dollars. — Mississippi.

To the State of Louisiana, three hundred and eighty-five thousand eight hundred and eighty-six and two-third dollars. — Louisiana.

To the State of Ohio, one million five hundred and sixty-seven thousand eighty-nine and one-third dollars. — Ohio.

To the State of Kentucky, seven hundred and thirteen thousand six hundred and ninety-five and one-third dollars. — Kentucky.

To the State of Tennessee, six hundred and sixty-nine thousand four hundred and ninety-eight dollars. — Tennessee.

To the State of Indiana, nine hundred and four thousand eight hundred and seventy-five and one-third dollars. — Indiana.

To the State of Illinois, one million one hundred and forty-six thousand five hundred and fifty-one and one-third dollars. — Illinois.

To the State of Missouri, seven hundred and sixty-one thousand one hundred and twenty-seven and one-third dollars. — Missouri.

To the State of Kansas, seventy-one thousand seven hundred and forty-three and one-third dollars. — Kansas.

To the State of Arkansas, two hundred and sixty-one thousand eight hundred and eighty-six dollars. — Arkansas.

To the State of Michigan, five hundred and one thousand seven hundred and sixty-three and one-third dollars. — Michigan.

To the State of Florida, seventy-seven thousand five hundred and twenty-two and two-third dollars. — Florida.

To the State of Texas, three hundred and fifty-five thousand one hundred and six and two-third dollars. — Texas.

To the State of Iowa, four hundred and fifty-two thousand and eighty-eight dollars. — Iowa.

To the State of Wisconsin, five hundred and nineteen thousand six hundred and eighty-eight and two-third dollars. — Wisconsin.

To the State of California, two hundred and fifty-four thousand five hundred and thirty-eight and two-third dollars. — California.

To the State of Minnesota, one hundred and eight thousand five hundred and twenty-four dollars. — Minnesota.

To the State of Oregon, thirty-five thousand one hundred and forty and two-third dollars. — Oregon.

To the Territory of New Mexico, sixty-two thousand six hundred and forty-eight dollars. — New Mexico.

To the Territory of Utah, twenty-six thousand nine hundred and eighty-two dollars. — Utah.

To the Territory of Washington, seven thousand seven hundred and fifty-five and one-third dollars. — Washington.

To the Territory of Nebraska, nineteen thousand three hundred and twelve dollars. — Nebraska.

Nevada. To the Territory of Nevada, four tnousand five hundred and ninety-two and two-third dollars.

Colorado. To the Territory of Colorado, twenty-two thousand nine hundred and five and one-third dollars.

Dakota. To the Territory of Dakota, three thousand two hundred and forty-one and one-third dollars.

District of Columbia. To the District of Columbia, forty-nine thousand four hundred and thirty-seven and one-third dollars.

Collection districts for assessing and collecting the tax. SEC. 9. *And be it further enacted,* That, for the purpose of assessing the above tax and collecting the same, the President of the United States be, and he is hereby, authorized to divide, respectively, the States and Territories of the United States and the District of Columbia into convenient collection districts, and

Assessors and collectors. to nominate and, by and with the advice of the Senate, to appoint an assessor and a collector for each such district, who shall be

Proviso. freeholders and resident within the same : *Provided,* That any of said States and Territories, as well as the District of Columbia, may, if the President shall deem it proper, be erected into one

Assessors and collectors not to be appointed before, &c. district : *And provided, further,* That the appointment of said assessors and collectors, or any of them, shall not be made until on or after the second Tuesday in February, one thousand eight hundred and sixty-two.

Collectors to give bond before entering upon duty. SEC. 10. *And be it further enacted,* That before any such collector shall enter upon the duties of his office he shall execute a bond for such amount as shall be prescribed by the Secretary of

Amount and sureties, &c. the Treasury, with sureties to be approved as sufficient by the Solicitor of the Treasury, containing the condition that said collector shall justly and faithfully account for to the United States, and pay over, in compliance with the order or regulations of the Secretary of the Treasury, all public moneys which may come into his hands or possession ; which bond shall be filed in the office of the First Comptroller of the Treasury, to be by him directed to be put in suit upon any breach of the condition thereof. And such collectors shall, from time to time, renew, strengthen, and increase their official bonds, as the Secretary of the Treasury may direct.

Collection district to be divided into assessment districts. SEC. 11. *And be it further enacted,* That each of the assessors shall divide his district into a convenient number of assessment districts, within each of which he shall appoint one 'respectable

Assistant assessors. freeholder to be assistant assessor ; and each assessor and assistant assessor so appointed, and accepting the appointment, shall, before he enters on the duties of his appointment, take and subscribe before some competent magistrate, or some collector to be appointed by this act, (who is hereby empowered to admin-

Oath. ister the same,) the following oath or affirmation, to wit : " I, A B, do swear, or affirm, (as the case may be,) that I will, to the best of my knowledge, skill, and judgment, diligently and faithfully execute the office and duties of assessor for, (naming the assessment district,) without favor or partiality, and that I will do equal right and justice in every case in which I shall act as assessor."

Certificate. And a certificate of such oath or affirmation shall be delivered to the collector of the district for which such assessor or assistant assessor shall be appointed. And every assessor or assistant as-

Penalty for acting without oath. sessor acting in the said office without having taken the said oath or affirmation shall forfeit and pay one hundred dollars, one moiety thereof to the use of the United States, and the other moiety thereof to him who shall first sue for the same; to be recovered, with costs of suit, in any court having competent jurisdiction.

SEC. 12. *And be it further enacted,* That the Secretary of the Treasury shall establish regulations suitable and necessary for carrying this act into effect; which regulations shall be binding on each assessor and his assistants in the performance of the duties enjoined by or under this act, and shall also frame instructions for the said assessors and their assistants; pursuant to which instructions the said assessors shall, on the first day of March next, direct and cause the several assistant assessors in the district to inquire after and concerning all lands, lots of ground, with their improvements, buildings, and dwelling-houses, made liable to taxation under this act by reference as well to any lists of assessment or collection taken under the laws of the respective States, as to any other records or documents, and by all other lawful ways and means, and to value and enumerate the said objects of taxation in the manner prescribed by this act, and in conformity with the regulations and instructions above mentioned. *(Secretary of Treasury to establish regulations under this act, and frame instructions. Assessors and assistants to follow them.)*

SEC. 13. *And be it further enacted,* That the said direct tax laid by this act shall be assessed and laid on the value of all lands and lots of ground, with their improvements and dwelling-houses, which several articles subject to taxation shall be enumerated and valued, by the respective assessors, at the rate each of them is worth in money on the first day of April, eighteen hundred and sixty-two: *Provided, however,* That all property, of whatever kind, coming within any of the foregoing descriptions, and belonging to the United States or any State, or permanently or specially exempted from taxation by the laws of the State wherein the same may be situated at the time of the passage of this act, together with such property belonging to any individual, who actually resides thereon, as shall be worth the sum of five hundred dollars, shall be exempted from the aforesaid enumeration and valuation, and from the direct tax aforesaid: *And provided, further,* That in making such assessment due regard shall be had to any valuation that may have been made under the authority of the State or Territory at any period nearest to said first day of April. *(Direct tax. Real estate. Valuation to be as of April 1, 1862. Exemptions.)*

SEC. 14. *And be it further enacted,* That the respective assistant assessors shall, immediately after being required as aforesaid by the assessors, proceed through every part of their respective districts, and shall require all persons owning, possessing, or having the care or management of any lands, lots of ground, buildings, or dwelling-houses, lying and being within the collection district where they reside, and liable to a direct tax as aforesaid, to deliver written lists of the same; which lists shall be made in such manner as may be directed by the assessor, and, as far as practicable, conformably to those which may be required for the same purpose under the authority of the respective States. *(Property owners to furnish lists upon request.)*

SEC. 15. *And be it further enacted,* That if any person owning, possessing, or having the care or management of property liable to a direct tax, as aforesaid, shall not be prepared to exhibit a written list when required, as aforesaid, and shall consent to disclose the particulars of any and all the lands and lots of ground, with their improvements, buildings, and dwelling-houses, taxable as aforesaid, then, and in that case it shall be the duty of the *(If owner has no list and will disclose, officer to make list.)*

officer to make such list, which, being distinctly read and consented to, shall be received as the list of such person.

Penalty for delivering or disclosing fraudulent list.

SEC. 16. *And be it further enacted,* That if any such person shall deliver or disclose to any assessor or assistant assessor appointed in pursuance of this act, and requiring a list or lists, as aforesaid, any false or fraudulent list, with intent to defeat or evade the valuation or enumeration hereby intended to be made, such person so offending, and being thereof convicted before any court having competent jurisdiction, shall be fined in a sum not exceeding five hundred dollars, at the discretion of the court, and shall pay all costs and charges of prosecution; and the valuation and enumeration required by this act shall, in all such cases, be made, as aforesaid, upon lists, according to the form above described, to be made out by the assessors and assistant assessors, respectively; which lists the said assessors are hereby authorized and required to make according to the best information they can obtain, and for the purpose of making which they are hereby authorized to enter into and upon all and singular the premises, respectively; and from the valuation and enumeration so made there shall be no appeal.

Lists, how to be made in such cases.

No appeal from valuation, &c.

Notice to owner to furnish list in certain cases.

SEC. 17. *And be it further enacted,* That in case any person shall be absent from his place of residence at the time an assessor shall call to receive the list of such person, it shall be the duty of such assessor or assistant assessor to leave at the house or place of residence of such person, with some person of suitable age and discretion, a written note or memorandum, requiring him to present to such assessor the list or lists required by this act within ten days from the date of such note or memorandum.

Proceedings when list is not given upon notice or request.

SEC. 18. *And be it further enacted,* That if any person, on being notified or required as aforesaid, shall refuse or neglect to give such list or lists as aforesaid within the time required by this act, it shall be the duty of the assessor for the assessment district within which such person shall reside, and he is hereby authorized and required, to enter into and upon the lands, buildings, dwelling-houses, and premises, if it be necessary, of such persons so refusing or neglecting, and to make, according to the best information which he can obtain, and on his own view and information, such lists of the lands and lots of ground, with their improvements, buildings, and dwelling-houses, owned or possessed, or under the care or management of such person, as are required by this act; which lists, so made and subscribed by such assessor, shall be taken and reputed as good and sufficient lists of the persons and property for which such person is to be taxed for the purposes of this act.

Property of absent owners, list how made.

SEC. 19. *And be it further enacted,* That whenever there shall be in any assessment district any property, lands, and lots of ground, buildings, or dwelling-houses, not owned or possessed by, or under the care and management of, any person or persons within such district, and liable to be taxed as aforesaid, and no list of which shall be transmitted to the assessor in the manner provided by this act, it shall be the duty of the assessor for such district, and he is hereby authorized and required, to enter into and upon the real estate, if it be necessary, and take such view thereof, and make lists of the same, according to the form prescribed; which lists, being subscribed by the said assessor, shall be taken and reputed as good and sufficient lists of such property under and for the purposes of this act.

DIRECT TAX. 11

SEC. 20. *And be it further enacted*, That the owners, possessors, or persons, having the care or management of lands, lots of ground, buildings, and dwelling-houses, not lying or being within the assessment district in which they reside, shall be permitted to make out and deliver the lists thereof required by this act, (provided the assessment district in which the said objects of taxation lie or be is therein distinctly stated,) at the time and in the manner prescribed, to the assessor of the assessment district wherein such persons reside. And it shall be the duty of the assessors, in all such cases, to transmit such lists, at the time and in the manner prescribed for the transmission of the lists of the objects of taxation lying and being within their respective assessment districts, to the assessor of the collection district wherein the said objects of taxation shall lie or be immediately after the receipt thereof; and the said lists shall be valid and sufficient for the purposes of this act; and on the delivery of such list, the person making and delivering the same shall pay to the assessor one dollar, which he shall retain to his own use. *(Lists how made of property in another collection district.)*

SEC. 21. *And be it further enacted*, That the lists aforesaid shall be taken with reference to the day fixed for that purpose by this act, as aforesaid; and the assistant assessors, respectively, after collecting the said lists, shall proceed to arrange the same, and to make two general lists, the first of which shall exhibit, in alphabetical order, the names of all persons liable to pay a tax under this act residing within the assessment district, together with the value and assessment of the objects liable to taxation within such district for which each such person is liable, and, whenever so required by the assessor, the amount of direct tax payable by each person on such objects under the State laws imposing direct taxes; and the second list shall exhibit, in alphabetical order, the names of all persons residing out of the collection district, owners of property within the district, together with the value and assessment thereof, with the amount of direct tax payable thereon as aforesaid. The forms of the said general list shall be devised and prescribed by the assessor, and lists taken according to such form shall be made out by the assistant assessors and delivered to the assessor within sixty days after the day fixed by this act, as aforesaid, requiring lists from individuals. And if any assistant assessor shall fail to perform any duty assigned by this act within the time prescribed by his precept, warrant, or other legal instructions, not being prevented therefrom by sickness or other unavoidable accident, every such assistant assessor shall be discharged from office, and shall, moreover, forfeit and pay two hundred dollars, to be recovered for the use of the United States in any court having competent jurisdiction, with costs of suit. *(Lists to be taken in reference to a day certain. List of residents, of non-residents. Assessor to devise form of lists. Penalty on assistant assessor for neglect of duty.)*

SEC. 22. *And be it further enacted*, That immediately after the valuations and enumerations shall have been completed as aforesaid, the assessor in each collection district shall, by advertisement in some public newspaper, if any there be in such district, and by written notifications to be publicly posted up in at least four of the most public places in each collection district, advertise all persons concerned of the place where the said lists, valuations, and enumerations may be seen and examined; and that during twenty-five days after the publication of the notifications, as aforesaid, appeals will be received and determined by him relative to *(Notice to be given when lists, valuations, &c., are completed.)*

12 DIRECT TAX.

Assessors to submit proceedings of assistants to inspectors. any erroneous or excessive valuations or enumerations by the assessor. And it shall be the duty of the assessor in each collection district, during twenty-five days after the date of publication to be made as aforesaid, to submit the proceedings of the assistant assessors and the list by them received or taken as aforesaid to the inspection of any and all persons who shall apply for that purpose; and the said assessors are hereby authorized to receive, hear, and determine, in a summary way, according to law and right, upon any and all appeals which may be exhibited against **To hear and determine appeals.** the proceedings of the said assessors: *Provided always*, That it shall be the duty of said assessor to advertise and attend, not less than two successive days of the said twenty-five, at the court-house of each county within his collection district, there to receive and determine upon the appeals aforesaid: *And provided, also*, That the question to be determined by the assessor, on **How valuations are to be determined.** an appeal respecting the valuation of property, shall be, whether the valuation complained of be or be not in a just relation or proportion to other valuations in the same collection district. And all **Appeals to be in writing, what to contain.** appeals to the assessors, as aforesaid, shall be made in writing, and shall specify the particular cause, matter, or thing respecting which a decision is requested; and shall, moreover, state the ground or principle of inequality or error complained of. And **Valuations may be re-examined and equalized, not to be increased without notice, &c.** the assessor shall have power to re-examine and equalize the valuations as shall appear just and equitable; but no valuation shall be increased without a previous notice, of at least five days, to the party interested, to appear and object to the same, if he judge proper; which notice shall be given by a note in writing, to be left at the dwelling-house of the party by such assessor or an assistant assessor.

If more than one collection district in a State, &c., the assessors may equalize, &c. Sec. 23. *And be it further enacted*, That whenever a State, Territory, or the District of Columbia, shall contain more than one collection district, the assessors shall have power, on examination of the lists rendered by the assistant assessors, according to the provisions of this act, to revise, adjust, and equalize the valuation of lands and lots of ground, with their improvements, buildings, and dwelling-houses, between such collection districts, by deducting from or adding to either such a rate per centum as shall appear just and equitable.

Assessors to make out lists of valuations and deliver to board of assessors. Sec. 24. *And be it further enacted*, That the assessors shall, immediately after the expiration of the time for hearing and deciding appeals, make out correct lists of the valuation and enumeration in each collection district, and deliver the same to the board of assessors hereinafter constituted in and for the States respectively. And it shall be the duty of the assessors in each State to convene in general meeting at such time and place as shall be appointed and directed by the Secretary of the Treasury. And **Board, how constituted.** the said assessors, or a majority of them, so convened, shall constitute, and they are hereby constituted, a board of assessors for the purposes of this act, and shall make and establish such rules and regulations as to them shall appear necessary for carrying such purposes into effect, not being inconsistent with this act or the laws of the United States.

Board of assessors to appoint clerks. Sec. 25. *And be it further enacted*, That the said board of assessors, convened and organized as aforesaid, shall and may appoint a suitable person or persons to be their clerk or clerks, but not more than one for each collection district, who shall hold his or their office or offices at the pleasure of said board of assessors, and whose duty it shall be to receive, record, and preserve all tax lists, returns, and other documents delivered and made to the said board of assessors, and who shall take an oath (or affirmation if conscientiously scrupulous of taking an oath) faithfully to discharge his or their trust; and in default of taking such oath or affirmation, previous to entering on the duties of such appointment, or on failure to perform any part of the duties enjoined on him or them, respectively, by this act, he or they shall, respectively, forfeit and pay the sum of two hundred dollars for the use of the United States, to be recovered in any court having competent jurisdiction, and shall also be removed from office. *[Number and duty of clerks. Penalty for acting without taking oath.]*

SEC. 26. *And be it further enacted,* That it shall be the duty of the said clerks to record the proceedings of the said board of assessors, and to enter on the record the names of such of the assessors as shall attend any general meeting of the board of assessors for the purposes of this act. And if any assessor shall fail to attend such general meeting his absence shall be noted on the said record, and he shall, for every day he may be absent therefrom, forfeit and pay the sum of ten dollars for the use of the United States. And if any assessor shall fail or neglect to furnish the said board of assessors with the lists of valuation and enumeration of each assessment district within his collection district within three days after the time appointed as aforesaid for such general meeting of the said board of assessors, he shall forfeit and pay the sum of five hundred dollars for the use of the United States, and, moreover, shall forfeit his compensation as assessor. And it shall be the duty of the clerks of the said board of assessors to certify to the Secretary of the Treasury an extract of the minutes of the board, showing such failures or neglect, which shall be sufficient evidence of the forfeiture of such compensation, to all intents and purposes: *Provided, always,* That it shall be in the power of the Secretary of the Treasury to exonerate such assessor or assessors from the forfeiture of the said compensation, in whole or in part, as to him shall appear just and equitable. *[Duty of clerks. Penalty on assessor for not attending general meeting of board, for failing to furnish lists. Secretary of the Treasury may exonerate assessor.]*

SEC. 27. *And be it further enacted,* That if the said board of assessors shall not, within three days after the first meeting thereof as aforesaid, be furnished with all the lists of valuation of the several counties and State districts of any State, they shall nevertheless proceed to make out the equalization and apportionment by this act directed, and they shall assign to such counties and State districts the valuation lists of which shall not have been furnished, such valuation as they shall deem just and right; and the valuation thus made to such counties and State districts by the board of assessors shall be final, and the proper quota of direct tax shall be, and is hereby, declared to be imposed thereon accordingly. *[Board to make out equalization and apportionment. Their valuation to be final, and the basis of taxation.]*

SEC. 28. *And be it further enacted,* That it shall be the duty of the said board of assessors diligently and carefully to consider and examine the said lists of valuation, and they shall have power to revise, adjust, and equalize the valuation of property in any county or State district, by adding thereto or deducting therefrom such a rate per centum as shall, under the valuation of the several counties and State districts, be just and equitable: *Provided,* The relative valuation of property in the same county shall not be changed, unless manifest error or imperfection shall appear in any *[Board of assessors to revise and adjust lists. Relative valuation not to be changed unless, &c.]*

14 DIRECT TAX.

of the lists of valuation, in which case the said board of assessors shall have power to correct the same, as to them shall appear just and right. And if, in consequence of any revisal, change, and alteration of the said valuation, any inequality shall be produced in the apportionment of the said direct tax to the several States as aforesaid, it shall be the duty of the Secretary of the Treasury to report the same to Congress, to the intent that provision may be made by law for rectifying such inequality.

Inequalities of taxation to be reported to Congress.

SEC. 29. *And be it further enacted,* That as soon as the said board of assessors shall have completed the adjustment and equalization of the valuation aforesaid, they shall proceed to apportion to each county and State district its proper quota of direct tax. And the said board of assessors shall, within twenty days after the time appointed by the Secretary of the Treasury for their first meeting, complete the said apportionment, and shall record the same; they shall thereupon further deliver to each assessor a certificate of such apportionment, together with the several lists by the assessors, respectively, presented to the board as aforesaid, and transmit to the Secretary of the Treasury a certificate of the apportionment by them made as aforesaid; and the assessors, respectively, shall thereupon proceed to revise their respective lists, and alter and make the same in all respects conformable to the apportionment aforesaid by the said board of assessors; and the said assessors, respectively, shall make out lists containing the sums payable according to the provisions of this act upon every object of taxation in and for each collection district; which lists shall contain the name of each person residing within the said district, owning or having the care or superintendence of property lying within the said district which is liable to the said tax, when such person or persons are known, together with the sums payable by each; and where there is any property within any collection district liable to the payment of the said tax, not owned or occupied by or under the superintendence of any person resident therein, there shall be a separate list of such property, specifying the sum payable, and the names of the respective proprietors, where known. And the said assessors shall furnish to the collectors of the several collection districts, respectively, within thirty-five days after the apportionment is completed, as aforesaid, a certified copy of such list or lists for their proper collection districts, and in default of performance of the duties enjoined on the board of assessors and assessors, respectively, by this section, they shall severally and individually forfeit and pay the sum of five hundred dollars to the use of the United States, to be recovered in any court having competent jurisdiction. And it is hereby enacted and declared that the valuation, assessment, equalization, and apportionment made by the said board of assessors, as aforesaid, shall be and remain in full force and operation for laying, levying, and collecting, yearly and every year, the annual direct tax by this act laid and imposed, until altered, modified, or abolished by law.

Board to apportion tax.

Other duties in regard to tax.

Assessors to make their lists conform.

Contents of lists.

Lists to be given to collectors.

Penalty on assessors, &c., under this section.

Valuation and apportionment to continue until altered.

SEC. 30. *And be it further enacted,* That there shall be allowed and paid to the several assessors and assistant assessors, for their services under this act: to each assessor two dollars per day for every day employed in making the necessary arrangements and giving the necessary instructions to the assistant assessors for the valuation, and three dollars per day for every day employed in

Pay of assessors and assistant assessors.

hearing appeals, revising valuations, and making out lists agreeably to the provisions of this act, and one dollar for every hundred taxable persons contained in the tax list, as delivered by him to said board of assessors; to each assistant assessor two dollars for every day actually employed in collecting lists and making valuations, the number of days necessary for that purpose to be certified by the assessor and approved by the commissioner of taxes, and one dollar for every hundred taxable persons contained in the tax lists, as completed and delivered by him to the assessor; to each of the assessors constituting the board of assessors, as aforesaid, for every day's actual attendance at said board, the sum of three dollars, and for travelling to and from the place designated by the Secretary of the Treasury, ten cents for each mile, by the most direct and usual route; and to each of the clerks of said board two dollars for every day's actual attendance thereon. And the said board of assessors, and said assessors, respectively, shall be allowed their necessary and reasonable charges for stationery and blank books used in the execution of their duties; and the compensation herein specified shall be in full for all expenses not otherwise particularly authorized, and shall be paid at the treasury, and such amount as shall be required for such payment is hereby appropriated. *Allowed for stationery and blank books.*

SEC. 31. *And be it further enacted,* That each collector, on receiving a list, as aforesaid, from the said assessors, respectively, shall subscribe three receipts; one of which shall be given on a full and correct copy of such list, which list shall be delivered by him to, and shall remain with, the assessor of his collection district, and shall be open to the inspection of any person who may apply to inspect the same; and the other two receipts shall be given on aggregate statements of the lists aforesaid, exhibiting the gross amount of taxes to be collected in each county or State district contained in the collection district, one of which aggregate statements and receipts shall be transmitted to the Secretary, and the other to the First Comptroller of the Treasury. *Collector on receiving list to give three receipts.*

SEC. 32. *And be it further enacted,* That each collector, before receiving any list, as aforesaid, for collection, shall give bond with one or more good and sufficient sureties, to be approved by the Solicitor of the Treasury, in the amount of the taxes assessed in the collection district for which he has been or may be appointed; which bond shall be payable to the United States, with condition for the true and faithful discharge of the duties of his office according to law, and particularly for the due collection and payment of all moneys assessed upon such district, and the said bond shall be transmitted to the Solicitor of the Treasury, and, after approval by him, shall be deposited in the office of the First Comptroller of the Treasury: *Provided, always,* That nothing herein contained shall be deemed to annul or in anywise impair the obligation of the bond heretofore given by any collector; but the same shall be and remain in full force and virtue, anything in this act to the contrary thereof in anywise notwithstanding. *Collector to give bond before receiving list. Form, penalty, &c., of bond. Proviso.*

SEC. 33. *And be it further enacted,* That the annual amount of the taxes so assessed shall be and remain a lien upon all lands and other real state of the individuals who may be assessed for the same during two years after the time it shall annually become due and payable; and the said lien shall extend to each and every *Tax assessed to be a lien for two years.*

part of all tracts or lots of land or dwelling-houses, notwithstanding the same may have been divided or alienated in part.

Collector may appoint deputies, and revoke appointments, &c.

SEC. 34. *And be it further enacted,* That each collector shall be authorized to appoint, by an instrument of writing under his hand and seal, as many deputies as he may think proper, to be by him compensated for their services, and also to revoke the powers of any deputy, giving public notice thereof in that portion of the district assigned to such deputy; and each such deputy shall have

Authority of deputy.

the like authority, in every respect, to collect the direct tax so assessed within the portion of the district assigned to him which is by this act vested in the collector himself; but each collector shall,

Collector responsible for moneys collected.

in every respect, be responsible both to the United States and to individuals, as the case may be, for all moneys collected, and for every act done as deputy collector by any of his deputies whilst acting as such: *Provided,* That nothing herein contained shall prevent any collector from collecting himself the whole or any part of the tax so assessed and payable in his district.

Collector to advertise that tax is due and payable, &c.

SEC. 35. *And be it further enacted,* That each of the said collectors shall, within ten days after receiving his collection list from the assessors, respectively, as aforesaid, and annually, within ten days after he shall be so required by the Secretary of the Treasury, advertise in one newspaper printed in his collection district, if any there be, and by notifications, to be posted up in at least four public places in his collection district, that the said tax has become due and payable, and state the times and places at which he or they will attend to receive the same, which shall be within twenty days after such notification; and with respect to persons who shall not attend, according to such notifications, it shall be the duty of each collector, in person or by deputy, to apply once

to demand at dwellings taxes not paid.

at their respective dwellings within such district, and there demand the taxes payable by such persons, which application shall be made within sixty days after the receipt of the collection list, as aforesaid, or after the receipt of the requisition of the Secretary of the Treasury, as aforesaid, by the collectors; and if the said taxes shall not be then paid, or within twenty days thereafter, it shall be lawful for such collector, or his deputies, to proceed to

to distrain, if not paid within, &c.

collect the said taxes by distraint and sale of the goods, chattels, or effects of the persons delinquent as aforesaid. And in case of such distraint, it shall be the duty of the officer charged with the

Duty of officer in case of distraint.

collection to make, or cause to be made, an account of goods or chattels which may be distrained, a copy of which, signed by the officer making such distraint, shall be left with the owner or possessor of such goods, chattels, or effects, or at his or her dwelling, with some person of suitable age and discretion, with a note of the sum demanded, and the time and place of sale; and the said officer shall forthwith cause a notification to be publicly posted up at two of the taverns nearest to the residence of the person whose property shall be distrained, or at the court-house of the same county, if not more than ten miles distant, which notice shall specify the articles distrained, and the time and place for the sale thereof, which time shall not be less than ten days from the date of such notification, and the place proposed for sale not more than five miles distant from the place of making such dis-

Property may be restored after distraint, on payment, &c., of tax, &c.

traint: *Provided,* That in any case of distraint for the payment of the tax aforesaid, the goods, chattels, or effects so distrained shall and may be restored to the owner or possessor if, prior to the sale thereof, payment or tender thereof shall be made to the proper officer charged with the collection, of the full amount demanded, together with such fee for levying, and such sum for the necessary and reasonable expense of removing and keeping the goods, chattels, or effects so distrained, as may be allowed in like cases by the laws or practice of the State wherein the distraint shall have been made; but in case of non-payment or tender, as aforesaid, the said officers shall proceed to sell the said goods, chattels, or effects at public auction, and shall and may retain from the proceeds of such sale the amount demandable for the use of the United States, with the necessary and reasonable expenses of distraint and sale, and a commission of five per centum thereon for his own use, rendering the overplus, if any there be, to the person whose goods, chattels, or effects shall have been distrained: *Provided*, That it shall not be lawful to make distraint of the tools or implements of a trade or profession, beasts of the plough necessary for the cultivation of improved lands, arms, or household furniture, or apparel necessary for a family. *If tax not paid, property to be sold.* *What exempted from distraint.*

SEC. 36. *And be it further enacted*, That whenever goods, chattels, or effects sufficient to satisfy any tax upon buildings, dwelling-houses, or lands and their improvements, owned, occupied, or superintended by persons known or residing within the same collection district cannot be found, the collector having first advertised the same for thirty days in a newspaper printed within the collection district, if such there be, and having posted up, in at least ten public places within the same, a notification of the intended sale, thirty days previous thereto, shall proceed to sell at public sale so much of the said property as may be necessary to satisfy the taxes due thereon, together with an addition of twenty per centum to the said taxes. But in all cases where the property liable to a direct tax under this act may not be divisible, so as to enable the collector by a sale of part thereof to raise the whole amount of the tax, with all costs, charges, and commissions, the whole of such property shall be sold, and the surplus of the proceeds of the sale, after satisfying the tax, costs, charges, and commissions, shall be paid to the owner of the property, or his legal representatives, or if he or they cannot be found, or refuse to receive the same, then such surplus shall be deposited in the treasury of the United States, to be there held for the use of the owner or his legal representatives, until he or they shall make application therefor to the Secretary of the Treasury, who, upon such application, shall, by warrant on the treasury, cause the same to be paid to the applicant. And if the property advertised for sale as aforesaid cannot be sold for the amount of the tax due thereon, with the said additional twenty per centum thereto, the collector shall purchase the same in behalf of the United States for the amount aforesaid: *Provided*, That the owner or superintendent of the property aforesaid, after the same shall have been, as aforesaid, advertised for sale, and before it shall have been actually sold, shall be allowed to pay the amount of the tax thereon, with an addition of ten per centum on the same, on the payment of which the sale of the property shall not take place: *Provided, also*, That the owners, their heirs, executors, or administrators, or any person on their behalf, shall have liberty to redeem the lands and other property sold, as aforesaid, within two years from

When personal property cannot be found sufficient to satisfy tax and costs, the real estate to be sold.

Provisions as to sale.

If real estate will not sell for enough to pay tax, the United States to take it.

Proviso.

Right of redemption.

Deed not to be given until, &c.

the time of sale, upon payment to the collector for the use of the purchaser, his heirs, or assigns, of the amount paid by said purchaser, with interest for the same, at the rate of twenty per centum per annum; and no deed shall be given in pursuance of such sale until the time of redemption shall have expired. And the collector shall render a distinct account of the charges incurred in offering and advertising for sale such property, and shall pay into the treasury the surplus, if any there be, of the aforesaid addition of twenty per centum, or ten per centum, as the case may be, after defraying the charges. And in every case of the sale of real estate which shall be made under the authority of this act by the collectors, respectively, or their lawful deputies, respectively,

Form, &c., of deed.

the deeds for the estate so sold shall be prepared, made, executed, and proved or acknowledged at the time and times prescribed in this act by the collectors, respectively, within whose collection district such real estate shall be situated, in such form of law as shall be authorized and required by the laws of the United States, or by the law of the State in which such real estate lies, for making, executing, proving, and acknowledging deeds of bargain and sale or other conveyances for the transfer and conveyance of real estate; and for every deed so prepared, made, executed, proved, and acknowledged, the purchaser or grantee shall pay to the

Cost thereof.

collector the sum of two dollars, for the use of the collector or other person effecting the sale of the real estate thereby conveyed.

Collection of tax on property of non-residents.

SEC. 37. *And be it further enacted*, That with respect to property lying within any collection district not owned or occupied or superintended by some person residing in such collection district, and on which the tax shall not have been paid to the collector within ninety days after the day on which he shall have received the collection lists from the said assessors, respectively, as aforesaid, or the requisition of the Secretary of the Treasury, as aforesaid, the collector shall transmit lists of the same to one of the collectors within the same State, to be designated for that purpose by the Secretary of the Treasury; and the collector who shall have been thus designated by the Secretary of the Treasury shall transmit receipts for all the lists received, as aforesaid, to the collector transmitting the same; and the collectors thus designated in each State by the Secretary of the Treasury shall cause notifications of the taxes due as aforesaid, and contained in the lists thus transmitted to them, to be published for sixty days in at least one of the newspapers published in the State; and the owners of the property on which such taxes may be due shall be permitted to pay to such collector the said tax, with an addition of ten per centum thereon: *Provided*, That such payment is made within one year after the day on which the collector of the district where such property lies had notified that the tax had become due on the same.

Property may be sold when tax has remained unpaid one year.

SEC. 38. *And be it further enacted*, That when any tax, as aforesaid, shall have remained unpaid for the term of one year, as aforesaid, the collector in the State where the property lies, and who shall have been designated by the Secretary of the Treasury,

Provision as to sale, &c.

as aforesaid, having first advertised the same for sixty days in at least one newspaper in the State, shall proceed to sell, at public sale, so much of the said property as may be necessary to satisfy the taxes due thereon, together with an addition of twenty per centum thereon; or if such property is not divisible, as aforesaid, the whole thereof shall be sold, and accounted for in the manner hereinbefore provided. If the property advertised for sale cannot be sold for the amount of the tax due thereon, with the said addition thereon, the collector shall purchase the same in behalf of the United States for such amount and addition. And the collector shall render a distinct account of the charges incurred in offering and advertising for sale such property, and pay into the treasury the surplus, if any, of the aforesaid addition of ten or twenty per centum, as the case may be, after defraying the said charges.

SEC. 39. *And be it further enacted*, That the collectors, designated as aforesaid by the Secretary of the Treasury, shall deposit with the clerks of the district court of the United States in the respective States, and within which district the property lies, correct lists of the tracts of land or other real property sold by virtue of this act for non-payment of taxes, together with the names of owners or presumed owners, and of the purchasers of the same at the public sales aforesaid, and of the amount paid by said purchasers for the same; the owners, their heirs, executors, or administrators, or any person in their behalf, shall have liberty to redeem the lands or other property sold, as aforesaid, within two years from the time of sale, upon payment to the clerk aforesaid, for the use of the purchaser, his heirs, or assigns, of the amount paid by such purchaser for the said land, or other real property, with interest for the same at the rate of twenty per centum per annum, and of a commission of five per centum on such payment, for the use of the clerk aforesaid. The clerks shall, on application, pay to the purchasers the moneys thus paid for their use; and the collectors, respectively, shall give deeds for the lands or property aforesaid to the purchasers entitled to the same, in all cases where the same shall not have been redeemed within two years, as aforesaid, by the original owners thereof, or their legal representatives, or any person in their behalf, and deposit such deeds with such clerk. And the said clerk shall be entitled to receive from the purchaser, for his own use, the sum of one dollar, in addition to the sum hereinbefore made payable to the collector, for every such deed, to be paid on the delivery thereof to such purchasers. And in all cases where lands may be sold under this act for the payment of taxes, belonging to infants, persons of insane mind, married women, or persons beyond sea, such persons shall have the term of two years after their respective disabilities shall have been removed, or their return to the United States, to redeem lands thus sold, on their payment into the clerk's office aforesaid the amount paid by the purchaser, with fifty per centum addition thereto, together with ten per centum interest per annum on the aggregate sum, and on their payment to the purchaser of the land aforesaid a compensation for all improvements he may have made on the premises subsequent to his purchase, the value of which improvements to be ascertained by three or more neighboring freeholders, to be appointed by the clerk aforesaid, who, on an actual view of the premises, shall assess the value of such improvements, on their oaths, and make return of such valuation to the clerk immediately. And the clerk of the court shall receive such compensation for his services herein, to be paid by and received from the parties, like costs of suit, as the court shall in that respect tax and allow.

SEC. 40. *And be it further enacted*, That the several collectors shall, at the expiration of every month after they shall, respect-

Treasury statement of collections, pay over quarterly, &c.

ively, commence their collections in the next and every ensuing year, transmit to the Secretary of the Treasury a statement of the collections made by them, respectively, within the month, and pay over quarterly, or sooner if required by the Secretary of the Treasury, the moneys by them respectively collected within the said term; and each of the said collectors shall complete the collection of all sums annually assigned to him for collection, as aforesaid, shall pay over the same into the treasury, and shall render his final account to the Treasury Department within six months from and after the day when he shall have received the collection lists from the said board of assessors or the said requisition of the Secretary of the Treasury, as aforesaid: *Provided, however*, That the period of one year and three months from the said annual day shall be annually allowed to the collector designated in each State, as aforesaid, by the Secretary of the Treasury, with respect to the taxes contained in the list transmitted to him by the other collectors, as aforesaid.

Proviso.

To be charged with amount of taxes receipted for by him.

SEC. 41. *And be it further enacted*, That each collector shall be charged with the whole amount of taxes by him receipted, whether contained in the lists delivered to him by the principal assessors, respectively, or transmitted to him by other collectors; and shall be allowed credit for the amount of taxes contained in the lists transmitted in the manner above provided to other collectors, and by them receipted as aforesaid; and also for the taxes of such persons as may have absconded, or become insolvent, subsequent to the date of the assessment, and prior to the day when the tax ought, according to the provisions of this act, to have been collected: *Provided*, That it shall be proved to the satisfaction of the First Comptroller of the Treasury that due diligence was used by the collector, and that no property was left from which the tax could have been recovered; and each collector designated in each State, as aforesaid, by the Secretary of the Treasury shall receive credit for the taxes due for all tracts of land which, after being offered by him for sale in manner aforesaid, shall or may have been purchased by him in behalf of the United States.

To be credited with what.

Proviso.

Delinquent collectors.

SEC. 42. *And be it further enacted*, That if any collector shall fail either to collect or to render his account, or to pay over in the manner or within the times hereinbefore provided, it shall be the duty of the First Comptroller of the Treasury, and he is hereby authorized and required, immediately after such delinquency, to report the same to the Solicitor of the Treasury, who shall issue a warrant of distress against such delinquent collector and his sureties, directed to the marshal of the district, therein expressing the amount of the taxes with which the said collector is chargeable, and the sums, if any, which have been paid. And the said marshal shall, himself, or by his deputy, immediately proceed to levy and collect the sum which may remain due, by distress and sale of the goods and chattels, or any personal effects of the delinquent collector; and for want of goods, chattels, or effects aforesaid, sufficient to satisfy the said warrant, the same may be levied on the person of the collector, who may be committed to prison, there to remain until discharged in due course of law; and furthermore, notwithstanding the commitment of the collector to prison, as aforesaid, or if he abscond, and goods, chattels, and effects cannot be found sufficient to satisfy the

Personal property to be seized and sold.

Arrest.

said warrant, the said marshal or his deputy shall and may proceed to levy and collect the sum which remains due, by distress and sale of the goods and chattels, or any personal effects, of the surety or sureties of the delinquent collector. And the amount of the sums due from any collector, as aforesaid, shall, and the same are hereby declared to be a lien upon the lands and real estate of such collector and his sureties, until the same shall be discharged according to law. And for want of goods and chattels, or other personal effects of such collector or his sureties, sufficient to satisfy any warrant of distress, issued pursuant to the preceding section of this act, the lands and real estate of such collector and his sureties, or so much thereof as may be necessary for satisfying the said warrant, after being advertised for at least three weeks in not less than three public places in the collection district, and in one newspaper printed in the county or district, if any there be, prior to the proposed time of sale, may and shall be sold by the marshal or his deputy; and for all lands and real estate sold in pursuance of the authority aforesaid, the conveyances of the marshals or their deputies, executed in due form of law, shall give a valid title against all persons claiming under delinquent collectors or their sureties aforesaid. And all moneys that may remain of the proceeds of such sale, after satisfying the warrant of distress, and paying the reasonable costs and charges of sale, shall be returned to the proprietor of the lands or real estate sold as aforesaid. *Sums due from collector to be a lien on his lands, and those of his sureties.* *Real estate may be sold.* *Title under tax deed.* *Balance, if any after, &c.*

SEC. 43. *And be it further enacted,* That each and every collector, or his deputy, who shall exercise or be guilty of any extortion or oppression, under color of this act, or shall demand other or greater sums than shall be authorized by this act, shall be liable to pay a sum not exceeding two thousand dollars, to be recovered by and for the use of the party injured, with costs of suit, in any court having competent jurisdiction; and each and every collector, or his deputies, shall give receipts for all sums by them collected and retained in pursuance of this act. *Penalty on collector and deputy for extortion, &c.*

SEC. 44. *And be it further enacted,* That separate accounts shall be kept at the treasury of all moneys received from the direct tax, and from the internal duties, or income tax, in each of the respective States, Territories, and District of Columbia, and collection districts; and that separate accounts shall be kept of the amount of each species of duty that shall accrue, with the moneys paid to the collectors, assessors, and assistant assessors, and to the other officers employed in each of the respective States, Territories, and collection districts, which accounts it shall be the duty of the Secretary of the Treasury, annually, in the month of December, to lay before Congress. *Accounts, how to be kept at Treasury Department, of moneys received.* *To be reported to Congress.*

SEC. 45. *And be it further enacted,* That the assessors, respectively, shall, yearly, and in every year, after the expiration of one year from the second Tuesday of February next, inquire and ascertain, in the manner by the fourteenth section of this act provided, what transfers and changes of property in lands, lots of ground, buildings, and dwelling-houses have been made and effected in their respective districts, subsequent to the next preceding valuation, assessment, and apportionment of the direct tax by this act laid; and within twenty days thereafter they shall make out three lists of such transfers and changes, and transmit one list to the Secretary of the Treasury, another list to the *Assessors to make out lists of transfers and changes of real estate.*

commissioner of taxes, and the third shall be delivered to the collector of the collection district. And it shall, yearly, and every year, after the said year one thousand eight hundred and sixy-two, be the duty of the Secretary of the Treasury to notify the collectors of the several collection districts the day on which it shall be the duty of the said collectors to commence laying and collecting the annual direct tax by this act laid and imposed, according to the assessment of the tax lists to them delivered by the said assessors, as aforesaid, subject only to such alterations therein as shall be just and proper, in the opinion of the Secretary of the Treasury, to conform to the transfers and changes aforesaid, ascertained by the assessors aforesaid ; and the said collectors shall, annually, in all respects, proceed in and conclude the collection of the said direct tax in the same manner and within the time hereinbefore provided and prescribed.

Duty of collectors.

SEC. 46. *And be it further enacted,* That in case any State, Territory, or the District of Columbia, after notice given of its intention to assume and pay, or to levy, collect, and pay said direct tax herein provided for and apportioned to said State, Territory, or District, shall, in any year after the taking effect of this act, fail to pay the amount of said direct tax, or any part thereof, as provided in this act, in such cases it shall be lawful for the Secretary of the Treasury of the United States to appoint United States assessors, assistant assessors, and collectors, as in this act provided, whose duty it shall be to proceed forthwith, under such regulations as the said Secretary of the Treasury shall prescribe, to collect all or any part of said direct tax the same as though said State, Territory, or District had not given notice, nor assumed to levy, collect, and pay said taxes, or any part thereof.

Proceedings if any State fails to pay, &c., her quota of the tax.

SEC. 47. *And be it further enacted,* That any person who shall be convicted of wilfully taking a false oath or affirmation in any of the cases in which an oath or affirmation is required to be taken by this act, shall be liable to the pains and penalties to which persons are liable for wilful and corrupt perjury, and shall, moreover, forfeit the sum of five hundred dollars.

Penalty for taking false oath or affirmation.

SEC. 48. *And be it further enacted,* That there shall be allowed to the collectors appointed under this act, in full compensation for their services and that of their deputies in carrying this act into effect, a commission of four per centum upon the first hundred thousand dollars, one per centum upon the second one hundred thousand dollars, and one-half of one per centum upon all sums above two hundred thousand dollars ; such commissions to be computed upon the amounts by them respectively paid over and accounted for under the instructions of the Treasury Department : *Provided,* That in no case shall such commissions exceed the sum of four thousand dollars for a principal officer, and two thousand dollars for an assistant. And there shall be further allowed to each collector their necessary and reasonable charges for stationery and blank books used in the performance of their official duties, which, after being duly examined and certified by the commissioner of taxes, shall be paid out of the treasury.

Pay of collectors and deputies.

Commissions.

Proviso.

Allowance for stationery, blank books, &c.

SEC. 49. *And be it further enacted,* That, from and after the first day of January next, there shall be levied, collected, and paid, upon the annual income of every person residing in the United States, whether such income is derived from any kind of property, or from any profession, trade, employment, or vocation

Income tax.

carried on in the United States or elsewhere, or from any other source whatever, if such annual income exceeds the sum of eight hundred dollars, a tax of three per centum on the amount of such excess of such income above eight hundred dollars: *Provided,* That upon such portion of said income as shall be derived from interest upon treasury notes or other securities of the United States, there shall be levied, collected, and paid a tax of one and one-half per centum. Upon the income rents, or dividends accruing upon any property, securities, or stocks owned in the United States by any citizen of the United States residing abroad, there shall be levied, collected, and paid a tax of five per centum, excepting that portion of said income derived from interest on treasury notes and other securities of the government of the United States, which shall pay one and one-half per centum. The tax herein provided shall be assessed upon the annual income of the persons hereinafter named for the year next preceding the time for assessing said tax, to wit, the year next preceding the first of January, eighteen hundred and sixty-two; and the said taxes, when so assessed and made public, shall become a lien on the property or other sources of said income for the amount of the same, with the interest and other expenses of collection until paid: *Provided,* That, in estimating said income, all national, State, or local taxes assessed upon the property, from which the income is derived, shall be first deducted.

Excess over $800.

Proviso.

Of what date to be assessed.

Lien.

Income, how to be estimated.

SEC. 50. *And be it further enacted,* That it shall be the duty of the President of the United States, and he is hereby authorized, by and with the advice and consent of the Senate, to appoint one principal assessor and one principal collector in each of the States and Territories of the United States, and in the District of Columbia, to assess and collect the internal duties or income tax imposed by this act, with authority in each of said officers to appoint so many assistants as the public service may require, to be approved by the Secretary of the Treasury. The said taxes to be assessed and collected under such regulations as the Secretary of the Treasury may prescribe. The said collectors, herein authorized to be appointed, shall give bonds, to the satisfaction of the Secretary of the Treasury, in such sums as he may prescribe, for the faithful performance of their respective duties. And the Secretary of the Treasury shall prescribe such reasonable compensation for the assessment and collection of said internal duties or income tax as may appear to him just and proper; not, however, to exceed in any case the sum of two thousand five hundred dollars per annum for the principal officers herein referred to, and twelve hundred dollars per annum for an assistant. The assistant collectors herein provided shall give bonds to the satisfaction of the principal collector for the faithful performance of their duties. The Secretary of the Treasury is further authorized to select and appoint one or more depositaries in each State for the deposit and safe-keeping of the moneys arising from the taxes herein imposed when collected, and the receipt of the proper officer of such depository to the collector for the moneys deposited by him shall be the proper voucher for such collector in the settlement of his account at the Treasury Department. And he is further authorized and empowered to make such officer or depositary the disbursing agent of the treasury for the payment of all interest due to the citizens of such State upon the treasury notes or other

Mode of assessing and collecting income tax.

Collector to give bond.

Pay.

Assistant collector's bond.

Depositaries.

Depositaries to be disbursing agents.

government securities issued by authority of law. And he shall also prescribe the forms of returns to be made to the department by all assessors and collectors appointed under the authority of this act. He shall also prescribe the form of oath or obligation to be taken by the several officers authorized or directed to be appointed and commissioned by the President under this act, before a competent magistrate duly authorized to administer oaths, and the form of the return to be made thereon to the Treasury Department.

Form of return.
Form of oath.

SEC. 51. *And be it further enacted,* That the tax herein imposed by the forty-ninth section of this act shall be due and payable on or before the thirtieth day of June, in the year eighteen hundred and sixty-two, and all sums due and unpaid at that day shall draw interest thereafter at the rate of six per centum per annum; and if any person or persons shall neglect or refuse to pay, after due notice, said tax assessed against him, her, or them, for the space of more than thirty days after the same is due and payable; it shall be lawful for any collector or assistant collector, charged with the duty of collecting such tax, and they are hereby authorized, to levy the same on the visible property of any such person, or so much thereof as may be sufficient to pay such tax, with the interest due thereon, and the expenses incident to such levy and sale, first giving thirty days' public notice of the time and place of the sale thereof; and in case of the failure of any person or persons authorized to act as agent or agents for the collection of the rents or other income of any person residing abroad, shall neglect or refuse to pay the tax assessed thereon (having had due notice) for more than thirty days after the thirtieth of June, eighteen hundred and sixty-two, the collector or his assistant, for the district where such property is located, or rents or income is payable, shall be, and hereby, is authorized to levy upon the property itself, and to sell the same, or so much thereof as may be necessary to pay the tax assessed, together with the interest and expenses incident to such levy and sale, first giving thirty days' public notice of the time and place of sale. And in all cases of the sale of property herein authorized, the conveyance by the officer authorized to make the sale, duly executed, shall give a valid title to the purchaser, whether the property sold be real or personal. And the several collectors and assistants appointed under the authority of this act may, if they find no property to satisfy the taxes assessed upon any person by authority of the forty-ninth section of this act, and which such person neglects to pay as hereinbefore provided, shall have power, and it shall be their duty, to examine, under oath, the person assessed under this act, or any other person, and may sell at public auction, after ten days' notice, any stock, bonds, or choses in action, belonging to said person, or so much thereof as will pay such tax and the expenses of such sale; and in case he refuses to testify, the said several collectors and assistants shall have power to arrest such person and commit him to prison, to be held in custody until the same shall be paid, with interest thereon, at the rate of six per centum per annum, from the time when the same was payable as aforesaid, and all fees and charges of such commitment and custody. And the place of custody shall in all cases be the same provided by law for the custody of persons committed for any cause by the authority of the United States, and the warrant

When income tax is payable.
Proceedings to enforce payment.
Levy.
Sale after notice.
Title under tax sale.
Examinations.
Sales of stocks, &c.
Penalty for refusing to testify.
Custody, place of.

of the collector, stating the cause of commitment, shall be sufficient authority to the proper officer for receiving and keeping such person in custody until the amount of said tax and interest, and all fees and the expense of such custody, shall have been fully paid and discharged; which fees and expenses shall be the same as are chargeable under the laws of the United States in other cases of commitment and custody. And it shall be the duty of such collector to pay the expenses of such custody, and the same, with his fees, shall be allowed on settlement of his accounts. And the person so committed shall have the same right to be discharged from such custody as may be allowed by the laws of the State or Territory, or the District of Columbia, where he is so held in custody, to persons committed under the laws of such State or Territory, or District of Columbia, for the non-payment of taxes, and in the manner provided by such laws; or he may be discharged at any time by order of the Secretary of the Treasury. *Custody, fees and expense of.*

Custody, discharged from.

SEC. 52. *And be it further enacted,* That should any of the people of any of the States or Territories of the United States, or the District of Columbia, be in actual rebellion against the authority of the government of the United States at the time this act goes into operation, so that the laws of the United States cannot be executed therein, it shall be the duty of the President, and he is hereby authorized, to proceed to execute the provisions of this act within the limits of such State or Territory, or District of Columbia, so soon as the authority of the United States therein is re-established, and to collect the sums which would have been due from the persons residing or holding property or stocks therein, with the interest due, at the rate of six per centum per annum thereon until paid in the manner and under the regulations prescribed in the foregoing sections of this act. *If any State is in rebellion, when this act goes into operation, act to be executed, when, &c.*

SEC. 53. *And be it further enacted,* That any State or Territory and the District of Columbia may lawfully assume, assess, collect and pay into the treasury of the United States the direct tax, or its quota thereof, imposed by this act upon the State, Territory, or the District of Columbia, in its own way and manner, by and through its own officers, assessors, and collectors; that it shall be lawful to use for this purpose the last or any subsequent valuation, list, or appraisal made by State or territorial authority for the purpose of State or territorial taxation therein, next preceding the date when this act takes effect, to make any laws or regulations for these purposes, to fix or change the compensation to officers, assessors, and collectors; and any such State, Territory, or District, which shall give notice by the governor, or other proper officer thereof, to the Secretary of the Treasury of the United States, on or before the second Tuesday of February next, and in each succeeding year thereafter, of its intention to assume and pay, or to assess, collect, and pay into the treasury of the United States, the direct tax imposed by this act, shall be entitled, in lieu of the compensation, pay per diem and percentage herein prescribed and allowed to assessors, assistant assessors, and collectors of the United States, to a deduction of fifteen per centum on the quota of direct tax apportioned to such State, Territory, or the District of Columbia levied and collected by said State, Territory, and District of Columbia through its said officers: *Provided, however,* That the deduction shall only be *Each State may collect and pay its quota of the direct tax in its own way.*

Proceedings in such case.

Deduction in such case of 15 per cent.

26   DIRECT TAX.

To what to apply. made to apply to such part or parts of the same as shall have been actually paid into the Treasury of the United States on or before the last day of June in the year to which such payment relates, and a deduction of ten per centum to such part or parts of the same as shall have been actually paid into the treasury of the United States on or before the last day of September in the year to which such payment relates, such year being regarded as commencing on the first day of April : *And provided, further,* That whenever notice of the intention to make such payment by the State, or Territory, and the District of Columbia, shall have been given to the Secretary of the Treasury, in accordance with *No assessors to be appointed in such case.* the foregoing provisions, no assessors, assistant assessors, or collectors, in any State, Territory, or District, so giving notice, shall be appointed, unless said State, Territory, or District shall be in default : *And provided, further,* That the amount of direct tax *State may pay its tax by releasing claim against the United States.* apportioned to any State, Territory, or the District of Columbia, shall be liable to be paid and satisfied, in whole or in part, by the release of such State, Territory, or District, duly executed, to the United States, of any liquidated and determined claim of such State, Territory, or District, of equal amount against the United *Proviso.* States : *Provided,* That, in case of such release, such State, Territory, or District shall be allowed the same abatement of the amount of such tax as would be allowed in case of payment of the same in money.

Duty of collectors to collect duties imposed by this act. SEC. 54. *And be it further enacted,* That it shall be the duty of the collectors aforesaid in their respective districts, and they are hereby authorized, to collect the duties imposed by this act, and to prosecute for the recovery of the same, and for the recovery of any sum or sums which may be forfeited by virtue of this *Fines and penalties, how recovered.* act ; and all fines, penalties, and forfeitures which shall be incurred by force of this act, shall and may be sued for and recovered in the name of the United States or of the collector within whose district any such fine, penalty, or forfeiture shall have been incurred, by bill, plaint, or information; one moiety thereof to the use of the United States, and the other moiety thereof to the use of such collector.

Debts due from collector to the United States to be a lien on his real estate and that of his sureties. SEC. 55. *And be it further enacted,* That the amount of all debts due to the United States by any collector, under this act, whether secured by bond or otherwise, shall and are hereby declared to be a lien upon the lands and real estate of such collector, and of his sureties, if he shall have given bond, from the time when suit shall be instituted for recovering the same ; and, for want of goods and chattels and other personal effects of such collector or his sureties to satisfy any judgment which shall or may be recovered against them, respectively, such lands and real estate may be sold at public auction, after being advertised for at least three weeks in not less than three public papers within the collection district, and in one newspaper printed in the county, if any there be, at least six weeks prior to the time of sale ; and for all lands or real estate sold in pursuance of the authority aforesaid, the conveyances of the marshals or their deputies, executed in due form of law, shall give a valid title against all persons claiming under such collector or his sureties, respectively.

Office of commissioner of taxes created. SEC. 56. *And be it further enacted,* That, for superintending the collection of the direct tax and internal duties or income tax laid by this act, an officer is hereby authorized in the Treasury

Department, to be called "Commissioner of Taxes," who shall be charged, under the direction of the Secretary, with preparing all the forms necessary for the assessment and collection of the tax and duties aforesaid, with preparing, signing, and distributing all such licenses as are required, and with the general superintendence of all the officers employed in assessing and collecting said tax and duties; said commissioner shall be appointed by the President, upon the nomination of the Secretary of the Treasury, and he shall receive an annual salary of three thousand dollars. The Secretary of the Treasury may assign the necessary clerks to the office of said commissioner, whose aggregate salaries shall not exceed six thousand dollars per annum, and the amount required to pay the salaries of said commissioner and clerks is hereby appropriated. *Authority, duty, salary. Clerks.*

SEC. 57. *And be it further enacted,* That in case of the sickness or temporary disability of a collector to discharge such of his duties as cannot, under existing laws, be discharged by a deputy, they may be devolved by him upon a deputy: *Provided,* Information thereof be immediately communicated to the Secretary of the Treasury, and shall not be disapproved by him: *And provided,* That the responsibility of the collector or his sureties to the United States shall not be thereby affected or impaired. *If a collector is sick, deputy may act, &c.*

SEC. 58. *And be it further enacted,* That in case a collector shall die, resign, or be removed, the deputy of such collector longest in service at the time immediately preceding, who shall have been longest employed by him, may and shall, until a successor shall be appointed, discharge all the duties of said collector, and for whose conduct, in case of the death of the collector, his estate shall be responsible to the United States. *If collector dies, resigns, &c., who to act in his place.*

Approved August 5, 1861.

AN ACT

For the collection of direct taxes in insurrectionary districts within the United States, and for other purposes.

Be it enacted by the Senate and House of Representatives of the United States of America in Congress assembled, That when in any State or Territory, or in any portion of any State or Territory, by reason of insurrection or rebellion, the civil authority of the government of the United States is obstructed, so that the provisions of the act entitled "An act to provide increased revenue from imports to pay interest on the public debt, and for other purposes," approved August fifth, eighteen hundred and sixty-one, for assessing, levying, and collecting the direct taxes therein mentioned, cannot be peaceably executed, the said direct taxes, by said act apportioned among the several States and Territories, respectively, shall be apportioned and charged in each State and Territory, or part thereof, wherein the civil authority is thus obstructed, upon all the lands and lots of ground situate therein, respectively, except such as are exempt from taxation by the laws of said State or of the United States, as the said lands or lots of ground were enumerated and valued under the last assessment *Act Aug. 5, 1861. Direct tax to be charged in insurrectionary districts to all lands. Lands to be valued.*

and valuation thereof made under the authority of said State or Territory previous to the first day of January, anno Domini eighteen hundred and sixty-one; and each and every parcel of the said lands, according to said valuation, is hereby declared to be, by virtue of this act, charged with the payment of so much of the whole tax laid and apportioned by said act upon the State or Territory wherein the same is respectively situate, as shall bear the same direct proportion to the whole amount of the direct tax apportioned to said State or Territory as the value of said parcels of land respectively bear to the whole valuation of the real estate in said State or Territory according to the said assessment and valuation made under the authority of the same; and in addition thereto a penalty of fifty per centum of said tax shall be charged thereon.

Lands to be charged with the tax according to valuation.

Penalty.

Proclamation declaring the districts in insurrection.

SEC. 2. *And be it further enacted,* That on or before the first day of July next, the President, by his proclamation, shall declare in what States and parts of States said insurrection exists, and thereupon the said several lots and parcels of land shall become charged respectively with their respective portions of said direct tax, and the same together with a penalty shall be a lien thereon, without any other or further proceeding whatever.

Owners may pay tax in sixty days after the amount is fixed.

SEC. 3. *And be it further enacted,* That it shall be lawful for the owner or owners of said lots or parcels of land, within sixty days after the tax commissioners herein named shall have fixed the amount, to pay the tax thus charged upon the same, respectively, into the Treasury of the United States, or to the commissioners herein appointed, and take a certificate thereof, by virtue whereof the said lands shall be discharged from said tax.

Title forfeited to United States or in purchasers.

SEC. 4. *And be it further enacted,* That the title of, in, and to each and every piece or parcel of land upon which said tax has not been paid as above provided, shall thereupon become forfeited to the United States, and, upon the sale hereinafter provided for, shall vest in the United States or in the purchasers at such sale, in fee simple, free and discharged from all prior liens, encumbrances, right, title, and claim whatsoever.

Tax commissioners appointed.

SEC. 5. *And be it further enacted,* That the President of the United States, by and with the advice and consent of the Senate, may appoint a board of three tax commissioners for each of said States in which such insurrection exists, with a salary of three thousand dollars each per annum, to give security in the sum of fifty thousand dollars each, in such form as the Secretary of the Treasury shall direct, and to be approved by him, for the faithful performance of all their duties as such, and to account for and pay over all moneys and other property coming to their hands: *Provided,* That said commissioners shall not receive pay under the provisions of this act until they shall have entered upon the discharge of their duties.

Salary.

Security.

Proviso.

Time of commissioners entering upon duty.

SEC. 6. *And be it further enacted,* That the said board of tax commissioners shall enter upon the discharge of the duties of their office whenever the commanding general of the forces of the United States, entering into any such insurrectionary State or district, shall have established the military authority of the United States throughout any parish or district or county of the same, and they shall open one or more offices for the transaction of business.

SEC. 7. *And be it further enacted,* That the said board of commissioners shall be required, in case the taxes charged upon the said lots and parcels of land shall not be paid as provided for in the third section of this act, to cause the same to be advertised for sale in a newspaper published in the town, parish, district, or county where situate ; and if there be no such newspaper published in said county, or if the publisher thereof refuse to publish the same, then in any other newspaper to be selected by said commissioners in said district, or in the city of Washington, for at least four weeks, and by posting notices of said sale in three public places in the town, parish, district, or county within which said lands are situate, at least four weeks previous to the day of sale ; and at the time and place of sale to cause the same to be severally sold to the highest bidder for a sum not less than the taxes, penalty, and costs, and ten per centum per annum interest on said tax, pursuant to said notice ; and the said commissioners shall, at said sale, strike off the same severally to the United States at that sum, unless some person shall bid the same or a larger sum ; who shall, upon paying the purchase money in gold and silver coin, or in treasury notes of the United States, or in certificates of indebtedness against the United States, be entitled to receive from said commissioners their certificate of sale ; which said certificate shall be received in all courts and places as prima facie evidence of the regularity and validity of said sale, and of the title of said purchaser or purchasers under the same : *Provided*, That the owner of said lots of ground, or any loyal person of the United States, having any valid lien upon or interest in the same, may, at any time, within sixty days after said sale, appear before the said board of tax commissioners in his or her own proper person, and, if a citizen, upon taking an oath to support the Constitution of the United States, and paying the amount of said tax and penalty, with interest thereon from the date of the said proclamation of the President mentioned in the second section of this act, at the rate of fifteen per centum per annum, together with the expenses of the sale and subsequent proceedings to be determined by said commissioners, may redeem said lots of land from said sale ; and any purchaser, under the same, having paid moneys, treasury notes, or other certificates of indebtedness of the United States, shall, upon such redemption being made, be entitled to have the same, with the interest accruing after said sale, returned to him by the said commissioners, upon surrendering up the certificates of sale : *And provided, further,* That if the owner of said lots of ground shall be a minor, a non-resident alien, or loyal citizen beyond seas, a person of unsound mind, or under a legal disability, the guardian, trustee, or other person having charge of the person or estate of such person may redeem the same at any time within two years after the sale thereof in the manner above provided and with like effect : *And provided, further,* That the certificate of said commissioners shall only be affected as evidence of the regularity and validity of sale by establishing the fact that said property was not subject to taxes, or that the taxes had been paid previous to sale, or that the property had been redeemed according to the provisions of this act.

SEC. 8. *And be it further enacted,* That at any time within one year after the said sale by said commissioners any person being the owner of any lot or parcel of ground at the passage of this act, who shall, by sufficient evidence, prove to the satisfaction of said board of commissioners that he or she, after the passage of this act, has not taken part in the present insurrection against the United States, or in any manner aided or abetted the same; and that, by reason of said insurrection, he or she has been unable to pay said tax, or to redeem said lands from sale within the time above provided for, the said board of commissioners may allow him or her further time to redeem the same, not exceeding two years from the day of sale; and for this purpose they may take the testimony of witnesses, and shall reduce the same to writing; and the United States, or any person claiming an interest in said lands, may appear and oppose the said application. From their decision the United States or any party in interest may appeal to the district court of the United States for said district, which is hereby authorized to take jurisdiction of the same, as in other cases involving the equity of redemption. And in case said board of commissioners should, for any cause, cease to act before the expiration of one year after said sales, the said district court shall have original jurisdiction of the proceeding for redemption, as herein provided, to take place before the said board of commissioners.

Commissioners may allow two years for redemption.

May appeal to district court.

SEC. 9. *And be it further enacted,* That in cases where the owners of said lots and parcels of ground have abandoned the same, and have not paid the tax thereon as provided for in the third section of this act, nor paid the same, nor redeemed the said lands from sale as provided for in the seventh section of this act, and the said board of commissioners shall be satisfied that said owners have left the same to join the rebel forces or otherwise to engage in and abet this rebellion, and the same shall have been struck off to the United States at said sale, the said commissioners shall, in the name of the United States, enter upon and take possession of the same, and may lease the same, together or in parcels, to any person or persons who are citizens of the United States, or may have declared on oath their intention to become such, until the said rebellion and insurrection in said State shall be put down and the civil authority of the United States established, and until the people of said State shall elect a legislature and State officers, who shall take an oath to support the Constitution of the United States, to be announced by the proclamation of the President, and until the first day of March next thereafter, said leases to be in such form and with such security as shall, in the judgment of said commissioners, produce to the United States the greatest revenue.

Proceedings in case of abandonment of land and non-payment of tax.

Commissioners to lease lands.

SEC. 10. *And be it further enacted,* That the said commissioners shall from time to time make such temporary rules and regulations and insert such clauses in said leases as shall be just and proper to secure proper and reasonable employment and support, at wages or upon shares of the crop of such persons and families as may be residing upon the said parcels or lots of land which said rules and regulations are declared to be subject to the approval of the President.

To make rules and regulations for support of families.

SEC. 11. *And be it further enacted,* That the said board of commissioners, under the direction of the President, may be authorized, instead of leasing the said lands vested in the United States, as above provided, to cause the same, or any portion thereof, to be subdivided and sold in parcels not to exceed three hundred and twenty acres to any one purchaser, at public sale, after giving due

May sell lands to officers, soldiers, sailors, & marines.

notice thereof, as upon the sale of other public lands of the United States, for sixty days, and to issue a certificate therefor; and that, at any such sale, any loyal citizen of the United States, or any person who shall have declared on oath his intention to become such, or any person who shall have faithfully served as an officer, musician, or private soldier or sailor in the army or navy or marine service of the United States, as a regular or volunteer, for the term of three months, may become the purchaser; and if upon such sale any person serving in the army or navy or marine corps shall pay one-fourth part of the purchase money, a certificate shall be given him, and he shall have the term of three years in which to pay the remainder, either in money or in certificates of indebtedness from the United States; and any citizen of the United States, or any person who shall have declared his intention to become such, being the head of a family, and residing in the State or district where said lands are situate, and not the owner of any other lands, may, under such rules as may be established by said board of commissioners, have the right to enter upon and acquire the rights of pre-emption in such lands as may be unimproved and vested in the United States, and as may be selected by said board of commissioners, under the direction of the President, from time to time, for such purpose. *Terms of sale.*

SEC. 12. *And be it further enacted,* That the proceeds of said leases and sales shall be paid into the treasury of the United States, one-fourth of which shall be paid over to the governor of said State wherein said lands are situated, or his authorized agent, when such insurrection shall be put down, and the people shall elect a legislature and State officers who shall take an oath to support the Constitution of the United States, and such fact shall be proclaimed by the President, for the purpose of reimbursing the loyal citizens of said State, or for such other purpose as said State may direct; and one-fourth shall also be paid over to said State as a fund to aid in the colonization or emigration from said State of any free person of African descent who may desire to remove therefrom to Hayti, Liberia, or any other tropical State or colony. *Disposition of the proceeds.*

SEC. 13. *And be it further enacted,* That in case the records of assessment and valuation of the lots of land mentioned in the first section of this act shall be destroyed, concealed, or lost, so as not to come within the possession of the said boards of commissioners, they shall be authorized to take evidence of the same, or to value and assess the same in their own judgment upon such evidence as may appear before them; and no mistake in the valuation of the same, or in the amount of tax thereon, shall, in any manner whatever, affect the validity of the sale of the same or of any of the proceedings preliminary thereto. *Commissioners authorized to take evidence of value.*

SEC. 14. *And be it further enacted,* That the said tax commissioners shall keep a book or books, in which they shall enter, or cause to be entered, the amount or quota of said direct tax assessed on each tract or parcel of land; which said amounts shall be distinctly stated in the advertisement, or notice of sale, together with a description of the tract to be sold, and an entry shall be made in said book, or books, of each tract sold, together with the name of the purchaser, and the sum for which the same may have been sold. A transcript or transcripts of said book or books, duly verified by said commissioners, and said books when said commis- *Commissioners to keep record of tax assessed. Entry of sale and amount sold for. Transcript to be sent to Secretary of the Treasury.*

sion shall expire, shall be filed in the office of the Secretary of the Treasury of the United States, and said books and transcripts, and copies of said books and transcripts, duly certified by the Secretary of the Treasury, shall be evidence in any court of the United States. The said commissioners may employ a clerk, whose compensation shall be twelve hundred dollars per annum.

Clerk's salary.

SEC. 15. *And be it further enacted,* That the thirteenth section of the act of August fifth, eighteen hundred and sixty-one, entitled "An act to provide increased revenue from imports to pay interest on the public debt, and for other purposes," shall be so construed as not to exempt from taxation property above the value of five hundred dollars, but to exempt from taxation property of the value of five hundred dollars, or less, owned by individuals, notwithstanding the provisions of said act.

$500 exempt from taxation.

SEC. 16. *And be it further enacted,* That this act shall take effect from and after its passage.

Approved June 7, 1862.

INDEX OF DIRECT TAX BILL

NOTE.—For modifications of so much of the act of August 5, 1861, as relates to the tariff, see the tariff act of 1862.

A

	PAGE
Ad valorem duties on imports,	4
Administrator, (see Executor.)	
Alabama, direct tax apportioned to,	7
Allowance, (see Drawback.)	
Appeals from valuation, made in cases of fraud, not allowed,	10
Assessors to hear and determine,	12
Arkansas, direct tax apportioned to,	7
Assessors for assessing, &c., for each district to be appointed,	8
When to be appointed and qualifications of,	8
To make list in cases of refusal or neglect,	9
Assessors to devise form of lists,	11
To give notice of the completion of lists for examination,	11
To hear and determine appeals,	12
To submit proceedings of assistants,	12
To revise lists made by the assistants,	12
Board of, how constituted,	12
Board of, to appoint clerks,	12
Penalty for not attending general meeting of the board,	13
Penalty for failing to furnish lists,	13
May be exonerated,	13
Board of, to make out equalization and apportionment,	13
Board of, to revise and adjust lists,	13
Board of, to apportion tax,	14
To make their lists to conform to the apportionment of the board of assessors,	14
Pay of,	14
To make out list of transfers of real estate,	21
Not to be appointed when States assume payment of tax,	26
Assessments of direct taxes on real estate, provisions concerning,	8, 27
Assistant assessors, for assessing, &c., to be appointed,	8
To make two lists of assessments,	11
Pay of,	14

C

	PAGE
California, direct tax apportioned to,	7
Cape of Good Hope, additional duties on imports in foreign vessels from beyond,	4
Clerk of the court, compensation of,	19
Clerks to assessors, how appointed,	12
Penalty for acting without taking the oath,	13
Duty of,	13
Clerk to commissioners of taxes in States in insurrection, to be appointed,	32
Salary,	32
Collection districts for assessing, &c., States and Territories to be divided into convenient,	8
Collectors for collecting, &c., to be appointed,	8
To give bonds and surety, and when filed,	8
To receive lists,	15
To be charged with taxes receipted for,	20
Delinquent, proceeding respecting,	20
Delinquent, property may be seized and sold,	21
Duty of, in relation to collection of taxes,	22
Compensation of,	22, 23
To give bond,	23
To collect income tax,	24
To commit to prison persons refusing to testify,	24
Not to be appointed where States assume payment of taxes,	26
To collect taxes, to prosecute and recover all penalties and forfeitures,	26
Real estate of, liable for debts due United States,	26
In case of sickness, deputy may act,	27
In case of death, oldest deputy to act,	27
Collectors to give bonds before receiving lists,	15
To appoint deputies, &c.	16
To advertise time when tax is due,	16
To demand tax at dwellings,	16
To distrain in case tax is not paid,	16
To give deeds for real estate sold,	18

INDEX OF DIRECT TAX BILL.

	PAGE
Collectors to deposit list of property sold with clerk of the court,	19
To transmit monthly statement of collections,	19
Colorado, direct tax apportioned to,	8
Commissioner of taxes, office created,	26
Authority and duty,	27
Salary,	27
Commissioners of taxes, to be appointed in States or parts of States in insurrection,	28
Salary,	28
Security to be given,	28
Time of entering upon their duties,	28
To give notice of the sale of lands in States or parts of States in insurrection,	29
May allow two years for redemption of lands in insurrectionary districts,	30
May lease lands,	30
To make provision for the support of families,	30
May sell lands instead of leasing,	30
To take evidence of the value of land,	31
To keep record of taxes assessed,	31
May appoint a clerk,	32
Connecticut, direct tax apportioned to,	6

D

Dakota, direct tax apportioned to,	8
Deduction allowed to States for collecting and paying direct tax,	25
To what to apply,	26
Deeds for real estate sold to be given by collector,	18
Delaware, direct tax apportioned to,	6
Depositaries to be selected by Secretary of the Treasury,	23
To be disbursing agents,	23
Depository, (see Depositary.)	
Deputy collectors to be appointed by collectors,	16
Authority of,	16
To act in cases of sickness or death of collectors,	27
Direct tax, amount laid, and how apportioned,	6
Amounts apportioned to several States and Territories and District of Columbia,	6
States and Territories, &c., to be divided into convenient collection districts,	8
Any State or Territory may form one collection district,	8
Assessors and collectors to be appointed for each district,	8
When to be appointed, and qualifications of,	8
Collectors to give bonds before entering on duties,	8
Amount and sureties of, and where filed,	8
Bonds may be increased,	8
To be charged in insurrectionary districts to all lands,	27
Owners of lands may pay in sixty days after amount is fixed,	28
Distraint to be made when tax is not paid,	16

	PAGE
Distraint, duty of officer in case of,	16
District of Columbia, direct tax apportioned to,	8
Drawback allowed on imports exported,	5
Duties, ad valorem, on imports,	4
On bonded goods, time payable,	5
Specific, on imports,	3

F

Florida, direct tax apportioned to,	7
Foreign vessels, additional duties on imports in,	4
Forfeitures and penalties for assessors and assistant assessors acting without taking oath,	8
To be prosecuted and collected by collector,	26

G

Georgia, direct tax apportioned to,	7

I

Illinois, direct tax apportioned to,	7
Imports, specific duties on,	3
Imports, ad valorem duties on,	4
Imports in foreign vessels, additional duty on,	4
Imports re-exported, allowance of drawback on,	5
Income tax, amount to be levied,	22
Income, how estimated,	23
Income tax, when payable,	24
Proceedings in cases of failure to pay,	24
Indiana, direct tax apportioned to,	7
Iowa, direct tax apportioned to	7

K

Kansas, direct tax apportioned to,	7
Kentucky, direct tax apportioned to,	7

L

Lands in insurrectionary districts to be charged with direct taxes,	27
To be valued according to last State valuation,	27
To be charged with taxes according to valuation,	28
Owners of, may pay tax in sixty days after amount is fixed,	28
To be forfeited to the United States for non-payment of tax,	28
In insurrectionary districts, commissioners to give notice of sale,	29
May be redeemed within sixty days,	29
Abandoned proceedings for the payment of taxes on,	30
Terms of the sale of,	31
Disposition of the proceeds of the sale of,	31
Commissioners may take evidence of the value of,	31
Lien for two years upon lands, &c.,	15

INDEX OF DIRECT TAX BILL. 35

	PAGE
Lists to be made out by property owners,	9
Assistant assessors to make, in case of refusal or neglect,	9
How to be made in cases of fraud,	10
To be furnished when required,	10
Of property of absent owners, how to be made,	10
Of property in other districts, how to be made,	11
When to be made,	11
When completed for examination, notice to be given,	11
Of assistants to be revised by assessors,	12
Penalty for assessors failing to furnish,	13
Board of assessors to revise and adjust,	13
Contents of,	14
Time for the delivery to collectors,	14
For purposes of internal revenue, persons to make list of goods, &c., liable to duty,	9
Louisiana, direct tax apportioned to,	7

M

Maine, direct tax apportioned to,	6
Maryland, direct tax apportioned to,	7
Massachusetts, direct tax apportioned to,	6
Michigan, direct tax apportioned to,	7
Minnesota, direct tax apportioned to,	7
Missouri, direct tax apportioned to,	7
Mississippi, direct tax apportioned to,	7

N

Nebraska, direct tax apportioned to,	7
Nevada, direct tax apportioned to,	8
New Hampshire, direct tax apportioned to,	6
New Jersey, direct tax apportioned to,	6
New Mexico, direct tax apportioned to,	7
New York, direct tax apportioned to,	6
Non-residents, tax of, how to be collected,	18
To have two years to redeem property sold,	19
North Carolina, direct tax apportioned to,	7

O

Oath of assessors and assistant assessors of direct taxes,	8
Certificate of,	8
Penalty for acting without,	8
Ohio, direct tax apportioned to,	7
Oregon, direct tax apportioned to,	7

P

Penalty for delivering or disclosing fraudulent list,	10
For neglect of duty by assessors, &c.,	11
For clerks acting without taking oath,	13
For assessors failing to attend general meetings of the board,	18
For assessors failing to furnish lists,	13
For failing to deliver lists to collectors,	14
For taking a false oath,	22
For refusing to testify as to Income,	24
Pennsylvania, direct tax apportioned to,	6

	PAGE
President, by proclamation, shall declare the States and parts of States in insurrection,	28
Proclamation, President by, shall declare the States and parts of States in insurrection,	28
Property exempt from assessment, amount of,	9
Property, owners to furnish list upon request,	9
May be returned after distraint,	16
To be sold when tax is not paid,	17
Exempt from distraint,	17
Personal, of delinquent collectors to be seized,	20

R

Real estate, valuation to be made	9
When to be sold for taxes,	17
Time for redemption,	17
Of delinquent collectors may be sold,	21
Assessors to make lists of the transfers of,	21
May be levied on for income tax,	24
Redemption of real estate, time for in case of sale,	17
Non-residents to have two years,	19
Of lands in insurrectionary districts may be redeemed within sixty days,	29
Rhode Island, direct tax apportioned to,	6

S

South Carolina, direct tax apportioned to,	7
Specific duties on imports,	3

T

Taxes, collector to make monthly statements of collection of,	19
Collector to be charged with amounts,	20
Commissioner of office created,	26
Commissioner's salary,	27
Commissioner's authority and duty,	27
Tax, income, how levied and per cent.,	22
When payable,	24
Tax, (see Duties.)	
Taxes, direct, to be charged to all lands in insurrectionary districts,	27
Commissioners of, to be appointed in States, or parts of States, in insurrection,	28
Commissioners of, time to enter upon their duty,	28
On abandoned land in insurrectionary districts, proceedings for the payment of,	30
Assessed, commissioners to keep record of,	31
A lien for two years upon lands, &c.,	15
Time when due to be advertised,	16
To be demanded at the dwelling,	16
Of non-residents how to be collected,	18
Taxation, inequalities to be reported to Congress,	14
Tennessee, direct tax apportioned to,	7

	PAGE		PAGE
Texas, direct tax apportioned to,	7	Valuations may be re-examined and equalized,	12
Treasury, Secretary of, to make rules and regulations,	9	By board of assessors to be final,	13
May exonerate assessors,	13	Relative, not to be changed,	13
To notify collectors the time to collect taxes,	22	Varnish, amount of duty on,	71
		Vermont, direct tax apportioned to,	6
To select depositaries,	23	Virginia, direct tax apportioned to,	7

U

Utah, direct tax apportioned to, . . 7

V

Valuations, how to be determined, . . 12

W

Washington, direct tax apportioned to, . 7
Warehouse, fire-proof, erected by a distiller, may be declared a bonded warehouse, ... 51
Wisconsin, direct tax apportioned to, . 7

www.ingramcontent.com/pod-product-compliance
Lightning Source LLC
Chambersburg PA
CBHW022134160426
43197CB00009B/1283